2495

The Capitalist
Revolution
in Latin America

The Capitalist Revolution in Latin America

Paul Craig Roberts

Karen LaFollette Araujo

The Institute for Political Economy
Washington, D.C.
The Independent Institute
Oakland, California

WITH A FOREWORD BY

Peter Bauer

Emeritus Professor
London School of Economics

New York   Oxford
OXFORD UNIVERSITY PRESS
1997

Oxford University Press

Oxford   New York

Athens   Auckland   Bangkok   Bogotá   Bombay
Buenos Aires   Calcutta   Cape Town   Dar es Salaam
Delhi   Florence   Hong Kong   Istanbul   Karachi
Kuala Lumpur   Madras   Madrid   Melbourne
Mexico City   Nairobi   Paris   Singapore
Taipei   Tokyo   Toronto

and associated companies

Berlin   Ibadan

Published by Oxford University Press, Inc.
198 Madison Avenue, New York, New York 10016

Oxford is a registered trademark of Oxford University Press

Roberts, Paul Craig, 1939–
The capitalist revolution in Latin America / by Paul Craig Roberts and Karen LaFollette Araujo.
p.   cm.
Includes bibliographical references and index.
ISBN 0–19–511176–1
1. Latin America—Economic policy.   2. Latin America—Economic conditions—1982–
3. Capitalism—Latin America.   I. Araujo, Karen LaFollette, 1960– .   II. Title.
HC125.R5415   1997
338.98—dc20   96–25073

1 3 5 7 9 8 6 4 2

Printed in the United States of America
on acid-free paper

Contents

Foreword

This book is about the transformation of Latin American economies from extensive state control to largely market-oriented economies. The primary focus is on Mexico, Chile, and Argentina. Within the Latin American context, Paul Craig Roberts and Karen LaFollette Araujo examine the background of the establishment of state-controlled economies in Latin America; the obstacles and opportunities facing the reformers; the people behind the reforms; and the consequences of the changes. Subsidiary themes include the operations and prospects of major international organizations, especially the World Bank.

The discussion is completely accessible to the general reader. At the same time, it should be valuable to readers who are familiar with Latin America, including its history, and also to those with some general knowledge of the reforms and their outcome.

Two completely different factors have contributed to the situation that faced the reformers. First, the legacies of 400 years of Spanish colonial rule and, second, the insistence on development planning in development literature during the postwar era.

Students of Latin America will know in a general way that Spanish colonial rule was accompanied by extensive state controls, which are vividly and informatively described in this book. But not many will know how pervasive and detailed these controls were. The system of economic controls, including the major state monopolies, reflected the influence of special interest groups and the bullionist and mercantilist theories of the sixteenth and seventeenth centuries. The account here of the operations of state economic controls in the Spanish Empire goes a long way to explain why the massive inflow of gold and silver did not serve to promote development in Spain.

In recent decades, the maintenance or renewal of state economic control was reinforced by the influential advocacy of government development planning. This also is well known, but here again few readers will be familiar with the emphatic insistence by prominent academics that development planning and foreign aid were indispensable for the economic advance of underdeveloped countries. Some of their statements quoted and discussed here are wholly unrelated to reality and are indeed bizarre. They often emanated from senior faculty members of leading universities and prominent figures in international organizations. This phenomenon shows how imperfectly the screening mechanism operates in academic social studies.

Some lessons of much interest emerge from the authors' account of the reform process. One of these is the critical role of a handful of clear-headed and determined persons operating successfully under unpropitious conditions. Another is the importance of promoting effective economic reform ahead of political reform in order to protect the former from special interest groups. This was conspicuous in Chilean experience, but was also present in Mexico and Peru. Failure to observe this sequence has exacerbated the difficulties of the reformists in post-Communist Eastern Europe.

It does not detract from the achievement of the Latin American reformers to recognize that the situation before the reforms was not so uniformly bleak as this book might at times suggest. Mexico exported large amounts of petroleum products. Moreover, there was significant viable manufacturing activity in the country. For instance, Syntex, one of the world leaders in pharmaceutical chemicals, operated in Mexico throughout the 1960s.

The account of the reform process, and the obstacles and opportunities facing the reformers, is pertinent beyond Latin America. Those hoping to reform the economies of Eastern Europe, to reduce state controls in India, and to remove legacies of the late colonial period in Africa, such as the state buying monopolies operating there, will find this book instructive.

A subsidiary theme in the book is a critical account of the operations of the World Bank. The authors suggest that the bank should be closed down and express hope that this would indeed come about as a result of public recognition that the bank has outlived whatever usefulness it may have had.

I think this hope is unfounded. The World Bank, like other so-called development banks, is not a bank as usually understood, but a political institution. The survival of the bank and of the International Monetary Fund will depend on the play of political forces, the influence of the various special-interest groups that benefit from their activities, and the vagaries of the climate of opinion. The bank serves as a role model for similar institutions elsewhere, such as the Asian Development Bank, the Inter-American Development Bank, and the more recently established European Bank for Reconstruction and Development. As I write this foreword (March 1996), the capital of this last named institution has just been doubled by the member governments.

This foreword provides only a very incomplete picture, of both the contents and the merits of this perceptive book. A wide range of readers—lay, academic, and technical—will benefit from careful perusal of *The Capitalist Revolution in Latin America.*

Peter Bauer

Emeritus Professor
London School of Economics

The Capitalist
Revolution
in Latin America

1

Latin America on the Rise

Any lingering doubt after the North American Free Trade Agreement (NAFTA) about Mexico's importance to the United States was dispelled by the unprecedented $50 billion U.S. bailout of Mexico in January 1995. The bailout, intended to rescue Mexico from an economic crisis set off by the decision to devalue the Mexican peso in December 1994, was organized by the Clinton Administration with support from Republican leaders in Congress. There were arguments for and against bailing out Mexico, but the fact that the money was spent on Mexico and not on the simultaneous bankruptcies of Orange County, California, and Washington, D.C., is testimony to the stake that the United States has in Mexico.

Mexico is a large country with a population approaching 100 million that is embarked on a process of marketization and democratization. As a result of NAFTA and GATT, the United States has expanded trade and investment ties with Mexico. Moreover, Mexico is a gateway on our border to Central and South America with a combined population of 460 million, a potential market larger than the United States and Canada or the European Community. As modernization takes root in Latin America, economic opportunities abound.

In the past, U.S. interest in Latin America was geographical and strategic. The Monroe Doctrine was propounded to keep European powers from entanglements in the region, and there have been occasions when U.S. military forces have intervened when it was believed, correctly or incorrectly, that U.S. interests were at stake. During the post World War II period, the United States was the major participant in aid programs that channeled $400 billion into the region. The aid generated some increased economic ties, but they were limited mainly to consultants and suppliers to government-financed and government-operated projects. It is only with the recent privatizations that the region has become genuinely open to foreign capital and international business.

United States businesses face a dazzling array of opportunities in Latin America's new climate, and U.S. corporations have snapped up shares of privatized firms and won majority shares (in conjunction with native partners) in a number of firms. They are providing capital and know-how to help modernize companies. They are investors in virtually every sector opened to foreign investment and are pushing to open holdout sectors such as petroleum in Mexico and mining in Brazil. Retailers and food products manufacturers, such as Price Club/CostCo and Walmart, are forming joint ventures with Latin American firms. Franchising of U.S. corporations is well under way, with Pizza Hut, McDonald's, KFC, and Subway among the dozens of franchises spotted in major Latin American cities.

Multinational firms are staking out strategic positions when they locate plant and equipment in Latin America. For example, telecommunications firms such as GTE, Bell Atlantic, and Bell South are flocking to Chile, which has the most deregulated telecommunications market in Latin America, to conduct experimental operations there in advance of what they believe will be increasingly deregulated telecommunications throughout South America. Citibank is positioning itself to sell investment products to privatized social security systems.

Magazines are springing up to cater to U.S. and Latin American businesses seeking to expand their exposure to markets in the region. One new monthly, Miami-based *U.S./Latin Trade,* takes the capitalist transformation of Latin America for granted. Its articles report the developing trade ties, major foreign investments, and the activities of the major players and industries.

The United States does not have Latin America to itself. European and Asian firms see opportunities and are acting on them. Writing in the April 1995 issue of *U.S./Latin Trade,* Mark Ludwig reported that during 1994 there were 521 announced mergers and acquisitions in Latin America and the Caribbean, involving companies from the

United States, Europe, Asia, and the region. The 1994 figure was up 27 percent from the 410 announced during 1993.

Many in the United States fear the growing economic ties with Latin America. Ross Perot, environmentalists, and labor unions fought the free trade treaty with Mexico. Perot struck a chord among millions of Americans with his metaphor of the "giant sucking sound" of cheap Mexican labor pulling jobs away from the United States.

Others in the United States hope that growing Mexican prosperity will stop the massive wave of illegal immigration that is changing the character of border states and burdening taxpayers with welfare benefits to illegals. The success in November 1994 of California's Proposition 187 banning state welfare benefits for illegals is a sign of the growing frustration over illegal aliens. For the foreseeable future, U.S. politics will continue to be affected by events in Latin America.

Trade, immigration, investment, and jobs are among the many reasons that Latin America has acquired a new importance to the United States. But the biggest reason of all is that Latin American countries are changing their politics, their economic policies, and their behavior. They are fast shedding the socialist/protectionist policies—what Hernando De Soto calls "mercantilism"—that kept out private foreign investors and reserved their economies for those with political connections who were able to obtain special business privileges and dispensations from the government. Economists call this kind of economic activity rent-seeking and contrast it with capitalist profit-seeking in which people must risk their property in open market competition. The latter produces a competitive environment in which those who are most innovative and most successful in meeting consumer wants rise to the top. The former distributes economic rewards on the basis of privileges conveyed by the state.

Latin America has long been plugged as the up-and-coming region, ripe for Yankee know-how and investment, yet in the past the region's potential languished. What makes today's situation different is that institutional, political, and cultural changes are reorienting the economies from rent-seeking to profit-seeking. Elite-run systems organized for insiders are being replaced by more open entrepreneurial societies. There are still elites and insiders, but the rules of the game have changed. Private capitalists and entrepreneurs are feted and celebrated, not shunted to the black market. This is the first time in the postwar period that there is capitalism in the region. For some countries, it is the first time in their history.

This is a big change from ten years ago. Then, privatization proposals still met with sneers and hostility. Until recently, foreigners were mainly viewed as exploiters. This attitude produced trade barriers that discouraged business relationships.

In this book, we show the changes in thinking and in institutions. Nobel Prize winner Douglass North defines institutions as the "rules of the game in a society," meaning the law, cultural attitudes, and other constraints that form the framework for human interaction. As North emphasizes, the path of institutional change determines the level of economic opportunity in a society. This book is about these societal transformations. The day-to-day management or mismanagement of macroeconomic policy, such as led to the peso crisis in December 1994, is not our focus.

In the nineteenth century, Latin American countries threw off Spanish and Portuguese rule, but kept the culture of a government-run economy. Now after 400 years Latin America is finally escaping from its rent-seeking past. The region is at last shedding the cultural attitude hostile to commerce, trade, and work that made it socially more acceptable to court privilege and peddle influence than to compete in markets.

While this book has a point of view—that markets and private property are liberating influences—we are explaining a real happening in an important region, not advocating on the basis of theory that Latin America adopt a set of policies that we favor. The statist institutions that shaped Latin American culture and hindered its economic development predate economic theory. But these anachronistic institutions gained a longer lease on life from economic theories of "market failure," which presumed a need for government power to redress exaggerated shortcomings of a market system.

In more recent years the work of economists such as Nobel Prize winners James M. Buchanan and Ronald Coase have leavened the old emphasis on market failure with awareness of government failure. The government failures in Latin America are so great that they are acknowledged even by the ruling parties and the international organizations that financed the failed experiment with publicly directed economic development. Many economists today understand that it is the presence of government—for example, agricultural subsidies—that causes market failures and that the pollution of air and water resources stems from the absence of private property rights, just as overgrazing is the fate of common pasture lands. Moreover, the collapse of Soviet central planning has taken the onus off the market as an institution prone to failure.

The arrival of capitalism in Latin America does not mean that there is no longer any risk in doing business in the region—all the usual business risks apply, plus others related to the instability of new institutions. Moreover, in the bloodless revolutions that are taking place in Latin America, people who are associated with the old order are not wiped out. They are still there, often in influential positions. If Latin American reforms do not maintain their momentum, then the natural inclination is for the old order to re-infect the system with rent-seeking forms of behavior, permitting privilege to supplant the market as the allocator of resources.

Mexico's transformation occurred during the twelve-year period 1982 to 1994, comprising the presidencies of Miguel De la Madrid and Carlos Salinas. Salinas's reputation was tarnished when his successor, Ernesto Zedillo, blamed the December 1994 peso devaluation on economic imbalances inherited from Salinas's policies. It does appear that Salinas's government permitted the money supply to grow too rapidly in 1994, an election year, especially in light of the impact on investor confidence of two political assassinations and the Chiapas revolt. Many believe that Salinas could have taken the heat off his successor by devaluing the peso before he left office in order to correct the trade deficit. Mexico, however, had had a sizeable trade deficit during the previous two years without ill effect. Successful developing countries often run trade deficits as the counterpart to capital inflows.

If Salinas deserves blame, he deserves it for not taking reasonable steps to shore up the peso's value. He could have tightened monetary policy while boosting the demand for pesos by announcing more privatizations and the opening of additional economic sectors to foreign capital. His successor, on taking office, had the same options. Many analysts maintain that by December Mexico had no choice but to devalue, as the country was running out of dollar reserves. However, visible actions to make pesos scarcer, while attracting foreign capital with privatizations, could have boosted Mexico's reserves and averted the crisis.

The consequences of the devaluation were harsh and spread to other Latin American countries. The crisis caused many to write off Mexico, but we see it as a stumble, similar to Chile's difficulty during 1982, from which Mexico will recover. Imbalances and mistakes are a part of the process. The important result is the transformation of the character of the Mexican economy.

In the event of serious difficulties, Mexico has an ace in the hole: it can privatize Pemex, the national oil company. Pemex has proven oil and gas reserves worth at least $100 billion in addition to pipelines, refineries, and petrochemical plants, but the state-owned company is so plundered that it lacks the resources to develop the country's hydrocarbons resources. Privatizing Pemex would kill two birds with one stone: it would help create a permanent demand for pesos by attracting large inflows of foreign capital, and it would rid Mexico of an inefficient company whose activities are a net drain on the economy.

In this book we begin with the future and go back to the past. This may make it seem like we are telling the story in reverse order, but the most important development is the reality of capitalism today in Latin America and the future to which it points. First we show how Latin America rescued itself, and then we show the nature of the rent-seeking culture that barred economic progress for centuries.

Chapter 2 describes the capitalist transformation in Chile, Mexico, and Argentina. These countries were the first to undertake the difficult economic and political transformation that freed resources from statist controls and created a climate conducive to free enterprise.

Chapter 3 tells why this difficult path was taken. These countries had become "blocked societies," and the only alternative to change was failure. Their economic and social systems were paralyzed by the networks of privileges that constitute the interventionist state. Privilege had checkmated privilege, and the societies were exhausted by rent-seeking.

Chapter 4 shows how U.S.-sponsored development planning spurred on rent-seeking activities until the economies were bound up tightly by privilege. The culture of government dependency overturned private property rights and shrunk the sphere of the market's allocation of resources. This is the real reason why the aid flows were unfortunate. They destroyed the possibility of a free economy. This misguided approach, institutionalized in the World Bank and the other development institutions, stymied real economic development by stimulating the pursuit of privilege.

Chapter 5 explains the economic history of Latin America in terms of the influence-peddling culture inherited from colonial rule. Spain governed its colonies by selling government jobs, which could be bought and sold for profit, while suppressing the development of markets for goods, services, and capital with regulation. The government-to-government loans that constituted the backbone of U.S. development aid in the postwar period strengthened the influence-peddling culture and delayed the necessary economic and political revolutions.

In Chapter 6, we address the question of what to do with the World Bank and the other development institutions now that development planning has been abandoned and private capital has taken over the investment role. We recommend that they either be privatized or closed.

In the last chapter, we describe the implications for U.S. economic policy of the capitalist revolution in Latin America. As Latin America becomes capitalist, and as Asia and the former Soviet bloc undergo the same transformation, the United States is no longer protected against the folly of its own policies by the blanket of socialism that smothered potential competitors in the rest of the world. Today there are many alternative locations where North Americans can take their human, financial, and physical capital. This means that policies in the United States will have to undergo fundamental change. Sacred cows such as progressive taxation, the double taxation of dividends, and a pay-as-you-go Social Security system financed by a tax on employment will have to be jettisoned.

One final word. The anticapitalist left has demonized General Augusto Pinochet, whose government ruled Chile for almost seventeen years and left as its legacy a constitutional democracy. During his reign, Pinochet had to confront organized terrorists. Repressions under his government were moderate compared to those that Castro inflicted on Cuba for example, or that characterized political violence in Argentina and Peru. Even Mexico's one-party rule has been highlighted by such harsh measures as the massacre of several hundred students in 1968 and the routine murder of political challengers to the ruling party. We believe Pinochet was singled out because he doubly sinned, adding marketization to political repression of the left. Nevertheless, Pinochet's reputation has tainted Chile's success, and some readers might feel that no story of Chile's development is complete without a denunciation of Pinochet.

The Pinochet story has been told and mistold many times. Whatever else occurred during his reign in Chile, the merits of his reforms are not debatable. After laying the foundations for a constitutional democracy, he stepped down, and the social democrats who followed him have not touched his reforms. The acceptance of his reforms by his critics is testimony to their worth. This book is about the economic transformation under way in Latin America, a story important in itself and best left uncluttered with attempts to sort out the conflicting claims of the violent power struggles that once were a hallmark of the region.

2

The Economic Transformation
of Latin America

As the twentieth century enters its final years, Latin America is enveloped in tumultuous change. Countries that had for decades relied on socialist development planning and inward-looking protectionist policies privatized, deregulated, and opened their economies to global trade. Like Hernán Cortés, who burned his ships behind him as he set off to conquer the New World, the new political leaders burned their bridges to the old order. They democratized political systems, and a civil society emerged independent of the state. From Mexico to Argentina, governments subjected themselves to standards of truth, morality, and justice, elevating the rights of the individual over privileges that had been seized by the state. The outcome of the reforms is a rebirth in all areas of life: economic, political, social, and spiritual.

This claim may seem excessive in view of the corruption charges made against the Salinas family and Carlos Menem's family. However, it would be a mistake to view the escalating corruption charges as a sign of rising corruption. Rather, the allegations indicate that a formerly untouchable class can now be held accountable. It is the success of Salinas and Menem in opening the political system that has made such allegations possible. The charges would be more appropriately viewed as signs of increased accountability and political competition.

The changes in Latin America caught the world off balance. The average North American was still thinking of Mexico in terms of a sombreroed peasant nodding off under the cactus when in July 1993 Barton Biggs, chairman of asset management at Morgan Stanley, recommended that United States investors take their money out of the United States and put it into Mexican stocks. Only a few years earlier Mexico did not even have a stock market worthy of the name, as most everything was owned by the government.

By 1993, Chileans had become global investors. Only twenty years earlier Chile had been completely demolished by socialism with its economy in a state of collapse. In 1993, however, hardly a week went by without news of a Chilean company snapping up companies and concluding business deals in Mexico, Argentina, Peru, and even China. At the same time, Argentina, best known for incredibly high rates of inflation, had its finances in order and inflation—at 11 percent instead of 1100 percent—under control for the first time in twenty-four years.

Mexico

The emergence of capitalist institutions in Latin America is a remarkable story and one with world ramifications. In the 1990s, Mexican stocks appeared in the portfolios of U.S. and Japanese investors. Mexico's president traveled the globe promoting trade agreements, and the country began to export an array of manufactured goods and agricultural products, rather than just people and petroleum as it had in the past. Growth rates were good, government finances were under control, and the government had resources to invest in infrastructure and people. Mexicans exuded confidence bordering on arrogance, a startling change from their past fatalistic xenophobia, even pursuing a free trade agreement with the "Northern Colossus." How did Mexico turn from an economic basketcase unable to service its debts into a successful country?

The real Mexican revolution began nearly seventy-five years after the pretense of 1910. Mexican President Miguel De la Madrid (1982–1988), a technocrat, seemed an unlikely revolutionary. Born in a small state in the Mexican southwest, De la Madrid left early in his life for Mexico City. He earned a law degree at the Mexican National Autonomous University, and entered the ruling party in 1963. Like Mikhail Gorbachev, he was a party man to the core, having spent nearly twenty years rising through the trenches of the PRI finance bureaucracy. Also like Gorbachev, a sophisticated veneer concealed the fact that he was a tough customer, since it is inconceivable that anyone without the personality of a pit bull could have ruled over the fierce thugs spawned by Mexico's one party state. Perhaps the only clue that he would be different was a master's degree in public administration from Harvard, a first for a Mexican president.

De la Madrid inherited the system in its moment of crisis. The country teetered on the edge of the abyss, confronting economic, political, moral, and social collapse. The Institutional Revolutionary Party (PRI) had dominated Mexico since 1929 and had increasingly concentrated property rights in government hands. The result was what development economist Peter Bauer calls the politicization of society, in which everyone sought favors and protection from the government. For decades, Mexicans turned a blind eye to the institutionalized corruption, but the debt crisis broke the unwritten social contract that had maintained the PRI in power. The government had guaranteed people a minimum standard of living to ensure survival, and in return Mexicans pledged their support to the PRI. When incomes fell in 1982, the PRI could not escape blame as it held the economy in its hands.

By the 1980s, the private business activity that had developed along the U.S. border, known as the *maquiladoras,* or offshore assembly plants, had stimulated the National Action Party (PAN), a political party led by active businessmen. PAN began to challenge PRI with growing popular support. PAN supporters advocated capitalism and democracy as an alternative to what they saw as the failed patrimonialist system—political elites managing national resources for their benefit at the expense of society.

Confusion reigned within the ruling party as De la Madrid and his staff considered their options. The World Bank and IMF, concerned with loan repayment, urged reforms that would add to political instability by squeezing hard-hit Mexicans. Moreover, the austerity reforms would leave intact the nepotistic economy that had brought Mexico to its knees. De la Madrid struck a new path. He privatized 122 companies.

Once De la Madrid began to privatize, he had to bring government regulations into harmony with private property. Privatized firms needed to be allowed to compete with each other and with remaining state enterprises. He began to open markets to foreign imports in order to force companies to increase efficiency and become more competitive. He changed laws to welcome foreign investment in the Mexican stock market and create a good business climate. He sold to private investors minority holdings in the banking system that his predecessor had nationalized. He cut the budget and crusaded for the "moraliza-tion" of the government, demanding a professional bureaucracy and the end of institutionalized corruption. He cut some taxes. To under-score the country's commitment to freer trade, Mexico joined GATT.

The changes were hesitant at first and focused on the economic sphere. President De la Madrid did not know what forces would be uncorked by his opening the closed Mexican society. Moreover, his staff, which included such talent as Budget Minister Carlos Salinas de Gortari and his deputy Pedro Aspe, had no experience in how to pri-vatize a socialist system.

Considerable resistance existed to reform and especially to privati-zation. Opposition to the divestitures was organized by the state-run universities, especially UNAM, the Mexican National Autonomous University, as well as by the labor unions and bureaucratic interests. Some private businessmen resisted the dismantling of protectionist trade barriers that had provided them with protected profits. In 1987, disgruntled elements of the PRI, who had grown rich from their ability to milk the economy, found their voice in a faction of leftists led by Cuauhtemoc Cárdenas that split off from the ruling party to resist the downsizing of the Mexican state.

By 1988, the country was on a new course. Mexico had a stock mar-ket that channeled domestic investment and attracted foreign invest-ment. Inflation was down, public spending was down, and the government budget registered an unprecedented surplus before inter-est payments on the debt. There were 200,000 more businesses in 1988 than in 1980, even after taking into account the bankruptcies that occurred during the crisis of 1982.

Remaining public companies operated better than they ever had in the past. It began to be the norm for government contracts to be opened to competitive bidding. State agencies started to undertake a regula-tory role and withdraw from the direct production of goods and ser-vices.

Imports were up, particularly of capital goods to help Mexican com-panies retool their operations. Exports of manufactured goods rose by more than 10 percent per year during the last three years of De la Madrid's rule. The number of international tourists choosing Mexico as a destination had doubled, growing to six million visitors by the end of the De la Madrid Administration. At the close of Miguel De la Madrid's presidency, thoroughgoing reform still lay ahead, but it was evident even to the opposition that Mexico was advancing as a coun-try and winning increased international respect.

Mexican presidents choose their successors. De la Madrid could have chosen a fence-sitter, or even an old-guard statist who would have reversed the modest reforms he had initiated. Instead, he chose Carlos Salinas de Gortari, a man who would burn the PRI's bridges to the old order.

Like De la Madrid, Carlos Salinas seemed an unlikely revolutionary. Born in Mexico City in 1948, he earned his Bachelors degree from the Mexican National Autonomous University and a doctorate from Harvard University. A De la Madrid protégé, Salinas spent fourteen years advancing through the PRI's finance bureaucracy, where learning the art of political compromise was paramount. Salinas is of medium height, light-skinned, trim, and balding. Paradoxically, for a Mexican his appearance was highly uncommon, but to the West he had something of a universal face, the kind that immediately blends into the crowd. Salinas lookalikes are frequently seen on the streets of Washington and New York, and, apparently, Moscow, as Mikhail Gorbachev's translator was a dead ringer for the Mexican president.

President Carlos Salinas undertook a whirlwind of reforms that improved the moral, economic, social, and political life of the country. His compatriots dubbed the program "Salinastroika," and, unlike Mikhail Gorbachev's perestroika, it was real. By 1993, Mexico was transformed.

Mexican presidents have historically been six-year dictators. Salinas used his powers for change. He flanked himself with a talented and patriotic staff committed to the vision of a new future for Mexico. Ironically, they were all U.S. educated and mostly graduates of schools where the ideal was a "mixed economy" in which government interventionism prevailed over free markets.

One of the group, Secretary of Finance Pedro Aspe, played a critical role in Mexico's transformation. Only thirty-eight when he joined President Salinas' cabinet, Aspe received his doctorate in economics from M.I.T. Aspe is a devout Catholic and a supply-side economist with a forceful, no-nonsense manner, commanding height, and vast political experience gained in the finance bureaucracy. Aspe's deputy Jacques Rogozinski was put in charge of privatization. Born in Paris of Polish parentage, Rogozinski was living proof of the adage that clever immigrants get ahead anywhere, even in a closed, nepotistic society like Mexico. He did undergraduate work at a prestigious Mexico City university, ITAM, and obtained his doctorate from the University of Colorado.

Another key figure in the Mexican transformation was Jaime Serra Puche, who had been an advisor to Salinas in the Finance ministry. Named Secretary of Commerce and Industry in December 1988, Serra earned a doctorate in economics from Yale University in 1979. Serra created the Deregulation Unit under the Secretariat he headed, and put ITAM professor Arturo Fernández in charge of it. An apostle of trade liberalization, Serra helped to bring trade barriers down from an average 100 percent in 1982 to just 10 percent by 1993.

Serra spearheaded the Mexican president's campaign for a North American Free Trade Agreement. He believed that the benefits of regional free trade would flow to all three countries, providing broader access to resources, inputs, services, markets, and technology, and he predicted that the resulting increased competition and new business opportunities would lead to "more jobs, lower costs and prices and greater competitiveness vis-à-vis the rest of the world."

Just ten years earlier, free trade with the United States would have been unthinkable. Surprisingly, Mexicans no longer feared being swallowed up by an economy twenty times the size of their own. Instead, Nafta's strongest opposition was led by U.S. presidential candidate Ross Perot and U.S. labor unions, who feared a massive loss of jobs to Mexico.

Salinas early recognized that a principal roadblock to the new economy was the incentive structure of Mexico's rent-seeking society. Rent-seeking is characterized by using political connections to obtain profits. The source of the profits varies—it could be licenses to import, a government-protected market, use of state resources for individual gain, or a regulation that bestows a special privilege on an individual or company. The profits allocated in this manner are known as rents.

In a rent-seeking society, most profit-making opportunities are allocated through the political process. Businesses succeed by lobbying the government for protection from competition and other special privileges. The emphasis is on how to divide and redistribute existing resources, not on expanding production or serving customers in markets. In a rent-seeking society, a large portion of the country's resources are dissipated in efforts to influence the government.

Nobel economist Douglass North has explained that societies are always characterized by a mixture of institutions, some that foster economic development and others that do not. What counts are competitive markets and low transaction costs. Transaction costs are the costs involved in economic exchange, such as information gathering to measure the value of what is being bought and sold, and the costs of protecting rights and enforcing agreements. North observes that if markets are incomplete, then transaction costs become significant.[1]

In Mexico, the leading institutions of society have been the lobbying associations formed by bureaucrats and bureaucratic go-betweens, powerful labor unions, rent-seeking business executives, and lawyers. Transactions costs rose as competing interest groups lobbied for more regulations and subsidies to offset those already on the books. Monopoly producers used government power to eliminate competitors and reserve protected profits for themselves. The only markets that existed in the true sense of the word were outside legal channels in the informal markets of the unofficial economy.

In addition to being economically inefficient, rent-seeking corrupts people's ethical behavior. With political decisions more important to individual success than personal effort, no means are spared in trying to achieve favorable outcomes. Bribery quickly emerges as the most efficient way to allocate resources, since bureaucrats and politicians are not entrepreneurs and cannot judge the best economic use of resources.

Salinas reasoned that in such a climate institutionalized corruption would defeat his reforms. Declaring that "the ends never justify the means," he sought a revival of religious morality to undergird a reformed economy and stimulate people to work better and more honestly. In his reasoning, he followed Mikhail Gorbachev, who saw the political, economic, moral, and spiritual spheres as "links in a single chain." Salinas made a well-publicized visit to the Vatican in 1991; to convey the message that his government would adhere to a higher moral standard, he restored relations with the Catholic Church that had been severed in 1917.

It is extraordinary that a few Mexican officials with supply-side ideas were able to implement a Reaganesque revolution that was more thoroughgoing than the Gipper's. Salinas and his staff privatized, deregulated, and cut government spending in nonessential areas. They further opened markets, cut taxes, cut tariffs, and liberalized investment laws to allow both foreign and domestic investors to invest in areas previously reserved for the state.

The divestment of government monopolies gave a great boost to the revival of civil society, deadened under decades of government expansion. Private companies multiplied as the government receded. Private community and charitable organizations sprang into existence, often headed by community-minded entrepreneurs. Privatization created wealth, fostered economic competition, and restored government finances.

Privatization Minister Jacques Rogozinski was given the green light to privatize as far and as fast as possible. Salinas was eager to be rid of the state-owned monopolies, because they lost tens of billions of dollars yearly, riddling government budgets with red ink. With 700 state companies slated for the divestment axe and opposition initially high, Rogozinski quipped that he had to strap on his safety belt to the hot seat every day at the office.

With Rogozinski's and Aspe's help, President Salinas freed vast swaths of the economy from the government. By 1993, they had sold off $24 billion of state-owned companies. They sold iron ore mining and steel companies, sugar refineries, and the two state airlines— Aeromexico and Mexicana de Aviación. They sold shipyards, manufacturers, chemical companies, and food distributors.

White elephants abounded among the companies the team privatized. For decades, the PRI had proclaimed that state-run companies were managed for the benefit of all Mexicans, but in fact the PRI had used foreign loans to build monumental mistakes and line officials' pockets. One large vegetable oil mill was a prodigious consumer of electricity, routinely causing power outages in the village where it was located. A Oaxaca-based sugar mill had to process 70,000 tons of cane to break even, but the region where it was located produced only 30,000 tons. Such companies incurred such high losses with so little hope of improvement that Rogozinski was quick to deed them gratis to prospective owners, before they could change their minds.

The privatizers encountered telling problems as they sold off state properties. The government had acquired properties according to no set criteria, merely at the whim of officials. Consequently, no complete registry of government properties existed. This permitted PRI officials to take advantage of the chaos and run enterprises as their own property, covering lavish expenses with public funds. In one case, the manager of a government-owned Acapulco hotel deeded the hotel swimming pool to his lover. This came to light after Rogozinski sold the hotel, when the private buyer returned to complain that a woman had shown up with a deed to the swimming pool.

Rogozinski presided over the divestment of two jewels of the Mexican government: the national telephone company, Telmex, and the country's banking system, nationalized in 1982 by López Portillo in the last act of Mexican socialism. Rogozinski won international renown in financial circles for his handling of those complex transactions. The sale of Telmex alone brought in $6.2 billion for the government.

The Telmex privatization helped to spur the rapid growth of Mexico's stock market and sell international investors on Mexico as a good place to do business. Rogozinski reversed the old nationalism and sold a controlling interest to a Mexican-French-U.S. consortium comprising the Mexican Carso Group, France Cable & Radio, and Southwestern Bell.

The Telmex privatization was also a critical step in improving the finances of the Mexican government. Finance Minister Pedro Aspe created a Contingency Fund in which revenues from the Telmex sale were applied to pay down the government's internal debt. Unlike U.S. budget directors, he recognized that revenues from privatization were one-time revenues and, therefore, should not finance ongoing expenditures. Aspe explained that using funds from privatization to pay down the internal debt enabled the government to permanently spend less on interest charges, freeing revenues to finance social expenditures.[2] Aspe continued this policy with resources obtained from subsequent divestitures.

In May 1990, President Salinas announced the privatization of the banking system. Mexico desperately needed a private banking system to finance the growth of the private businesses that had begun to appear now that the government no longer prevented their emergence with regulations and state-owned monopolies. Since the 1982 nationalization, the government had used the banks to finance its huge deficit. Many state-owned banks were poorly managed, and very little credit was available to the private sector.

Between 1990 and 1992, Rogozinski sold all eighteen banks, obtaining $7.4 billion for the government contingency fund. Naysayers on Wall Street were astounded that the Mexican government sold the banks for a price 3.1 times their net worth and 14.7 times profits, exceeding their goal of selling banks at one to two times book value.

Privatization created wealth. Many privatized companies rapidly increased in value, especially the banks. During the first quarter of 1992, the privatized Banamex's earnings were up 38 percent in real terms from a year earlier. Another privatized bank, Bancomer S.A., saw its first-quarter 1992 earnings rise an inflation-adjusted 84 percent from a year earlier.

For some companies, private ownership produced a stunning turnaround. Telmex was a prime example. In 1988, when the Mexican government still held a majority share of the telephone company, it generated sales of only about $1.5 billion, and its stock price languished. The market value of the firm was about $1.5 billion. Only four years later, sales were well over $4 billion, the stock had soared, and the firm was valued at almost $30 billion. In a short time, the private phone company was worth twenty times the socialized one.

A few companies continued to show losses after privatization. In the Mexican press there was much hand-wringing over the fate of companies such as the privatized mining concern, Cananea, and the privatized Mexicana de Aviación, but Mexican taxpayers were no longer responsible for covering their deficits. The realization that entrepreneurs in a free economy must sink or swim on their own merits slowly began to take root.

By 1991, public opinion had swung in favor of privatization. Mexicans began to view the privatizations as an opportunity for personal advancement. A December 1991 poll conducted for the Mexican monthly *Este País* revealed that a growing number of Mexicans believed that they would benefit from the privatizations. In all, 56 percent of the population were favorably disposed or neutral toward the government's reorientation of the economy to the private sector.[3]

In mid-1993, only about 150 state companies remained, and most of them, including some subsidiaries of the oil company, Pemex, the last state-owned sacred cow, were slated for divestment.

Mexican privatization filled government coffers with revenues. Between 1988 and 1993, privatization receipts totaled $24 billion. Freed from having to print money to finance the deficits of state companies, Aspe was able to cut inflation to 11.9 percent in 1992 and run a budget surplus. The internal debt was slashed almost in half as a percent of GDP between 1991 and 1992, falling from 15 percent of GDP to 8.7 percent. Interest rates dropped as the government reduced its debt servicing requirements.

These sensible changes were not achieved without drama. There were powerful interests who were losers from privatization, among them the gang running Pemex, the state oil company. The labor union had, in effect, privatized Pemex and turned it into a fiefdom. The chief warlord, the PRI, had delegated this power to the union in exchange for faithful support of the PRI.

President Carlos Salinas assumed the mantle of the Mexican presidency amid widespread allegations of electoral fraud, which weakened his mandate. The opposition saw Salinas as a modernizer and vowed to fight to thwart further reform. The socialists regrouped around

Cuauhtemoc Cárdenas, leader of the breakaway leftist PRI faction, and powerful labor leaders. The most prominent of these was Joaquín Hernandez Galicia, known as "La Quina," who, as head of the Pemex Union, the country's largest, essentially ran the state oil monopoly. Another prominent opponent was Fidel Velázquez, octogenarian boss of the 4.5 million-member Confederation of Mexican Workers.

De la Madrid's reforms had been necessarily limited because the situation was not ripe for taking on the unions. The Pemex union not only stood in the way of overhauling operations of the huge state oil monopoly, which generated 28 percent of government revenues, but also had the power, in solidarity with the other unions, to block further privatization. It was a pillar of the old order, and no real modernization could take place prior to taming the unions.

La Quina was a powerful thug who delivered votes for the PRI in exchange for the right to carve a vast personal empire out of Pemex. La Quina ran the union like his own principality, using the union's legal right to a 2 percent commission on Pemex contracts to amass a personal fortune in supermarkets, stores, ranches, farms, factories, and construction and trucking companies. He sold jobs at Pemex for highly lucrative kickbacks, inflating the Pemex payroll by between 30 to 50 percent. With some 210,000 workers under his control, and a personal army to rival that of the government, La Quina was a formidable foe.

Beset by turmoil within the PRI, Salinas limped through his first six weeks of office unable to advance his reform agenda. Then on January 10, 1989, he picked up the powerful scepter of the Mexican presidency and sent it crashing down on the heads of the old guard. In an early morning raid, federal troops blasted open the door of La Quina's home with a bazooka and arrested the labor leader and twenty of his top associates. The attorney general's office charged La Quina and his gang with "corruption, gangsterism, and arms trafficking." La Quina was a sitting duck for prosecution as he had set up a series of oil service companies that defrauded the government of hundreds of thousands of dollars in taxes.

News of the arrests riveted Mexicans. The country held its breath and waited for massive strikes and civil unrest, but none came. Pemex workers walked off the job the day after La Quina's arrest in protest, but by the following day most were back at work. It was too late for the diehard left, who lacked popular support. The country already had a new spirit.

President Carlos Salinas used the authority he gained from jailing the big fish to steamroll his critics and push his agenda forward.

Salinas and his team broke union strangleholds over state companies in industry after industry. They appealed to members' self-interest and enabled workers to purchase shares of privatized industries. If negotiations failed, they took their cue from the action against La Quina. Before they could sell the country's largest mine, the army had to be called in to subdue its rebellious union.

Opposition to privatization continued until 1990, when Rogozinski created the divestment unit of the Secretariat of Finance, a sixteen-member team that served as a holding company for the state enterprises. With Rogozinski as chairman and cabinet members on the board, the bureaucracy had to submit.

Serra and Fernández deregulated broad areas of the economy to provide privatized firms with a framework in which to operate. They sought to stimulate competition among the growing private sector while forcing remaining state enterprises to compete on a level playing field. Between 1988 and 1991, they fully or partially opened many activities, including telecommunications, transportation, technology transfer, ports, mining, and fishing to competition and market forces. They amended the foreign investment laws to allow unlimited foreign investment in the Mexican stock exchange and they implemented regulations promoting the private provision of public services, such as concessions to private companies to maintain highways, bridges, and ports.

The deregulators revised the regulatory framework governing Telmex, helping to increase its market value; they permitted the free import and market of sugar, complementing the privatization of state sugar mills; and they reclassified petrochemicals products to allow increased private property in secondary petrochemicals, a prelude to complete privatization of Pemex.

The benefits of deregulation quickly became apparent. In December 1992, Arturo Fernández reviewed the impact of deregulation on several economic sectors. Fernández found that in the trucking sector alone, the breakup of the oligopoly that had controlled the trucking industry throughout the country and the introduction of competition in the sector had resulted in a net transfer to the rest of the economy of $1 billion per year. New entrants began to flock to the trucking industry, thereby helping to lower rates and eliminate the monopolistic rents formerly enjoyed by the few.

Finance Minister Aspe implemented supply-side tax reforms in Mexico. Aspe established a tax system that encouraged saving and investment while beefing up enforcement. Aspe cut the maximum corporate income tax rate from 42 percent to 35 percent and reduced the maximum individual rate from 60.5 percent to 35 percent. There was no tax on capital gains for publicly traded firms, unlike in North America. Moreover, Aspe phased out state and local taxes, earmarking instead a 20.5 percent share of federal tax revenues to the localities.

Supply-side tax reforms quickly brought favorable results. The simplified system with lower rates, fewer taxes, and tougher enforcement produced government revenues that were up 33 percent in real terms by 1992, and the reforms achieved their aims of expanding GDP and the tax base. One-third of the increased revenue was due to increased economic activity. The lower tax rates encouraged Mexicans to pay their taxes, something they had paid bribes to avoid in the past.

With revenues from privatization and a growing economy, President Salinas was able to increase spending on people rather than on deficits of state enterprises. The government began to focus on providing basic services to taxpayers, such as education, health care, infrastructure, and potable water and sewerage facilities. In 1989, Salinas created an innovative countrywide program known as "Pronasol" or "Solidarity" to provide social services to the poor. During the crisis-ridden 1980s, the level of social spending did not rise, and the existing programs, imposed from above, were riddled with corruption and served as pork-barrel projects that benefited the political elite.

Salinas had come to the conclusion that public works projects did not necessarily win votes. Projects that were ill-conceived or imposed on a community actually increased opposition to the government. Salinas concluded that the central government needed to delegate to the responsible local officials the necessary resources to undertake public spending projects.

Solidarity emphasizes self-help and local community participation. By 1991, 63 percent of village governments had their own public works budgets. Solidarity also extended property deeds to 1.5 million squatters, and joint efforts between the government and local residents paved over 3,200 kilometers of roads in low-income areas and provided three million more Mexicans with electricity.

Unlike earlier presidents, Salinas's claims for his government's achievements in the social area were real. In 1993, Mexicans were astonished by the rapid proliferation of government services. On any given day around the Mexican capital, a new highway was being inaugurated, a new school dedicated, and potable water service went on line in yet another neighborhood, while the delivery of electricity was noticeably improving.

The Salinas government was accused of using the poverty program to shore up support for PRI political hegemony in Mexico. There was certainly evidence to support the allegation, as the Solidarity program was enormously popular throughout the country and was in part responsible for the PRI's fairly won electoral wins of the 1990s. In a 1991 poll, more than 60 percent of respondents had a favorable image of Solidarity.

The Mexican government was finally making significant strides toward providing basic public services, and the motives for doing so did not lessen the achievements. As Mexican investment lawyer Miguel Jauregui told the *Wall Street Journal*, "The public deficit is lower than ever, inflation is falling, and Solidarity isn't being funded by printing money, so how can you criticize it?"[4]

The Salinas team began reform of the public education system, a necessary step in order to create a competent and productive work-force. Public spending on schools and teachers greatly increased, and efforts were initiated to change the curriculum content to reflect the requirements of a modern society. The example of the Mexican history curriculum is illustrative. The way Mexican history has traditionally been taught has tended to coarsen the character of children spoonfed the constant message of Mexico as victim, continually betrayed throughout its history beginning with betrayal by *La Malinche,* the Indian consort of Cortez, then by Spanish colonialists, and finally by North American imperialism. Mexicans taught their children to be pro-fessional victims decades before this stance was adopted by preferred minorities in the United States. As recently as the early 1980s, the coarsest of words were used even in polite society to describe histori-cal relations between the United States and Mexico.

New textbooks were written emphasizing individual achievement and elevating the presidencies of Benito Juárez and Porfirio Díaz, two leaders who expanded civil and economic rights and fostered prosper-ity in Mexico. However, left-wingers in Mexican universities mounted fierce opposition to the deemphasis of the Mexican Revolution, forcing the Salinas Administration to shelve the new books and leave further education reform for the next government.

In the 1990s, Mexico was still in effect a one-party state, and polit-ical reform was just beginning. Salinas often pointed out that if Gor-bachev had reversed the order of his reforms, putting economic reform ahead of political reform, he might have held on to the presidency of the Soviet Union. Allowing people to speak their minds before they were able to fill their bellies was undoubtedly a recipe for instability.

By 1993, President Salinas had loosened political controls to the extent that he could point to some achievements.

First and foremost, Salinas worked to establish a rule of law in Mexico. Previously, as in the Soviet Union, the law had been whatever served the PRI. From the outset of his government, President Salinas said that he "would not tolerate any form of impunity whatsoever, that no one was above the law, and that the law could not benefit individuals who violated human rights."[5] Salinas established the National Human Rights Commission which works with international human rights agencies to protect Mexicans from human rights violations committed by Mexican authorities. In 1991, the Commission received 3,374 complaints, of which half were satisfactorily resolved. Abuses continued in the 1990s, but there was a discernible downward trend.

Salinas used administrative reform and constitutional changes to establish universal rules in government agencies. Salinas and his team began by streamlining and reordering the financial and economic bureaucracies. By 1993, they had reorganized the fishing, education, and agriculture bureaucracies as well. By means of an amendment to Mexico's Constitution, in 1992 President Salinas even extended private ownership and market forces into the inefficient, collectivist *ejido* system of agriculture, traditionally a sacred cow. In 1993, an amendment to Mexico's Constitution established the independence of the Central Bank, in order to prevent future Mexican presidents from resorting to printing money to finance a budget deficit.

The Federal Law for Economic Competition went into effect in July 1993. The law repealed the 1934 regulatory statutes of the Mexican Constitution pertaining to monopolies. The old law granted various monopolies. The new law aims to promote economic efficiency and protect the competitive process and the free flow of goods. It also establishes an antitrust policy with respect to conglomerates.

While reform has by no means percolated to every sector and activity, the changes have served to reduce incentives for competing groups to carve up pieces of the government for themselves. The Mexican business climate has been enhanced by the resulting increased sphere of individual action and lower transactions costs for firms and individuals.

In 1989, the PRI ceded the governorship of a major state, Baja California, to the opposition party PAN after the people vociferously protested the fraudulent win of the PRI. In 1991, after another fraudulent win, the PRI also gave way to the PAN in Guanajuato state. The PRI has been ceding electoral wins in some local elections to the opposition, both to the PAN and the Democratic Revolution Party (PRD). At one time, the PRI stifled dissent by killing its opposition, not unlike the Chinese or Soviet communists, albeit on a smaller scale. In 1968, police massacred several hundred protesting students whose demands included that the government adhere to the democratic principles of the 1917 Constitution. Despite continuing abuses, the changes of the 1990s were a great improvement.

The consequences of Mexico's economic transformation have been profound. At long last Mexico has given birth to freedom. The country came alive as the patrimonialist state was dismantled. The change captured attention. Entrepreneurs began to seize opportunities formerly reserved for favored elites. They began to move in to develop resources and compete with each other to serve consumers. Foreign investors started to put their money in Mexico, attracted by the favorable business climate created by Salinas and his team. Foreigners sent over $40 billion to Mexico between 1988 and 1993 alone, of which $10 billion was direct foreign investment. Between 1989 and 1991, Mexicans themselves brought back almost $15 billion in flight capital, signifying a strong vote of confidence in the country's economic reforms. The Mexico-U.S. border region has been the fastest growing region on earth.

In 1993, Mexico had one of the best performing stock markets in the world. By December 1992, foreign investment in the Mexican stock exchange totaled an astounding $29 billion, a source of trouble two years later when devaluation spurred capital flight. Capitalization of the Mexican stock market as a whole experienced exponential growth, from a paltry $15 billion in 1988 to $146 billion at the end of 1992. Trading volume quintupled between 1990 and 1992.

Firms that had formerly benefited from the protectionist barriers, whose monopoly position had allowed them to pad payrolls with legions of bureaucratic facilitators and charge high prices for shoddy goods, were suddenly forced to compete with highly efficient international firms. They were compelled to deal with issues of their competitiveness and productivity and seek strategic alliances abroad to obtain the technology and know-how to compete in the global market.

It was not all roses, and companies that could not adjust to the new circumstances failed. Hundreds of thousands of bureaucrats lost their jobs and were forced to develop marketable skills for the private sector. The rapid pace of change was disorienting, and many older adults, who had spent twenty or thirty years working in the old way, found it difficult to adjust. No miracle cure, the market economy succeeds because, unlike socialism, it does not subsidize failures until they bleed a nation dry.

By the 1990s, somnolent Mexicans had become risk-takers. Between 1985 and 1992, the number of businesses grew by 100 percent, from 619,059 businesses to 1.4 million. By 1991, Mexico's private sector was so fluid that Pedro Aspe observed that no one could project the list of Who's Who in business five years into the future.

With the U.S. congressional approval of NAFTA in November 1993, a market was created of 360 million consumers and $6 trillion in output. In 1994, U.S., Canadian, and Mexican companies were beginning to take advantage of the opportunities created by the agreement.

Salinas managed to de-socialize without disrupting the economy. Growth rates were good, averaging 3.5 percent yearly between 1989 and 1992. Visual evidence of a booming economy abounded, from construction crews to the ubiquitous cellular phone.

Signs of a newfound efficiency proliferate. A telling indicator of real reform is often an overhaul of operations of a country's embassies overseas. In 1994, Mexico's embassy in Washington bustled as staff efficiently and eagerly processed outside requests for official data. This was a far cry from the Mexican Embassy of even five years earlier, when outside requests would be met with a profusion of smiles, melodious words, and total inaction.

The change in attitude has made the telephone a much more useful instrument. In the xenophobic pre-reform climate, no inquiry would produce results without a strong personal recommendation. Today even telephone inquiries receive prompt and courteous responses.

In 1986, some analysts considered Mexico to be so hopelessly mired in crisis that they feared it would become the next domino to fall to communism. Seven years later, a survey of residents of twelve major cities in Mexico found that 80 percent of Mexicans believed that the performance of President Salinas' administration was good or very good. Sixty-five percent of the population thought that the political and economic situation would improve in the near future.

In December 1994, Mexicans had a setback. The incoming Zedillo Administration devalued the peso by 15 percent, touching off a run on the currency and a 40 percent drop in its value. There were imbalances before the devaluation, but the decision to devalue seems to have caused a larger crisis. The devaluation broke the contract governing the peso's dollar value and shattered investor confidence, thus leading to a larger devaluation just as Salinas's finance minister, Pedro Aspe, had warned.

The U.S.-sponsored peso bailout, which carries conditions that hurt the Mexican economy, could be counterproductive. Mexico needs to deepen reforms to stimulate its private sector, not impose high interest rates and tax increases that cripple business and industry. The difficult recession of 1995 resulted from the implementation of misguided economic advice.

Perhaps the worst consequence of the currency problem is that Mexico is once again in the clutches of the U.S. Treasury and the IMF. The view that is institutionalized in the U.S. Treasury and the IMF is that a trade deficit for a developing country is a sign of economic weakness and a source of currency instability. To correct the trade imbalance, the IMF urges devaluations and domestic austerity to curtail aggregate demand and, thereby, the demand for imports. The notion is that by devaluing the currency the country's exports will become more attractive and, thereby, rise, while domestic austerity curtails imports, thus permitting a trade balance. This scheme has a certain logic, but it is difficult to resolve this logic with the actual reality of a developing country.

It is normal for a developing country to have a trade deficit as a counterpart to capital inflows. Such inflows mean that the country's development policy has succeeded in retaining its own capital or attracting foreign capital to new opportunities. The problem is not the trade deficit, but maintaining confidence in the currency.

Mexico's worst policy mistake was to devalue precisely at the point in time when investors' confidence in the currency was under pressure, thereby confirming investors' worst fears. Instead, Mexico should have restored confidence in the currency with monetary tightening and additional privatizations to attract foreign capital. Announcing the privatization of Pemex, the state oil company, would have averted the crisis.

Having made the mistake of devaluing, Mexico acquired two economic problems. The country lost investor confidence and simultaneously came under austerity policies of the IMF that decimate the economic opportunities that had been unfolding with development. Moreover, the unemployment and increase in debt produced a political reaction to the opening of the economy. Those who prefer the old order blame Salinas's reforms for the hard times.

If Mexico is to reap the benefits of marketization started by De la Madrid and Salinas, the country must resist the temptation to finance development with domestic money creation and push on with privatizations that attract foreign capital. The combination of capital inflows with control over the money supply will solve the peso problem.

There could be a saving grace in the gratuitous peso debacle if it rids the region once and for all of the impulse to solve problems by reducing currency values. The benefits of devaluation can be outweighed by the costs of lost trust, economic chaos, and inflation. As the *Wall Street Journal* noted, the devaluation caused such a crisis that nobody can now doubt the economic value of the intangible "business confidence."

In the midst of the crisis, the outcome of the February 1995 gubernatorial election in Jalisco, Mexico's second most populous state, gave cause for optimism. The most capitalist party in the country, the National Action Party (PAN), won 55 percent of the vote. The PRD, the leftist stronghold of disgruntled interventionists, garnered less than 5 percent. The vote suggests that Mexicans do not blame the crisis on market reforms. The outcome also demonstrates a new commitment to democracy on the part of the PRI, which quickly conceded defeat rather than steal the election, as it would have done in the past.

By supplanting rent-seeking, capitalism is creating a civil society. The appeal of meritocracy over privilege has become a beacon to other countries in the hemisphere. The sight of the PRI disavowing its socialist handiwork, wrought over five decades, has had a powerful impact on Latin America.

Chile

Mexico was not the first country in Latin America to reform. Chile began its thoroughgoing reforms a decade earlier and went much further, setting itself as the model for the entire world. Not only did Chilean reformers create an independent central bank, they audaciously privatized social security and national health. The extraordinary story of Chile's recovery from ruin is not generally known because it was achieved by a military dictator, General Augusto Pinochet, who opened the economy to foreign markets, while implementing political reforms designed to consolidate a free society. Leftwing hostility to Pinochet and to capitalism produced a worldwide antagonism to Chile that kept this remarkable story untold and out of the news.

Chile was the first country in the world to privatize social security. José Piñera played the key role. Holding a doctorate in Economics from Harvard, Piñera was Chile's Minister of Labor and Social Security between 1978 and 1980. Only thirty years old on his appointment, Piñera was a devout Catholic, trim and fastidious, with a straight, sharp nose and dark hair. His job was no cakewalk. Powerful interest groups lined up against pension reform, and even within Pinochet's military there were many opponents. Few of Chile's traditional politicians supported an expansion of individual liberty into the social sphere, preferring to rely on the nanny state.

By 1980, Chile's state pension system, a pay-as-you-go system, as in the United States, was broke. The government was forced to bail out the system to the tune of $658 million yearly. The system served powerful interest groups that carved out lavish benefits for their constituents. Interest groups were able to exploit the system because it was premised on the redistribution of income. Politically connected elites were able to establish over 100 programs that provided different levels of benefits for different types of workers, while the majority of Chileans paid up to 50 percent of their taxable salaries into the system in exchange for meager benefits. The system's inability to pay out benefits in proportion to an individual's contribution created a high level of popular discontent. The previous four governments had proposed reforms, but entrenched interest groups had successfully fought off change.

José Piñera and his team crafted a privatized pension system based on monthly individual contributions to a professionally managed pension account with a private company. The activities of the AFPs, as the pension investment managers are known, are regulated and directed to prudent investments in the private sector. The accounts are owned by the employees, who are required to save at least 10 percent of their gross salary in the pension account. Workers can contribute up to an additional 10 percent to augment their retirement fund. People receive monthly statements and watch their retirement funds accumulate. At retirement, the worker can opt for monthly stipends calculated on the basis of life expectancy from the amount accumulated in the account or buy an annuity.[6]

Retirement ages are set at sixty years for women and sixty-five for men. This eliminated the unfair privilege of early retirement that some had received, paid for by the rest. A worker with a minimum of twenty years in the labor force over his or her lifetime is guaranteed a minimum pension by the state in the unlikely event that the amounts in the private accounts at retirement do not exceed the minimum pension.[7]

The new system expanded individual choice, as workers who had participated in the old pay-as-you-go system could opt for the new private system or continue in the old. Workers with claims on the old system who opted for the private system were given a bond representing their claims for deposit in the new system.[8] All new entrants into the work force are required to participate in the private system.

Other attractive features include the fact that the account is portable. When workers change jobs, they do not need to lose their pensions. Neither are they locked into a plan. An employee can change the plan participation with thirty days notice. Since accounts are private, amounts left in them after the owner's death revert to heirs.

Piñera first announced the new system on Labor Day, May 1, 1980, and met with a firestorm of criticism. Distracted by an upcoming plebescite on a new Constitution, which would ascertain the level of public support for military rule, the military government shelved pension reform.

Piñera bided his time and pounced on his opportunity. In September 1980, 66 percent of Chileans voted for the new Constitution, signifying solid support for the military's free market reforms. The following day, Piñera convinced General Pinochet to seize his golden moment and put his political capital on the line in behalf of pension reform. Pension reform was resuscitated, and so were the attempts to quell it.

In his memoirs, Piñera recounted how he was feted, cajoled, and threatened by people who had a stake in the old system. One private sector association offered him use of their luxurious accommodations in Reñaca, an exclusive beach resort close to Santiago. Others told him they would ensure that his proposal came to naught, just like every previous reform project. Even when the system was almost assured of approval, a group of thirty of Chile's leading labor leaders made a last-ditch attempt to hijack it for themselves. Their meeting with the minister in October 1980 illustrates the pressures reformers faced and Piñera's mettle as labor minister.[9]

The group spokesman informed Piñera that they believed that the pension reforms would "jeopardize the interests of the workers," and they found it "alarming that private consortiums are to manage the money of Chilean workers."[10] The labor leaders acknowledged that it was too late to stop reform, and therefore they wanted to change just one detail of the new system: "The new pension system should not be a matter of individual decision, but rather the unions should decide where the workers should invest their money."[11] The union leaders said that the workers were incapable of deciding for themselves such an important matter as their pensions. They lacked the judgment and probably even the interest to do it, since "many people are illiterate and can scarcely understand numbers." According to them, labor leaders were much better educated and better able to choose the most advantageous institutions for the workers.[12]

Piñera wrote that he was dumbfounded by the labor leaders' breathtaking contempt for the workers they led and their utter disregard for individual liberty. His response showed a sense of humor. He said that he would have appreciated their support on pension reform but that he was unable to accept their proposal, because he was "concerned about the salvation of [their] souls."[13]

To exclamations of "what in the name of God do you mean?," Piñera replied that he meant that if the decision of where workers were to affiliate was placed in the hands of labor leaders, they would face intense pressures that would make it difficult to preserve the integrity of their decisions. He noted that pension institutions would find it much easier to buy the favorable decisions of labor leaders in order to control the pension savings of large groups than to advertise and contract salespeople. He concluded: "I cannot accept this because I do not wish to foster immorality among you."[14]

This confounded the labor leaders and the meeting soon adjourned. With such a facility for sidestepping pressure tactics without utterly alienating important groups, Piñera soon obtained approval of the pension reform. The new private system took effect on Labor Day, May 1, 1981.

Twelve pension administrators had been authorized to accept pension accounts on May 1. In order to foster competition among equals, Piñera decided to create new private companies to run the system rather than allowing existing financial institutions to operate it. From the first, the system was a great success. A virtual avalanche of workers—25 percent—who had the option to change to the new system did so in the first month. Officials had expected at most 20,000 workers, or 1 percent of the relevant labor force, to switch in the first month, with possibly 20 percent affiliating by the end of the first year.[15]

The new pension system boosted the savings rate to 26 percent of GDP and quickly provided great stimulus to the capital markets. As a result of the high participation rate in the new system and the superior returns earned on retirement investments, the retirement funds grew rapidly. In 1995, the pension funds administered about $23 billion in funds and were the largest investors in Chile. The 1995 data showed that the funds had earned an average annual real rate of return (adjusted for inflation) of 14 percent since 1981.

As of 1995, the government had authorized twenty private investment companies to administer and invest the individual accounts. Individuals shopped for a pension fund manager as they would any other bank service. Those with the highest earnings, lowest commissions, and best service won the most customers.

The private pension system has contributed to the depoliticization of Chilean society. Since benefits under the new system have been entirely dependent on individual contributions to retirement accounts, there has been no opportunity for pressure groups to demand special benefits from the social security system. Also, through their pension investments, citizens have been developing a substantial ownership stake in Chile's private businesses. Workers have begun to support policies that are protective of private property and free markets.

The reform provided additional impetus for the government to implement measures to reduce public expenditures, such as selling off deficit-ridden public companies, in order to finance the growing deficit of the former state pension system. Retirees and persons nearing retirement at the time of implementation of the new system were grandfathered under the state pay-as-you-go system, but the tremendous popularity of the new system drastically reduced the number of payees into the state system. Pensions of grandfathered retirees increasingly had to be covered out of general government revenues.

Privatizing the pension system would have been enough to earn José Piñera his place in history, but he also oversaw the privatization of health care. The labor minister put Hernán Büchi in charge of designing a new health care system. Büchi's Beatle-style haircut and casual work attire caused consternation within the military government, but he had studied mineral engineering in Chile and obtained a master's degree in business administration from Columbia University. As a member of the team of pension reformers, he had gained a reputation for innovative private sector solutions.

As early as 1974–1975, Chile's reformers had begun a reorganization of the state-run health care system in an effort to improve efficiency and control costs. They decentralized management of government-run clinics and hospitals to the regional and municipal levels. They changed the method of financing public health services and relied more on fee-for-service charges. They established incentives to stimulate the private provision of health services. Reformers aimed to gradually downsize the state-run system, and it has been reoriented to serve mainly primary health care needs of lower-income participants, with a focus on preventive care.

In 1981, Hernán Büchi set up a system of private insurance to compete with the state health sector. Workers could choose between enrollment in the state-run system or enrollment in the private system. Members of the private system contribute a minimum 7 percent of their salary to private insurers, who offer a wide variety of insurance plans and levels of coverage. These insurers face strong competitive incentives, since members can choose to terminate their affiliation and select another private insurer or return to the state system.

Since the quality of care is much higher in the private system and members of the public system must pay contributions according to income in any case, enrollment in the private system has been steadily increasing. By 1988, 25 percent of the workforce was in the private system, and by 1992, one-third of the workforce was covered by private insurance. The number of private health care institutions expanded as well, from 700 in 1984 to about 1,100 in 1988.

One of the most promising aspects of the system is that, over the long term, retirees, whose health care needs are often extensive and costly, nevertheless have incentives to choose the private system. In the 1990s, lower income retirees, who receive a guaranteed minimum monthly pension through the state-run pension system, tend to choose the state-run health system. Increasingly, however, workers will begin to retire with rich pensions accumulated under the privatized pension system. Millions of workers who have spent their working lives contributing a portion of their salaries to a pension account, which they own, will be able to afford the private health care plans. On retirement, they can negotiate a contract with private health insurers.

In the 1990s, Chile's growing private health care system intertwines with pension reform to consolidate market reform and improve living standards. In the United States, the cost of Medicare and Medicaid programs is exploding, yet basic health indicators have not improved in cities such as Washington, D.C. In Chile, as the public sector's share in the health care system declined, population health indicators greatly improved. Infant mortality rates have fallen to 17 deaths per 1,000 births in 1992, from 74 deaths per thousand in 1970, and the malnourished population fell from 15 percent in 1975 to 8.6 percent in 1988.

The Chilean reforms succeeded because they empowered individuals to make their own choices regarding matters of vital importance to them. They sidelined government and gave decision-making power to individuals.

The establishment of an independent central bank was another breathtaking accomplishment. Chile's 1980 Constitution embedded a long-term guarantee against high inflation by prohibiting the Central Bank from financing ongoing government expenditures.[16] This alone was unheard of in Latin America, where governments routinely run the printing press to finance their budget deficits. Chile went still further, however. The country's October 1989 Central Bank Law established the Central Bank as an autonomous institution with its main responsibility to safeguard the stability of the currency and ensure the normal flow of internal and external payments. Except in the situation of war, the law prohibits the Central Bank from "directly or indirectly financing" spending by, or loans to, the government or government institutions and restricts financing only to banking institutions.[17] The reform aims at preventing a future government from using the Central Bank to fund increases in government expenditures.

Chileans now enjoy more legal safeguards than U.S. citizens with regard to stability of the currency. While the Federal Reserve is independent of the Executive Branch, how it is run depends on the individuals who make up the Federal Reserve Board. There are no safeguards to prevent the Fed from inflating the currency.

United States reformers scarcely dream of such accomplishments as Chile has achieved. What explains Chile's success? Perhaps University of Maryland professor Mancur Olson has the answer. Olson says that periods of instability weaken existing establishments and, thereby, provide opportunities for profound change.[18] Chilean reformers had an opportunity to remake their society, because socialism had created a general state of disorder.

In September 1973, Chile was in shambles. President Salvador Allende, an avowed Marxist who had taken office in 1970, had used his term to socialize the economy and dismantle Chile's democratic institutions. His attempt to impose communism on Chile was as thoroughgoing as Lenin's "war communism," and the results were as disastrous.

Through legal and illegal means, Allende brought more than 500 companies under government control, including nineteen commercial banks. Once under state control, the companies became politicized and were used to provide jobs for supporters and promote government policy. Allende politicized the judiciary, and radicals infiltrated Chile's civil institutions to try to bring them under government control. They targeted labor unions, universities, the Catholic Church, charitable organizations, and schools.

Production collapsed. The exponential growth of the public sector precipitated administrative chaos within the government, while simultaneously disorganizing the private sector. Buying power of salaries was cut in half over three years, the balance of payments was in chronic deficit, international reserves disappeared, and a moratorium was declared on the payment of the foreign debt. Foreign trade was paralyzed. By September 1973, state companies registered losses of more than $500 million, a huge sum for Chile. Allende resorted to printing money to cover public-sector deficits, and inflation soon reached 1,000 percent. Chile's economic and political institutions had turned into battlefields as resistance mounted to the paralyzing lawlessness.

Allende had brought in 14,000 foreign terrorists, Cuban troops, and Soviet advisors to ensure his hold on power while he undertook the revolution. But Chileans wanted no part of it and took matters into their own hands. By the winter of 1973, the majority of Chileans were demanding that their military step in and stop Allende. In August, the Chilean Parliament had arrived at an historic accord that denounced the unconstitutionalities committed by the Allende government. The final straw that convinced the Chilean military to act was a public demonstration by Chilean women demanding that the military save the country.

Pinochet responded to the call. Strikers returned to work, markets reopened, and shoppers were able to purchase produce that they had not seen in months. Labor groups urged solidarity with Pinochet's government, and indeed, some transport workers even volunteered to work free of charge in order to get consumer goods to the public as fast as possible. Rebuilding the economic, social, and political foundations that had been shattered by Allende was viewed as a national project.

Pinochet saw his mission as reviving the basic institutions of Chilean society and establishing a free market economy based on private property. Chile's pathbreaking social and monetary reforms were part of a free market revolution that was the most thorough break from socialism that the world had seen at that time. Even Margaret Thatcher's privatizations in Britain were small-scale in comparison.

Beginning in 1974, General Pinochet began to use constitutional reforms to lay the foundations for a free market economy. The economy was opened to foreign competition and foreign investment, state companies were privatized, and a broad range of reforms were implemented. Government spending was slashed.

Having little experience in economics or politics, Pinochet's government recruited the best talent in the country. The regime was fortunate in that there were a number of gifted individuals in Chile who espoused free market ideas. In the 1950s the Catholic University of Chile began a scholarship program for doctoral studies with the University of Chicago. The program was contingent on the graduates' agreement to return to Chile. By the 1970s, the "Chicago Boys" headed the economics departments of leading Chilean universities and were a presence in Chile's business sector as well. Recruited from their ranks and from the traditional center-right, the list of officials of the military government over the years reads like a *Who's Who* of Chile: Sergio De Castro, Carlos Cáceres, Jaime Guzmán, José Piñera, Hernán Büchi, Hernán Errazuriz, María Teresa Infante, and Sergio Onofre Jarpa, to name just a few.

Sergio De Castro began privatization in Chile. The intellectual leader of the Chicago Boys, De Castro was the central figure of the Pinochet economic team. He had earned a reputation for toughness while dean of the Economics Department of the Catholic University, a trait that served Chile well during his stints as Economy Minister (1974–1976) and Finance Minister (1976–1982).

Between 1974 and 1981, De Castro returned most of the private companies and corporations that had been nationalized under the Allende government to their original owners in a massive reprivatization program. In addition, he privatized other state companies that had been in the public sector prior to the Allende government. His team divested state firms through public bidding, liquidation, and direct sales.[19] With most Chileans appalled at how state firms had been run under Allende, opposition to privatization was negligible. The companies had been so mismanaged that many were able to increase production with only a fraction of their previous staffs.

Minister De Castro reduced public spending by half in relation to GDP between 1973 and 1978. He freed prices, forced public companies to compete with private firms on equal terms, and eliminated government subsidies to public companies. By 1978, De Castro had pruned the ranks of government employees by 67,000 individuals in an effort to uproot planning from the Chilean economy. In the agricultural sector, the economic team returned land to expropriated owners, and privatized the remainder.[20]

Allende had wrought a budget deficit of epic proportions. It reached 24 percent of GDP in 1973. Under De Castro's ministrations, the deficit dropped to a mere 0.8 percent of GDP by 1978. Inflation fell as the Chicago Boys stemmed the red ink.

De Castro opened the economy to foreign trade. Again he faced little effective opposition. Private companies that could have resisted were caught off balance and were scrambling to restructure the businesses they had recently bought or recovered. In 1973, tariff barriers had averaged 94 percent and sometimes reached 500 percent. By 1979, Chile had one of the most open economies in the world, with a maximum tariff of 10 percent. The economic team reasoned that competition with efficient international firms would force companies to become more competitive and help to lower prices.

The reformers relied on an export promotion strategy to generate high levels of growth in a country with a small domestic market. They eliminated relative price distortions that penalized exporters, and their tariff reforms were accompanied by customs, tax, and exchange-rate reforms. Private property and competition were introduced in the ports and transportation sectors, lowering costs for producers.

Chile's export strategy quickly bore fruit. Between 1973 and 1985 exports of agroindustry products grew at an astounding annual rate of 24 percent. During the same period, the volume of industrial exports grew at 19 percent annually, albeit starting from a very low base. The growth of industrial and agricultural exports permitted Chile to reduce its reliance on copper exports. Although copper exports composed 82 percent of all exports in 1973, they had fallen to 42 percent of the total by 1986. New export industries arose, such as forestry products, fish and fish by-products, and fruit products.

The economic team deregulated the banking industry. They phased out credit controls, including credit ceilings, maximum interest rates, reserve requirements, and ceilings on foreign borrowings by banks. They regulated specific operations across the board, so the distinctions among institutions tended to disappear.

The Chicago Boys modernized the legal framework and implemented favorable foreign investment laws. Laws regulating corporations and public offerings of commercial paper and long term debt were liberalized. They introduced new institutions to the market, such as securities firms and mutual funds in addition to the private pension funds. They boosted existing institutions including the stock exchange and the insurance industry.

Many mistakes were made in Chile, in part because the country began its reforms ahead of everybody else. Chile had no role model—rather it became the textbook case for other reforming countries who sought to copy the best of the Chilean experience and avoid the pitfalls.

During 1982 and 1984, external shocks pushed the Chilean peso off the fixed exchange rate. The government's popularity plummeted, and the Chicago Boys were roundly criticized. The entire free-market development model was called into question. The military government began to reimpose trade barriers and reregulate the financial markets.

The economy did not improve with the new measures, and opposition mounted. The Chilean government could have gone down in history as just another Latin American military government if Pinochet had not appointed Hernán Büchi Finance Minister in 1985. Büchi rescued them from a renewed mercantilism and put the reforms back on track, fostering high growth rates.

Büchi launched a supply-side strategy to overcome the crisis. He aimed to give a big boost to the export sector and increase investment in Chile to 20 percent of GDP. Measures included a one-time tax rebate for exporters, deregulation of financial markets to increase credit availability (which had been restricted during the crisis), tax cuts, and legal reforms to further stimulate foreign investment. Büchi reasoned that the savings rate in Chile was low because taxes and public spending were too high, crowding out the private sector. He cut public spending, established a tax system that taxed consumption rather than saving, and cut corporate taxes.

During 1985 and 1986, Büchi introduced a program to reprivatize companies brought down by the crisis. In a program known as "popular capitalism," Büchi sold small packages of stocks to a large number of investors, thereby recapitalizing the enterprises. Small investors were offered advantageous terms to encourage their participation. The renewed privatization effort was another important step in building popular support for securing private property and helped bolster the capital market.[21]

Between 1987 and 1989, Büchi undertook the privatization of major government-owned companies that had never been privately held—mainly utilities in the electrical and telecommunications sectors. By 1989, few state companies remained, among them the national copper company, Codelco.

To help stimulate cautious foreign investors and at the same time ease Chile's crushing foreign debt, Minister Büchi launched an innovative debt-for-equity swap program in May 1985. Authorized under Chapter 19 of the Chilean Central Bank's foreign exchange regulations, the program enabled foreign investors to purchase certain Chilean foreign debt obligations and convert these obligations into equity investments in Chilean enterprises. During 1985–1989, the Chilean government used the program to reduce the government's foreign commercial bank debt by $7.5 billion.[22]

Chile successfully resolved its debt crisis. The country's high growth rate combined with restructuring and the debt-equity swap program enabled Chile to lower its total foreign debt, government and private, from the peak of $21 billion in 1986 to $19.6 billion in February 1994. The figure would be much lower except that the rapidly growing private sector is borrowing abroad to modernize plant and equipment, while the public-sector share of the debt has been declining. The value of Chile's public foreign debt significantly increased in the secondary debt market, lessening the attractiveness of the debt-equity swaps as an investment vehicle, while the immense popularity of the program led to a shortage of eligible Chilean debt obligations. Consequently, the central bank ended the program in January 1993.

Pinochet reasoned that once a free-market economy was in place, the political consensus would move toward the center. By 1989, when he called free elections and handed over power to civilian rule, Chile's economy was roaring and a democratic constitution was firmly in place.

Patricio Aylwin's democratically elected government took office in 1990. The democrats did not throw out the work of the general. President Aylwin built on Pinochet's reforms and consolidated them. Finance Minister Alejandro Foxley and other members of the coalition government accepted the free-market model and retained many of the Pinochet government's highly competent employees. In 1991, Foxley rolled back the tariff increases of the previous decade to an 11 percent rate on most imports, and sought a free trade agreement with the United States, telling U.S. audiences that Chile wanted "trade not aid."

The fundamental transformation in the economy has wrought profound changes. Between 1974 and 1995, Chile attracted over $13.5 billion in foreign investment, a large achievement for a country with a market limited by a small population of 13.7 million inhabitants. In 1995, according to Chilean government figures, a record $3.5 billion in new foreign investment entered Chile.

Chilean growth statistics have been impressive. Statistics are often unreliable, but the Chilean figures were corroborated by visual evidence of a dynamic, growing economy. Between 1984 and 1995, the Chilean economy grew at a real average annual rate of 6.3 percent. Chile's annual inflation rate in 1995 was 8.2 percent.

In 1995, the Chilean government reported that the Chilean economy expanded by 8.2 percent, following eleven years of uninterrupted growth.[23] Moreover, after five years of falling inflation, the country appeared to have broken the cycle of inflationary booms followed by sharp recessions characteristic of the region. Santiago's skyline was a proliferation of construction cranes and shimmering new buildings framed by the Andean foothills. Unemployment, at 5.4 percent in 1995, was very low. Help wanted ads were displayed on many shop windows in every town.

Decades of government-sponsored development never trickled down to Chile's poor. In contrast, the bottom-up development created by Chilean capitalism is gradually bettering the lives of all Chileans. A lengthy article appeared May 31, 1992, in the leading newspaper *El Mercurio*, documenting the rising purchasing power of a burgeoning middle class. A study by a Chilean think tank examined consumption patterns in different sections of Santiago and found that consumption is rising fastest among middle-income citizens.[24] For example, sales of grocery products from 1990 to March 1992 rose 28 percent in middle-class communities and 8 percent in upper-class communities. Purchases of new cars, designer clothes, and electronics showed a similar pattern.[25]

Skyrocketing consumption was made possible by a growing economy and the employment stability it brought. Moreover, the privatized pension system enabled people of modest means to obtain credit. Miguel González, Santiago manager of a pension fund, told *El Mercurio* that every worker affiliated with the fund, whatever his or her salary, has the right to obtain credit. The newspaper observed that people believe their jobs are secure and thus are willing to use credit to finance purchases.[26]

The poor also benefited by any traditional liberal progressive measure, as the growing economy furnished the revenues to expand social spending targeted at the poor. In 1995, the Chilean government reported that social spending on education, training, and social infrastructure constituted 70 percent of the budget, the highest level ever.[27]

In the 1990s, Chileans exude confidence. Chilean entrepreneurs have expanded their horizons and traverse the world looking for investment opportunities. Chilean investments abroad are growing in exponential leaps, from a paltry $11 million in 1991 to $2 billion in 1995. Economist Andrés Benítez captured the new positive outlook in his 1991 book, *Chile on the Offensive*. Benítez told the Santiago-based *El Mercurio* newspaper that

> We are emerging from our corner of the world and today we think in global terms. We are leaving behind our history, full of moral triumphs, that led to generalized stagnation.... Today Chile is competing on a grand scale, taking the offensive and is not satisfied with moral victories.[28]

The "moral triumphs" disparaged by Benítez were the socialization of private property and the redistribution of income and wealth that had brought Chile to the brink.

Those reflecting Chile's new optimism believe an even brighter future awaits. Benítez concluded that Chileans "now recognize that there is a unique opportunity to overcome the state of underdevelopment that has characterized the country since its founding."[29]

By the 1990s, former Pinochet government officials, once objects of derision in the international press, had become leading citizens in democratic Chile. Their achievements proclaimed, José Piñera, Hernán Büchi, and the others have become the ambassadors of the new order, and they are sought as advisors by forward-thinking politicians throughout Latin America and in the former communist states.

Argentina

In 1989, extraordinary graffiti appeared on Buenos Aires apartment walls: "Viva Pinochet!" Argentine inflation reached 200 percent monthly in July, on top of 114 percent in June and 70 percent in May. Living standards had plummeted, and capital had vacated the country. Another socialist state was dying a violent death, and Pinochet, who had resurrected Chile, was seen as a miracle worker and not as a tyrant.

At the turn of the century, Argentina was one of the seven richest countries. It had been a capitalist wonder during 1860–1914, enjoying phenomenal growth rates and rising prosperity. The country opened its doors to a massive influx of European immigrants, whose human capital contributed in no small measure to the country's progress.

Argentina's past greatness made its downward slide during the twentieth century that much more painful. As elsewhere, the Depression of the 1930s precipitated rising state intervention in Argentina. The government began to socialize industries and create government agencies to regulate the economy and restrict trade. Gradually, rising state controls coalesced into a strategy of import substitution.

Beginning in 1946, Juan Perón expanded import substitution and turned Argentina into a rent-seeking society. He nationalized and closed off Argentina behind high tariff walls in the belief that he was creating a brave new "Argentina for the Argentines." Perón created state companies in the industries he wanted to promote—steel, petrochemicals, and automobiles, and he stimulated the growth of existing state companies. He seeded trade unions in the state sector and made them subservient to the government. He financed Argentina's inward-looking industrialization by heavy taxation of the country's agroindustrial base. In 1947, Juan Perón cemented his strategy by asserting Argentina's "economic independence" from the "capitalistic foreign powers" that had been "dominating the national economic sources."[30]

Perón turned Argentina into a welfare state. He made union membership mandatory and required employers to finance expensive health care and pension programs, run by the unions. He regularly increased wages and froze prices, decapitalizing Argentine industry.

Perón ruled Argentina for a total of ten years, and a succession of military and civilian governments could not undo the Peronist legacy: thousands of inefficient and deficit-ridden state companies, the calamitous decline of Argentina's infrastructure and public services, and a factionalized population split into rent-seeking coalitions that all demanded privileges and protection.

Socialist economic policies continued through the 1970s and 1980s and fostered high inflation as successive governments ran the printing press to finance Argentina's gargantuan state sector. The chaotic economy led to instability, stimulating a leftwing insurgency that fed from the chaos and grew to become the biggest terrorist threat in South America. The Argentine military responded to the guerrilla tactics with a "dirty war" of its own, and by the 1970s the country was in a state of virtual civil war.

Argentines lurched from one inflationary crisis to the next. There was a hyperinflationary crisis during 1975–1976, which coincided with a peak in Argentina's war against terrorism. From 1980 on, inflation was seldom below 100 percent. It averaged 400 percent a year from 1981 to 1985, dropped to around 100 percent during 1986–1987, and hit 340 percent in 1988.

In 1989, inflation exploded, temporarily reaching an annual rate of 100,000 percent in the second quarter of the year. The currency became worthless. Production came to a virtual standstill, and capital stampeded out of the country. Argentinians were forced to cope simultaneously with hyperinflation and depression-era levels of unemployment. Argentina had little to show for its $65 billion foreign debt except notoriously corrupt and deficit-ridden state enterprises. The population was demoralized after having suffered through a series of IMF-inspired austerity plans, none of which slowed inflation. On paydays, the great class equalizer was the rush to convert australs into dollars. The crisis could not be blamed on the foreign debt, as the country had not paid interest in a year. In May 1989, there were food riots, and large mobs raided supermarkets in Buenos Aires, Córdoba, and Rosario. Police troops had to quell the disturbances, and a nationwide state of siege was declared.

Perhaps the worst affront of all to Argentines, endowed as they are with an extremely well-developed sense of national pride, was seeing their nation's descent to just another seedy Latin country in the minds of foreigners. The humiliation came in 1989, when the World Bank reclassified Argentina's income status and grouped the country with the Dominican Republic, Nicaragua, and crisis-ridden Peru.

Ironically, Argentina's savior turned out to be a new and different leader of the Peronist party. From the outset, President Carlos Menem's policies strained the support of traditional Peronists, but Menem concluded early in his term: "Better that the people insult me for a year and applaud me for a century, rather than the other way around." On taking office, President Menem astounded the electorate by proposing the dismantling of the socialist system. Perhaps the only clue of Menem's intentions could be gleaned from his comments during a trip to the Soviet Union prior to his election, in which he stated that if Gorbachev can reform seventy-five years of Soviet communism, Argentina can reverse Peronism.

Like Mikhail Gorbachev, who told his compatriots that "if we do not get out of the system we're in—excuse my rough talk—then everything living in our society will die," Menem used the crisis as his opportunity to remake society.

His public works minister, Roberto Dromi, announced a sweeping project to privatize Argentina's deficit-ridden state enterprises in order to combat the country's huge budget deficit, amounting to 15 percent of GDP in 1989. Menem realized that the only way to control inflation was to get rid of the socialized companies whose deficits had to be financed by printing money. To preside over this task, President Menem turned to the business community and the opposition party. He made Alvaro Alsogaray, the opposition free-market party's presidential candidate, his economic advisor. He appointed Mr. Alsogaray's daughter, María Julia, an opposition politician in her own right, director of ENTEL, the state telephone company, and told her to privatize it.

For his economics minister, Menem chose Domingo Cavallo. Cavallo's crowning achievement is the Convertibility Act, which made Argentina's currency, at the time the virtually worthless austral, fully convertible to the dollar. The Act also requires that the monetary base be 100 percent backed by gold and hard currency reserves, a measure that prevents the central bank from printing new currency without a corresponding rise in the nation's gold and hard currency reserves. In January 1992, Cavallo lopped four zeros off the currency and renamed it the peso, making it worth exactly one dollar.

The Convertibility Act restored confidence in the currency and diminished inflationary expectations. Argentines were again willing to hold cash, thus reducing the velocity or turnover rate of money that had fueled hyperinflation. Interest rates tumbled to an annual rate of 10 percent—their lowest in thirty years—a sign that Cavallo's policy had worked. He told the *Wall Street Journal* in September 1992 that "what convertibility did was send a clear signal that Argentina has a currency."

During the first half of 1991, the government liberalized investment laws, cut some taxes, and reduced some public utility charges, while halting the inflationary printing of money to pay public salaries. In November 1991, Cavallo announced a broad-ranging deregulation program to build on the earlier reforms and stimulate the economy. He took aim at the bribes and high "Argentine cost" of doing business. By eliminating the cozy protectionist deals that businesses negotiated with the government, he made industry more competitive.

Argentina's jingoistic socialists grouped protectively around the state oil industry, but Menem brushed them off by declaring: "I would rather have Exxon's money here working for Argentina than Argentine money in a Miami bank."[31] By November 1993, the Argentine government had sold most state-owned companies, including the national oil company.

The effects of the confidence-building reforms were quickly felt. Argentina became the third Latin American "miracle." Inflation tumbled, economic growth spurted, and the capitalization of the Buenos Aires stock market jumped 900 percent in eighteen months. Revenues from privatizations produced unheard of budget surpluses in 1992 and 1993. Equally important, as President Menem told Argentines in August 1993, "by doing away with debt-ridden state-owned enterprises, we have eliminated very important pockets of corruption."

Argentines are proud of the rapid progress their country has made. "We're in the middle of a capitalist revolution," said Argentine venture capitalist Lisandro Bril, who bragged to the *Wall Street Journal* that "we're doing more, more deeply and faster than our neighbors. We're doing in three years what Chile did in 10 years and Mexico in five to seven."[32]

Cavallo says that the capitalist policies have caused a broad cultural change: "We were used to transferring our problems on to someone else, so we didn't try to solve them."[33] Companies passed on costs to consumers, consumers got higher wages, and the government printed money to cover the public deficit, but now "instead of having a million Argentines asking for subsidies, we have a million Argentines trying to resolve their problems."[34]

Menem's reforms were put to the test in May 1995 when Argentines voted overwhelmingly to stay on the free market path and rewarded Menem with a second presidential term. "This is a ratification of the work of a government that has changed Argentina," declared Cavallo. According to the Reuters News Agency, the once powerful Radical Party, whose candidate campaigned against the reforms, "was left teetering on the brink of political irrelevance."

Pinochet was never appreciated by progressive opinion, but, as time passes, his reforms appear to have become the economic role model for Latin America. A few years ago, a Peruvian diplomat in Washington was fired for publicly articulating the view that his crisis-ridden country needed a Pinochet. The diplomat was not politically correct, but he was in tune with his own country's graffiti, which proclaimed: "Pinochet, we need you, too!"

When democratically elected President Alberto Fujimori took office in July 1990, he found that he was unable to reform the Peruvian state because democracy, combined with the interventionist state, had turned government into a vehicle for dividing up the spoils of a patrimonialist state. Realizing that the demand for reform now exceeded the desire for spoils, he illegally disbanded the corrupt Congress and judiciary in April 1992. Fujimori used the military and summary justice to break the back of the Shining Path insurgency, which had benefited from economic turmoil and political and judicial corruption. International opinion howled, but decisive action and the return of stability paid off. An approving public bestowed on him the nickname "Chinochet." The sobriquet is a construction from "chino" ("Chinese man"), reflecting Fujimori's oriental lineage and the former Chilean dictator's name.

Fujimori's approval rating shot to 70 percent, and his party won a majority to form a new Congress. The editors of *El Comercio*, the largest newspaper, refused to make an issue of the questionable constitutionality of the new Congress. What matters, said the newspaper, is that Congress draft a Constitution that elevates the rights of individuals over the state.

With the old spoils system dismantled, privatization got under way. By December 1995, ninety-eight enterprises had been privatized, including the state telephone company that served Lima, a major bus company, copper refineries, the iron ore mining and steel company, Hierro-Peru, zinc refineries, other mining companies, banks, the national electric company, and the national airline.

Peru has adopted many Chilean reforms, including a privatized pension system that runs alongside the state system, and which in February 1996 controlled $1 billion in assets. Financial reforms and changes in investment laws caused investors to take notice of Peru and capital is flowing into the country.

By 1994 Peruvian economic growth was roaring along at 12.7 percent, according to the government. There was much visual evidence to back up the government's claims, and old-timers were astounded to see more economic activity in Lima than they had ever witnessed in their lifetimes. With most foreign investment longterm, Peru was little affected by the Mexican crisis, and in 1995 the government reported a growth rate of 6.9 percent. Despite mounting opposition to major privatizing of the state oil company, President Fujimori vows to rapidly conclude the privatization of the rest of Peru's state companies and consolidate market reforms. If Fujimori achieves his intentions, he will have transformed Peru.

Brazil, the largest country in South America, has been lagging the transformations that have occurred in Mexico, Chile, and Argentina. Perhaps under the government of Fernando Henrique Cardoso, who took office in January 1995, Brazil, the perpetual "land of tomorrow," has finally turned a corner. Cardoso was elected on the strength of the success of his Real Plan, initiated on July 1, 1994, that introduced a new currency, the real, and made it fully convertible to the dollar. Inflation fell from 45 percent per month in June to 2 percent per month in September 1994. During 1995, inflation averaged 19 percent, a low rate not attained since 1973.

Cardoso plans to cut government spending and amend the Brazilian Constitution to facilitate the large-scale privatization necessary if the country is to win the long-term battle against inflation and create a thriving market economy. Whether or not the government achieves its ambitious goals, the mentality has changed. If Brazil succeeds, Latin America's capitalist revolution will be complete.

Many American policymakers believe that democracy is a prerequisite for economic development. Without democracy interjecting social welfare programs and regulating businesses, they believe the economy develops along too narrow a path that only benefits a limited strata of the population. These policymakers were disturbed by Pinochet, as they are today by Fujimori. The "democracy first" model has suffered also at the hands of Mexico's reformist presidents, De la Madrid and Salinas, who used the dictatorial powers of the Mexican presidency to privatize the economy and push for a rule of law. Menem is also a strong executive, who presses the Argentine congress to rubber stamp his reforms.

The success of strong executives and the relative failure of democracies with weak presidents, such as Brazil and Venezuela, have led some to the conclusion that democracy is an obstacle to economic development. The year 1994 began with news reports that the Brazilian military wanted President Franco to take the extra-constitutional step of dissolving, with the military's backing, Brazil's congress, which was seen as an obstacle to reform. The generals confused the form of government with problems associated with the size of the state, whatever its form, and they forgot the role played by Brazil's former military junta in socializing Brazil's economy.

Chile's success was not due to dictatorship, but to the policy of economic liberty that Pinochet's government espoused. The vast bureaucracies that blocked human action were curtailed, and individuals were unleashed to find their potential. Today Chile's democracy and economy are the most secure, while countries still afflicted with oversized public sectors built up by development planning are wracked by instability.

The true lesson to be learned is that once government becomes too large to be watched, even democracy succumbs to corruption. Large interventionist states are inconsistent with participatory democracy, because they serve to divert public funds to organized special interests. When government is small, it attracts honorable people who want to serve their country. But once government is large, there is a lot to steal. Careers are made out of divvying up the spoils and transferring income and rights from unorganized to organized interests. In effect, those who have are plundered by those who are organized.

The demand for education, paved roads, sewers, and potable water in Latin America is real. It is part of Chile's and Mexico's success that they have shrunk government while expanding social spending. The focus on long-neglected poor populations is commendable, as is the sizeable share of government funding allocated to the private provision of public services. But if social spending gets out of hand, new organized interests will grow up around the state, and a new wave of rent-seeking will commence. Perhaps fearing as much, in March 1992, Mexican President Salinas denounced the "new reactionaries" who "would like to see the return of the excessively proprietary, expansive state."[35]

Whereas the marketization of Chile was thoughtfully undertaken, some Mexican writers have expressed concern that their own country's reforms were based more on expediency than on a true commitment to a free economy. Mexican economist Roberto Salinas has perhaps best expressed this view.

According to Roberto Salinas, Mexican privatization was conducted mainly to improve government finances by purging the state of deficit-ridden state enterprises.[36] Therefore, officials focused on obtaining the highest possible sale price. The purchase of protection from competition in the near term was included in the sale price of some major enterprises such as Telmex and the banks. In the post-privatization period, telephone service has not yet noticeably improved, while consumer costs have risen. The banking sector is still characterized by poor service and high costs.

Considerations of efficiency and competition were secondary in some large privatizations, according to Salinas. Therefore, privatization is gaining a reputation for having served the elite business-sector cronies of the government, turning some into billionaires, while the population has yet to see much benefit.[37]

It is true that some state companies were not privatized in an optimum manner, both in Mexico and elsewhere. The Argentine telephone company, privatized into two private regional monopolies, also comes to mind. Still, their transfer to private hands has reaped benefits for the public in terms of taxpayer savings, creating a hospitable climate for private investment. Foreign competition and an inflow of foreign capital will help to widen markets and push the government to deregulate remaining monopolies, both public and private.

Perhaps Mexico could not have initiated a program of widespread share distribution among the population at the time that it privatized Telmex. Leftist opponents of privatization were screaming that officials were planning to sell off the national patrimony at bargain-basement prices. In the mid-1990s, a percentage of shares of the remaining state enterprises could be distributed among the population to help widen private property rights and give the public a greater stake in the reforms.

In analyzing their own situation, Mexicans should be careful that they do not mislead themselves by focusing only on the dislocations produced by the reforms and the unevenness of development. It is easy to see what is going wrong, but they should also notice what is going right—in particular a more independent business sector and a rising level of accountability in the public sector.

The Latin American experience has shown that austerity must be imposed on the government sector, not the private sector. IMF-imposed austerity plans have often resulted in higher taxes on the private sector in order to maintain the voracious state and to service foreign debt. The ensuing recession shrinks the private sector and prejudices the success of privatization plans. Even the old Spanish monarchy, not known for its prowess in economic policy, had the wits not to over-tax the industries it wanted to create, such as gold and silver mining.

Countries that have shed their allegiance to development planning and undergone a capitalist revolution have advanced the furthest in integrating their economies with others both within and outside the region. Nothing ever came of the development planners' schemes to integrate the region's economies, despite the creation of expensive international bureaucracies that were supposed to do just that.

Today Latin American countries no longer hide behind protectionism. "Trade, not aid," is the catchphrase. In the 1990s, the tables are turned as Mexico and Chile anxiously seek free-trade agreements with the United States, while protectionist ideas are alive and well in U.S. policy circles funded by labor unions and environmental extremists.

In the 1990s, Mexico, Chile, and Argentina have a newfound confidence. No longer afraid of the Northern Colossus, they are willing to trade freely with the Yankee, because they are building the economic institutions that make competitive achievement possible. Chile, with its privatized social security and health care systems, can be said to have a more advanced form of capitalism than the United States.

The economic transformation of Latin America is an encouraging development. Despite powerful organized interests of which they were part, Latin politicians are determined to dismantle the rent-seeking societies that they built with Western development advice and loans in the post-World War II period. The development-planning approach substituted government borrowing for private investment so that the state could control the investment process and plan the economy's development. The result was the growth of government and the emergence of the "blocked society."

Notes

1. Douglass North, *Institutions, Institutional Change and Economic Performance* (Cambridge: Cambridge University Press, 1990), 95.
2. Federico Reyes Heroles y René Delgado, "Una buena noticia . . . y una mala," interview with Pedro Aspe Armella in *Este País*, December 1991, 18–23.

3. "Privatización del sector público," *Este País*, (Mexico City), December 1991, 16.
4. Matt Moffett, "Mexico's Popular Anti-Poverty Program Brings Renewed Support to Ruling Party," *Wall Street Journal*, 6 August 1991.
5. Third State of the Nation Speech by President Carlos Salinas de Gortari, November 1, 1991, in *Latin America Daily Report*, Foreign Broadcast Information Service, 13 November 1991, 13.
6. José Pablo Arellano, "Elementos Para el Análisis de la Reforma Previsional Chilena," *Estudios Cieplan*, December 1981, 5–44.
7. Ibid.
8. Ibid.
9. José Piñera, *El Cascabel al gato: la batalla por la Reforma Previsional* (Santiago: Empresa Editora Zig-Zag, S.A., 1991), 94–98.
10. Ibid., 95.
11. Ibid.
12. Ibid., 96.
13. Ibid.
14. Ibid.
15. Ibid., 123–29.
16. *Political Constitution of the Republic of Chile 1980*, Chapter XII, 49–50.
17. Presidencia de la República, Secretaría General de Gobierno, "The New Central Bank," *Chile 1991*, in "U.S. Market Access in Latin America: Recent Liberalization Measures and Remaining Barriers (With a Special Case Study on Chile)," Report to the Committee on Finance of the United States Senate on Investigation No. 332–318 Under Section 332 of the Tariff Act of 1930, June 1992, 5–8.
18. See Mancur Olson, *The Rise and Decline of Nations* (New Haven: Yale University Press, 1982).
19. See Dominique Hachette, Rolf Luders, Guillermo Tagle, et al., *Seis Casos de Privatización en Chile* (Washington, D.C.: Inter-American Development Bank, Working Documents series, March 1992), 2–5; and Felipe Larraín, "Public Sector Behavior in a Highly Indebted Country: The Contrasting Chilean Experience," in Felipe Larraín and Marcelo Selowsky, eds., *The Public Sector and the Latin American Crisis* (San Francisco: ICS Press, 1991), 89–136.
20. Larraín, "Public Sector Behavior," 89–136.
21. José Piñera, "The Path to Privatization in Chile," in William Glade, ed., *Privatization of Public Enterprises in Latin America* (San Francisco: ICS Press, 1991), 22.
22. See Melanie Tammen, "Energizing Third World Economies: The Role of Debt-Equity Swaps," Heritage Foundation Backgrounder, 8 November 1989; and Barbara Durr, "Chilean Debt Swaps Soar in First Half," *Financial Times*, 20 July 1989.

23. "Chile Balance 1995," report of the Chilean General Secretariat of the Government Ministry, December 1995.
24. The standard of living of middle-income Chileans cannot be compared to that of the prosperous U.S. middle class. In the past, middle-income Chileans have had a living standard lower than that obtainable by the North American working class.
25. Carolina Gazitua, "El Otro Consumo," Santiago *El Mercurio*, 31 May 1992.
26. Ibid.
27. "Chile Balance 1995," report of the Chilean General Secretariat of the Government Ministry, December 1995.
28. Paulo Ramírez, "El Chile Que Se La Juega," Santiago *El Mercurio*, 15 December 1991. Book title in Spanish: *Chile al Ataque*.
29. Ibid.
30. "Act of the Declaration of Economic Independence," in *Peron Expounds his Doctrine* (Buenos Aires: n.p., 1948), Appendix 1, 115–17.
31. "Going Private with No Holds Barred," editorial, *Business Week*, 24 September 1990, 60.
32. Thomas Kamm, "Talk of Buenos Aires Is That Latest Revival in Economy Is for Real," *Wall Street Journal*, 11 September 1992.
33. Ibid.
34. Ibid.
35. Address by President Carlos Salinas de Gortari on the sixty-third anniversary of the Institutional Revolutionary Party (PRI), Mexico City, in Mexico City *La Jornada*, Supplement "Perfil de la Jornada," 5 March 1992, I-III.
36. Roberto Salinas-Leon, "Mexican Privatization: The Road Not Taken," *Mexico Insight*, 29 May 1994.
37. Ibid.

3

The Blocked Society

By 1980, development planning in Latin America had reached a dead end. This was not instantly recognized. As late as 1982, Mexican President José López Portillo was still praising public spending as "the fundamental instrument of the State to direct the economy," as "the instrument by which plan targets are attained," and as "the best mechanism to achieve the redistribution of income for social development."[1]

López Portillo's eulogy to the government-controlled economy was the last gasp of Mexican socialism. He himself was to shortly ride away with a billion dollars of redistributed income in his pocket.[2] Within a few years, his successor would say that "the state took all the properties, leaving the people with all the needs." The system was crumbling. Mexico had built up a redistribution system that funneled revenues supplied by foreign loans and high petroleum prices to elites. When oil prices fell and foreign loans dried up, Mexico could not finance the payments that kept the government-controlled system afloat. The only thing Mexico had to show for its $100 billion foreign debt was 1,000 deficit-ridden state enterprises.

The crisis would provoke extraordinary changes. The interaction between the interventionist state and favored interest groups had spawned a web of controls that reserved economic opportunity for a minority and closed the system to everyone else. Elites prospered by siphoning revenues from the state. Resiliency was gone, and artificially constructed economies were cracking. One Brazilian summed up the common experience: "We've been living through a permanent assassination of our hopes."

In the twentieth century, Marxist and socialist parties denigrated private profits for exploiting workers and stripping countries of resources. Mexicans were influenced by this thinking and opted to establish a "more humane" system. Their experience shows that if a society does not seek profits, then it will seek something else, such as subsidies and privileges from the government. Private capitalists are said to be greedy, but at least they must earn their money by serving wants. Mexico's political elites, as the record shows, have been far more greedy than their private sector counterparts—and at public expense. The outcome was not any one person's fault, but was the result of a system based on perverse incentives. Socialism, whether in Mexico or the Soviet Union, inevitably leads to rent-seeking, or lobbying the government for privileges, as it concentrates economic opportunities in the hands of the state.

Mexico had vast natural resources, an enterprising population, and plenty of outside money to finance development. Yet, the country did not progress. Instead of building a private, profit-seeking economy that provided a tax base, Mexico created a subsidy-dependent system of rent-seeking. Mexican elites were encouraged to build up the state by foreign advisors, who provided aid to the Mexican government to underwrite development planning. The flow of aid put the government in charge of investment in accordance with a national plan. The World Bank and IMF convinced commercial banks that governments that followed the planning model were good credit risks, and the banks lent billions to Mexico.

With government handouts more attractive than private profits, society came to be organized around maximizing political benefits and not economic efficiency. Property rights were strong in government and not in the private sector, stimulating redistribution of existing resources instead of the production of new ones.

In short, Mexico built the wrong institutions. According to economist Douglass North, a country's success depends on its legal system, the official regulations and informal rules governing individual and corporate behavior, and the organizations that are created to take advantage of the incentives in the rules. Economic development will suffer if private property is disadvantaged, markets are uncompetitive, and transactions costs are high.

The State as Dominatrix

In a market economy, the role of government is to provide a legal framework and enforce the rules. This leaves the production and marketing of goods and services to those who can make profits in meeting wants. Failure results in removal and frees up resources for those who put them to more successful use. This rational process is destroyed when government becomes a producer and marketer. Losses no longer exhaust the firm's capital and terminate its inefficient use of resources. State firms are important to government for political reasons, and subsidies are used to keep them alive. Indeed, the political uses of the firms can overshadow their economic importance to such an extent that economic performance is irrelevant to the firms' existence.

This is the way it was in Mexico. The leading economic institutions of society were state companies—1,155 of them by 1982. This meant that rent-seekers and bureaucrats organized the leading sectors of the economy. With the approval of Western advisors, Mexico had bureaucracies running the oil industry, steel production, mining, telecommunications, marketing of basic foodstuffs, airlines, hotels, and even a bicycle factory. Agriculture was partly collectivized, and rural landholders were dependent on a centralized bureaucracy that dictated how and what to produce and set prices for farm output. There were private companies, a few of them huge conglomerates, but they depended on the government.

In the fall of 1981, a Mexican professor who was also an economist for the Ministry of Planning and Budget, admonished students against trying to use economic analysis to understand Mexico. He said that the leading sectors of the economy were run by the government, completely distorting supply and demand. He contended that the Mexican economy was based on political influence and not economic laws, and had to be analyzed in terms of who has political favor.

In Mexico, the private sector retreated as the state expanded. Nationalization and the extension of rent-seeking destroyed wealth, prohibited economic competition, and ruined government finances. The money channeled through the system generated a false sense of prosperity, even while politicians were wielding it to expropriate and dislodge the most productive segments of society. Civil society was deadened as government privilege trampled the rights of individuals. Individual action was blocked by the government and government-awarded monopolies. Rent-seeking demolished the spirit of enterprise as people came to realize that their success depended on political connections and not on their own efforts.

By 1980, the central government directly controlled 37 percent of GDP.[3] When state and municipal government and the Mexico City subway system were taken into account, government must have accounted for over half of the nation's national product. The system was extremely expensive. Money-losing state enterprises absorbed tens of billions of dollars that could have been channeled into productive job-creating ventures or needed infrastructure. Mexican jurist Luis Pazos estimated that for every superfluous make-work government employee, two real jobs were lost due to the subsidies required to maintain that job.[4]

With so much in the hands of the state, the government became a vast rake-off operation in which the ruling party tried to deal a share to everyone who counted. Government resources were redistributed according to political favor. People obtained money for the wrong reasons—for political connections, not by being efficient in the use of resources and successful in serving consumers.

Public Choice analysis demonstrates that ambitious individuals in government benefit from modes of behavior that have a negative impact on society as a whole. This is easily seen in the behavior of state firms, which are political entities organized to maximize political benefits. They mainly do not operate on commercial principles, but on the political principle of providing patronage to supporters. They are a source of plum jobs and lucrative contracts for politically connected elites. State firms have no owners, but there is much property for the taking. Fierce competition develops to determine who will control the firm and its component parts, because with power comes property. With few effective controls and little accountability, the fortunate few who end up controlling the state firms by virtue of their proximity to political power are given a license to personally profit from their positions.

In Mexico, the dominant role of the PRI meant that political competition took place between groups and personalities within the party. Princeton University Professor Peter Smith conducted an in-depth study on the rise to prominence of 2,008 top Mexican government officials, the Mexican political elite, between 1946 and 1971. Smith found that nepotism and currying favor with superiors were the critical determinants of individual success.[5]

Presidential favor was key, since so many appointments were made by the president. The best method of advancement was to personally know or be related to a president. Barring this, political operatives aimed to attract the support and favor of political superiors, and eventually the president. One study showed that none of the high officials of Conasupo, the government agricultural supply monopoly, had obtained their positions without some sort of introduction or contacts. Of the mid-level administrators in Conasupo, 80 percent had gotten their jobs through personal connections.[6]

The Mexican economy was dominated by state companies whose officials faced incentives to decapitalize the firms they ran in order to pay off political favors and enrich themselves and their circle of intimates. Government-dependent unions in the state firms lobbied for high salaries and perks for their members, raising costs in the state sector, while they pushed for high taxes and burdensome regulations to hobble the private sector. Within the government, the modus operandi was "robar pero obrar," which means literally "steal but build." There was a culture of acceptance toward the institutionalized corruption. Somebody would say "PRI functionary so-and-so stole millions," while another person would reply, "Yes, but he built the municipal buildings and opened the local state-owned sugar mill."

In the early 1980s, at the height of the revenue flows from oil and foreign loans, the creed was shortened simply to "steal," as government payrolls exploded and projects were undertaken willy-nilly at the whim of officials. A few companies, such as Pemex, the state oil firm, made profits. The rest ran deficits and survived by means of transfers from lucrative areas such as oil, or foreign loans.

Some examples give the flavor of Mexico's government-run system. Mexico's nationalized oil industry showcases the perverse incentives inherent to government firms. Petróleos Mexicanos, or Pemex, was formed in 1938 after the expropriation of foreign oil companies. The PRI planned to foster industrialization of the country by channeling revenues from nationalized oil to other government enterprises in sectors deemed to be strategic.

From the start, there was a property problem in the company. It had no owner, and, therefore, no one could be held accountable. This was Mexico's potentially largest and most important industry, and it was critical that it make a profit. The problem was dealt with by turning over management of the company to the oil workers' union. It was understood that union leaders could effectively privatize Pemex, cutting themselves in for a large share of the profits, in return for keeping the workers in line and producing profits for the government.

The relationship between top politicians and Pemex union leaders was a symbiotic one. Pemex directors were invariably presidential cronies, and presidential appointees filled management positions. The government gave the union a 2 percent commission on every Pemex contract and the right to assign half of all Pemex contracts, which did not have to be opened to competitive bidding. In 1980, Pemex director Jorge Díaz Serrano conceded to union leaders property rights to the export of a grade of oil known as "slop." Private companies run by Pemex union leader Joaquín Hernandez Galicia, known as "La Quina," and senator Salvador Barragán Camacho, among others, earned $900,000 in an April 1983 sale of "slop" alone. Also in 1980, union leaders were granted purchasing rights to barium oxide, used in drilling oil wells. They obtained illicit earnings in excess of $95 million by creating a triangular trade through phantom enterprises that raised costs 45 percent above the real level.[7] Union leaders enjoyed many other perks and privileges and built their own business empires with diverted Pemex revenues. Union companies, in reality owned by La Quina and his top associates, landed up to 20 percent of all Pemex contracts in 1985.

Conflicts of interest abounded in Pemex. In the United States, even the appearance of conflict attracts a special prosecutor, but in Mexico public officials blithely let government contracts to their own companies. Pemex officials tailored specifications to advantage their own companies and those of their friends and relatives. Moreover, Pemex officials wore many hats. For example, senator Salvador Barragán Camacho was a PRI senator, a Pemex union leader, and the owner of a number of private companies both in and out of the oil business. The opportunities for personal enrichment inherent in his positions were virtually limitless. Pemex officials sat on government commissions and on joint public sector–private sector commissions. With ownership of Pemex technically still in state hands and no private competition allowed, Pemex officials faced strong incentives to decapitalize the enterprise to the extent tolerated by the political leadership, rather than to act like entrepreneurs and reinvest profits.

State firms are inherently irrational because they are based on political considerations, not economic ones. The only way Pemex could function and produce profits was through the property rights given to the union, but this meant that every transaction came to require a payoff, or tribute, exacted by the union.

Pemex union officials showed their gratitude for the private fiefdoms they built courtesy of the PRI by delivering revenues to the government for use in presidential schemes to extend state control over the economy, as well as delivering worker votes for PRI candidates. Pemex's oil served as collateral for much of the huge debt amassed by the government between 1970 and 1982. Pemex itself borrowed some $22 billion on behalf of the government between 1976 and 1981.[8] The importance of oil to the Mexican economy and the fact that PRI operatives depended on the union leadership for votes and revenues allowed a thug like La Quina, who took over leadership of the oil union in 1961, to amass a personal fortune and extend his influence over the entire country.

This use of Pemex was not in the best interests of society. Free from the pressures of competition, Pemex managers had few incentives to make the best use of resources and modernize equipment. The large-scale waste and theft of resources was a deadweight loss to society, and Pemex's monopoly blocked the emergence of real entrepreneurs who would have raised productivity in the petroleum sector.

Moreover, as the largest foreign exchange earner in the country, Pemex is arguably the single entity most responsible for entrenching rent-seeking in Mexico—outside of the political party that created it. Throughout the decades, all companies, whether state or private, that have endeavored to secure contracts from Pemex have been forced to pay bribes and kickbacks to company officials. The vast scale of Pemex operations helped to set the framework for transacting throughout the country.

By the early 1980s, over a third of the economy was in the hands of privileged elites in government monopolies. Billions of dollars were redistributed to build up state enterprises such as CFE, the state power company, Sidermex, the state steel company and its affiliates, the state railway company, and the conglomeration of agricultural enterprises including Conasupo, the state agricultural supply company, and Banrural, the agricultural development bank. These enterprises were hailed as the harbingers of Mexico's economic development. However, the investments were not guided by profitability, and costs were not controlled. Funds were diverted to private pockets and wasted on uneconomic projects.

Most countries that adopted the planning model sought to emulate the Soviet Union and develop heavy industry. Mexico was no exception. Mexican leaders were afflicted with Stalinist megalomania and built huge steel complexes and mines, regardless of cost and economic viability. They were undertaken for political reasons: to create jobs and social services in politically strategic areas and to magnify the egos of presidents. The World Bank and Inter-American Development

Bank went along with this mindset, claiming in the 1970s and 1980s that it was less important for projects they financed to earn an economic return than to impact the social sector.

By the early 1980s, the country was littered with expensive white elephants. Examples included the electric company's nuclear reactor at Laguna Verde, begun during the early 1970s. By 1986, its real cost in dollars was calculated to be ten times higher than originally projected.[9] The Las Truchas steelworks complex, recipient of $314 million in multilateral development bank loans[10] and completed in 1977, had overrun its cost estimates by half a billion dollars. The complex was poorly constructed and a prodigious user of electricity, which greatly increased costs.[11] In 1986, the state entity that owned the steelworks owed over $1 billion to foreign creditors. It was finally privatized in 1989. The state sugar industry, which ran fifty-two sugar mills, went bankrupt in the early 1980s.

The case of the national power company, CFE, demonstrates how there could be so much expenditure and so little to show for it. Throughout the 1970s and 1980s, the CFE spent billions of dollars in the name of building an integrated power system based on developing hydroelectric, geothermal, coal, and nuclear energy resources. CFE received $1.4 billion in World Bank loans between 1972 and 1990. In 1972, the World Bank celebrated its own role in building up CFE, noting that the World Bank had made its first power loan to the Mexican power company in 1949, and by 1972 the state enterprise was one of the World Bank's largest borrowers.[12]

Despite all the resources at its disposal, CFE could not make a profit and ran large deficits. In 1972, the Mexican power company relied on government subsidies and foreign loans totaling 10,479 million pesos. By 1978 its needs had risen sixfold, to 69,309 million pesos. That year, 75 percent of CFE expenditures were financed through government transfers and foreign loans. A year later, CFE's interest payments on its foreign debt alone were higher than its net income from energy sales.[13]

Like any other parastatal, the Mexican power company pursued political objectives and served political elites first and foremost. It was the government's policy to subsidize electricity prices with a view to fostering the growth of domestic industry. It was also the government's policy to use the company to serve the politically powerful and favored. Having the CFE install a power generator in one's home at taxpayer expense was considered a status symbol. President López Portillo had the CFE erect an electrical substation large enough to run a medium-sized town to power his mansion complex overlooking Mexico City.[14] With López Portillo's brother-in-law established as a senior manager at CFE, many friends and relatives of the president built luxurious homes using materials, labor, and vehicles provided by CFE, along with electricity service.[15]

Pemex and CFE were the rule, not the exception. The leading sectors of the economy were run as political, not economic, ventures. The bigger the state firms grew, the more inefficient and costly to society they became.

Government control of the economy was undergirded by Mexico's legal and regulatory system with its roots in the colonialist past. An interventionist mentality dating from the time of Spanish rule has persisted for centuries.

In Mexico, nothing flowed as freely as regulations, and the flow grew with the number of public officials. The bureaucrats in the government ministries and agencies, which were formed to oversee state property holdings, dictated regulations that served to entrench state and private monopolies, set wages and prices, and establish protectionist tariff barriers against imports in favor of domestic firms. The predictable result was production disruptions and higher costs for consumers. This was of little concern to the bureaucrats who administered the rules, however, since their interest lay in making the rules and regulations as complex as possible in order to extract higher bribes to overlook the rules.

The example of Conasupo, the agricultural supply company, illustrates how the burgeoning public sector, with its accompanying rules and regulations, served to undermine private property and markets in agriculture, all in the name of helping the poor. Created in 1965,[16] the stated aims of Conasupo were to guarantee farmers a decent income, provide low-income urban consumers with basic goods at reasonable prices, and handle the distribution and storage of agricultural products more efficiently than the private sector.

Conasupo was given both regulatory authority and authority to be an active participant in agricultural markets, a clear conflict of interest. Commonplace in the Mexican government, this was akin to granting the U.S. Securities and Exchange Commission the right to broker stock trades. The organizational interest lay in promulgating regulations that favored the expansion of Conasupo activities and the elimination of private sector competitors.

Conasupo set price guarantees for farmers on basic foodstuffs such as corn, wheat, sorghum, rice, and beans. It subsidized consumer prices for basic foodstuffs, selling them below market cost through a network of supermarkets mainly in urban areas. It had monopoly rights to import and export basic foodstuffs. Conasupo set up distribution networks, and built massive silos to warehouse products to prepare for times of shortages. As the organization expanded, it took on additional functions including transportation via a fleet of trucks that sported the Conasupo logo, financing, insurance, and agricultural extension and training. To further its goal of supplanting private intermediaries, Conasupo officials believed that they needed to provide ever more services to farmers. In the early 1980s, Conasupo even offered medical care. Fourteen subsidiary companies were created to oversee these expanded functions. No thought was given to the cost effectiveness of these activities, since Conasupo deficits were covered by the Mexican government.[17]

Over the years, most studies on the impact of its activities were undertaken by the organization itself. The organization measured its effectiveness in terms of inputs—the expansion of its activities—rather than evaluating the impact of these activities. Not surprisingly, Conasupo judged its efforts to be of benefit to farmers and consumers alike, and attributed problems to private "speculators." Conasupo invariably recommended expansion of its own activities.

As Conasupo's activities expanded, employment exploded within the state entity. Between 1971 and 1974 alone, the number of employees at Conasupo headquarters grew by 69 percent. The Conasupo budget quintupled for the five-year period ending in 1975, and grew to represent 5.4 percent of the entire federal budget. With the help of $2 billion in multilateral development bank loans to Mexican agriculture, Conasupo continued to grow even during the crisis-ridden 1980s. During the period 1981–1984, its expenditures grew an average 80 percent yearly, well above the rate of inflation.[18]

As Conasupo grew, Mexican agriculture declined. There were existing rigidities due to the *ejido* system of collective farms, but Conasupo played a large role in the demise of Mexican agriculture. The political goal of providing cheap basic foodstuffs to urban consumers gradually took precedence over elevating the incomes of farmers. Prices for many basic goods remained fixed in real terms for long periods, eroding farmer incomes. The real level of price support for farmers progressively deteriorated between 1965 and 1983.[19] The disincentives faced by farmers resulted in falling production of basic foodstuffs. In 1967, production was falling at an accelerated rate and, by 1970, Mexico imported more than 750,000 tons of corn.[20] In 1984, Conasupo imported more than eight million tons of foodstuffs that it had once exported, such as beans and rice.[21]

Conasupo's subsidized prices undercut private retailers of basic foodstuffs. For example, in 1984, packaged beans in Conasupo's 12,500 stores sold for 7 cents a pound, while private retailers sold the beans at 11 cents a pound. The private supermarkets were forced to buy the beans in bulk from Conasupo for the same price that the beans were sold in state markets.[22]

In a 1987 study on the economic impact of Conasupo, Mexican economist Oscar Vera Ferrer found that between 1970 and 1983 on average only 14.2 percent of the subsidy channeled through Conasupo actually reached the groups it was intended to benefit.[23] Most of it was spent on salaries or diverted to private accounts, while Conasupo regulations mainly benefited agency employees. Milk was often unavailable in Conasupo supermarkets at the controlled price of 20 cents per liter, because it was sold for higher prices by Conasupo truck drivers who saw an opportunity for profit.[24]

Perhaps the greatest cost of Conasupo is the wasted time and energy of farmers. With Conasupo as the largest single participant in the market for basic foodstuffs, farmers have spent more time and money reacting to and anticipating its policies and trying to influence Conasupo officials than in planning how best to produce and meet the needs of consumers.

Virtually every sector of the economy was subjected to the kind of minute regulation that served to undermine agricultural markets. Mexican laws, for example, divided the trucking industry into regional private monopolies, thereby outlawing independent truckers. Upstart entrepreneurs were hauled off to jail for trying to compete. Television broadcasting was reserved for the government and one private company, Televisa. This ensured mediocre programming and blocked many aspirants to television careers from competing.

Nafinsa, the National Finance Agency, has been a central component in Mexico's rent-seeking state. Nafinsa is the conduit of government funding to state firms and favored private firms. Founded in 1934, Nafinsa has channeled tens of billions of dollars for infrastructure development, agricultural and tourism projects, and promotion of government and private industry. Nafinsa has been by far the largest recipient of multilateral development bank loans in Mexico, having distributed over $9.8 billion in World Bank and Inter-American Development bank loans between 1970 and 1992.

A politicized agency from the beginning, Nafinsa operated and continues to operate in the 1990s according to political criteria. Like any other government agency, it has been rife with fraud and waste. In the 1980s, foreign private firms that wished to bid on multilateral development bank projects in Mexico were discouraged when they learned that the borrower was Nafinsa rather than a state company that actually carried out works. With another layer of bureaucracy in the distribution of the funds, there was no telling how much money would arrive at the implementing agency and be available for equipment purchases and consulting services.

The state firms were a shaky foundation on which to base an economy. In the 1970s and early 1980s, they accumulated debt at an astonishing pace. Between 1970 and 1984, Mexican state enterprises borrowed $9.4 billion from the World Bank and Inter-American Development Bank alone.[25] Total public sector debt, only $3.8 billion in 1970, grew to $72 billion in 1983.[26]

As the multiplying state firms displaced more efficient private firms, shoddy goods at high prices became the norm. The substandard output of one firm was the input of another, contributing to generalized decline. The public was forced to put up with telephones that did not work, undrinkable water, plodding rail service, and erratic mail delivery. To make matters worse, arrogant bureaucrats frustrated one's every attempt to get anything done. In Mexico, the most prominent firms were not those that best served consumers, but rather those that had a high place in the government hierarchy such as Pemex and the state electric company.

In an economy dominated by state firms, private firms were disconnected from the realities faced by firms in a market system. They did not have to please shareholders and accounting firms or underwrite their expansion with their own funds or costly borrowed capital. Efficiency was not essential to well-connected firms that could obtain subsidies and lucrative contracts from the government. The success of firms did not depend on product innovation or other types of innovation that make or break their counterparts in a market system such as technological innovation, managerial innovation, or marketing innovation. Rather, their success depended on their access to government officials.

Political decisions were more important to a private firm's operations than its own production. This was because with one stroke the government could alter the firm's environment. It could create a state monopoly to run the sector in which the firm operated and thereby force the firm out of business, or, alternatively, create a protected niche for the firm. The best connected firms in the country could rely on the personal friendships of their directors with political leaders and officials of the Secretariat for Commerce and Industry for access to government favors. Other firms had to organize to protect themselves. Putting the bureaucrats in charge meant that every transaction came to require a bribe and made guiding people through the bureaucratic maze the most useful business activity.

The contrast between a rent-seeking society and a market society is sharp. In a market society, profits are earned by businesses competing to serve consumers. The entire society benefits as the needs of consumers are served. The rent-seeking society, on the other hand, works well only for the powerful with government connections. The entire society is the loser as elites sew up existing opportunities for themselves, thereby blocking others from competing, and resources are drained in unproductive activities to influence the government.

Suppose you are a bona-fide entrepreneur in the Mexican system. You invest capital and labor to manufacture a good product and market it, and you do everything right to make the business a success. You took the risk and it paid off. What do you have? Your property rights are uncertain since you could be taxed or expropriated at the whim of government officials. There is no rule of law and no impartial contract law. The only way to resolve a dispute in your favor is to pay the higher bribe to public officials or hire an "enforcer" to physically intimidate the other party.

If yours is a small business, such as a mom-and-pop restaurant, you could probably evade close scrutiny by the authorities and most likely they would not think your establishment worth expropriating. But the government would not do anything to help you. Myriad regulations and taxes apply to your business and you must pay bribes to the officials who come knocking at your door demanding compliance or payment.

If you become a wealthy industrialist, look out. You are a sitting duck for expropriation and confiscatory taxes. You have sunk much capital into immovable assets and your wealth is there for all to see. It is not possible for you to operate without lobbying the government and colluding with officials. The personal risks of ignoring government power are simply too great.

Knowing these realities beforehand, you have little incentive to risk everything to create a successful business when it is uncertain whether you will be able to keep the profits earned. Taxation and regulation are arbitrary, and it is not possible to predict what laws will actually be enforced one or two years hence.

If you do decide to go ahead against all odds and try to build a successful business through hard work and market savvy, it is best to stay small to avoid too much official notice and to invest capital that is moveable. You could join thousands of others operating outside the regulated official economy in the underground economy. Your property rights would still be insecure and your taxation would consist of bribes. With little legal recourse, you try to insulate your business with trusted family members and friends.

Most business people reacted logically to the incentives of the system and devoted energy and resources to seeking protection and privileges from the government. In pre-1990 Mexico, private sector dependence on the government was symbolized by the National Confederation of Chambers of Commerce (the Concanaco) and the Confederation of Industrialists (the Concamin). These business associations, with obligatory membership for firms with over 500 pesos in capital, behaved as "autonomous public institutions" rather than as aggressive representatives of private interests. Their representatives served on numerous government commissions, such as the National Commission on the Minimum Wage, and the National Commission on Tariffs. Even informal market vendors joined the National Chamber of the Industry of Transformation, Canacintra, to gain visibility and influence with the government. These organizations were rarely openly critical of government policy. Rather, they worked behind closed doors to influence policy from the inside.[27]

Professional success in Mexico was more dependent on political skills and social skills than business acumen. Those who achieved prominence were successful "fixers," people who could maneuver around bureaucratic obstacles and get things done. It was important to be a good social host, to have the right people attend one's parties, and to mix and mingle to make sure that the event flowed smoothly and the important people were entertained. This is not to say that social and political skills are not useful to firms everywhere, but in a market economy they are not enough to determine success.

The business sector in Mexico was dominated by about a dozen investment groups known by the names of their leaders or dominant families. Groups such as those owned by Luis Legorreta, Raúl Baillerés, Emiliano Azcarraga, Luis Aguila, and the Garza Sada clan had complex webs of interest in finance, industry, the media, commerce, and real estate. The emergence of the strong state allowed these groups to achieve predominance and keep control of the firms within family dynasties. The collusion between business and government walled off the firms from competition and gave them access to government loans and subsidies.

With few exceptions, Mexico's business sector saw itself as a weak social group that required government protection. Until the 1970s, most business executives were content with the prevailing arrangement in which the government provided protected spheres of operation for privileged companies, and in return these executives provided revenues to the government and refrained from seeking public electoral office or positions within the government bureaucracy.

They enjoyed tariff protections on imports that averaged over 100 percent across-the-board in 1982, and obtained special import licenses that allowed them to obtain needed inputs duty-free. With the business sector generally facing high taxation and minutely regulated, the well-connected obtained special exemptions from specific taxes and regulations. Such privileges did not come cheaply, but were often in exchange for bribes and favors to officials or a muzzling of criticism.

Favored businesses could obtain loans from the National Finance agency, Nafinsa. The agency has funneled socialized credit to thousands of private companies. Often, it was an equity participant and came to own stock in many companies. As early as 1966, businessmen accused the Nafinsa of lending to companies owned by influential people simply because of their position. They cited the instance of Nafinsa's purchase of a failing airline from ex-president Miguel Alemán.[28]

Companies that borrowed from Nafinsa did not have to worry excessively about loan repayment. Since Nafinsa had been given the task of promoting the industries that the government saw as necessary to the country's development, it had a vested interest in those firms, both public and private, to which it had lent funds. Government-aided firms were under much less pressure than firms that had obtained credit from the private sector when they found themselves unable to repay loans. Such firms were naturally more inclined to take on a higher percentage of debt than non-aided firms. A 1966 study found that Nafinsa borrowers took on an average of 20 percent more debt than private firms without access to government loans.[29] Dependent on government loans, many Nafinsa borrowers found themselves in dire straits in the early 1980s when the crisis hit.

With political concerns paramount and the line between the state and private sector muddled, there was little accountability. Companies garnered easy profits and prospered greatly due to their protected position. Insulated from competition, they did not need to control costs or focus on quality. As in the state sector, the result was a proliferation of shoddy goods at high prices. With capitalism underdeveloped, stock markets were very rudimentary.

While they were dependent on the government, Mexican business executives were not utterly dominated by it. They had some recourse to unfavorable policies: they could withdraw their investment capital from the country or wait until the next change of administration. They had some advantages in their dealings with the Mexican government: businessmen were not subject to the six-year change in administration, and the stability in the upper reaches of the private sector allowed them to develop the expertise and technical skills to influence bureaucrats. Within the bureaucracy, turnover was so high that often if one bureaucrat was uncooperative, a firm only had to wait a year or so to deal with that person's successor.[30]

There was a downside for business in the high government turnover, however. Special licenses or permits, once granted, were easily revoked. Successor bureaucrats were not bound by the bribes that had convinced their predecessor. One Mexican businessman had this complaint:

> The price of containers, both metal and cardboard, is excessive in Mexico. In Mexico, metal containers for food cost approximately double their price in America. At one stage I was allowed to import cans in bond but the permit was not renewed and I had to fall back on the high-priced domestic article. ... Were the government to allow the import of Japanese sheeting the price of cans would be halved.[31]

Businessmen had to spend time and money cultivating contacts with many up-and-coming officials within every ministry who had power over their fate. It was advisable to attend as many government functions as possible and meet a wide circle of officials, since bureaucratic appointments did not depend on merit and technical qualifications, but on connections. Officials bounced back and forth between ministries, and their training usually had little to do with the position they held.[32]

Businessmen could exploit the fact that the government was not a monolith with cohesive, well-defined interests. Often, agencies viewed each other as rivals and were antagonistic. By the same token, the interests of private firms did not necessarily coincide either. For example, a special concession given to one firm, such as protection from imports of a certain product, was detrimental to another, which used the product as a production input. The government was often able to take advantage of the rivalries between private firms and thus divide and conquer.

Intermediaries or go-betweens were critical in rent-seeking Mexico. On May 5, 1982, the *Wall Street Journal* reported on the intermediary role that four Mexican business executives from Grupo Industrial Delta, S.A. had played in helping two U.S. firms, Crawford Enterprises and Ruston Gas Turbines, secure contracts worth $647 million to supply gas compression equipment to Pemex. The Delta executives received $45 million in fees for acting as a middleman, which was deposited in two personal Swiss bank accounts. Part of that sum (5 percent of the total contracts plus $200,000) covered kickbacks to Pemex officials. Probably due to the publicity the case received in the United States, the Mexican executives were arrested. They were not accused of bribery—a laughable charge in Mexico—but for evading taxes on the payment. The U.S. firms were hauled before the Justice Department, accused of violating the Foreign Corrupt Practices Act.[33] In Mexico, such transactions were commonplace and viewed as part of the cost of doing business.

Throughout the decades of growing state control over the economy, there were some independent businessmen. The strongest group was found in the city of Monterrey, near Mexico's border with Texas. In 1929, Monterrey industrialist Luis Sada founded the Confederation of Employers of Mexico, known as Coparmex, in order to organize employers to defend their interests against the highly militant labor movement.[34]

A private association, the Coparmex has been (for Mexico) an outspoken free-market critic of the government. It has been less influential than the public institutions dominating the private sector, in part because of its independent stance and also because of its nature as a private institution. A thorn in the side of various presidents, it adopted free-market principles and embraced individual liberties when these positions were anathema to mainstream thought in Mexico. Coparmex business executives early positioned themselves against growing state interference and in the 1970s launched attacks on President Echeverría's nationalization fervor.[35]

Mexico's *maquiladora*, or offshore assembly industry, has been another exception in rent-seeking Mexico. In 1961, Mexico began a Border Industrialization Program that gave rise to the thriving offshore assembly industry in the Mexican border states. A special regulatory arrangement has governed the plants. Mexico has allowed the temporary duty-free entry of components and raw materials for their assembly in Mexico and reexport as final products. The program has also allowed 100 percent foreign ownership of the Mexican subsidiary as well as exemption from export taxes. In some cases, firms could sell up to 20 percent of their production in Mexico. On the U.S. side, tariff regulations have permitted return of the U.S. component portion duty-free, taxing only the value added in Mexico. Foreign companies could choose between establishing a wholly owned facility, a joint venture with a Mexican firm, or a subcontracting arrangement.[36] With the passage of Nafta in November 1993, the special advantages of the offshore assembly industry were removed.

Relatively free of the extensive government controls prevailing in the rest of the economy, Mexico's *maquiladora* industry has been a phenomenal success. Between 1966 and 1989, the industry grew at an average rate of 23 percent annually in terms of the number of plants, from 12 in 1966 to 1,500 in 1989. The total number of employees in the industry grew from 3,000 in 1966 to an estimated 350,000 at the end of 1989. In 1990, the *maquiladora* industry contributed an estimated $2 billion to Mexico's economy and was the country's second largest source of foreign exchange earnings.[37]

The offshore assembly plants and the market-oriented border businesses were viewed as anomalies in Mexico's government-run economy. They were suspect because they were too close, both physically and in mindset, to the so-called U.S. imperialists.

In rent-seeking Mexico, leading private companies benefited from government favors, but with private property rights inherently insecure, their position was precarious. President Luis Echeverría (1970–1976), an avowed Marxist, set out to socialize the economy, and dislodge both foreign and domestic companies. Echeverría buttressed his agenda on the privileges reserved for the state in Mexico's Constitution.

By late 1972, Mexico's private sector was embattled and fighting for survival. Business executives broke with their tradition of behind-the-scenes maneuvering and used the December 1972 visit of Chilean President Salvador Allende to Mexico to launch a public counterattack. Eighty business associations in the northern border region and the central region published a proclamation in Mexico's national press the day of the Chilean president's arrival. In it, the businessmen stated that they would grudgingly accompany Dr. Allende in some protocol functions out of respect for the country he represented, but they avowed their respect for democratic principles. In a direct affront to President Echeverría, the businessmen applauded the Chilean people for "their extraordinary fight for these principles, defending themselves from the imposition of communizing socialism that threatens their traditionally free and democratic life."[38]

Over the next two years, the battle escalated. In 1973, labor leaders allied with the government blamed rising inflation on business-sector fraud and greed. The CTM, the largest labor union in the country, led by Fidel Velázquez, announced its intention to launch a general strike for October 1. The Minister of Labor backed the unions and applauded the "uniting of cause, ideology, the power of the labor movement, and the revolutionary current in the country."

There were many damaging strikes against private firms. President Echeverría backed the unions every time and applauded their attacks on private businesses. Business executives accused Echeverría of fomenting terrorism and violence in the country. After one particularly brutal strike in August 1974, in which 180,000 workers participated, shutting down many businesses, Echeverría refused to listen to the pleas of industrialists and instead announced his support for labor's absolute right to strike at any time. This emboldened labor leaders to harden their stance and call for "revolutionary strikes to change the economic and social structures of the country."[39] Business leaders contended that, with Echeverría's approval, leftwing radicals organized strikes in order to bankrupt private firms and make it easier for the state to take them over.

The September 17, 1973, assassination of Eugenio Garza Sada, a strong government critic and leader of the Monterrey industrialists, escalated the war of words. The official version blamed leftwing terrorists for the assassination, but the private sector blamed the Echeverría government. At the industrialist's funeral, which the president attended, Ricardo Margáin, president of the Consultative Council of Monterrey industrialists, blamed Garza Sada's death on the government-sponsored attacks on the private sector.[40]

Most business groups were not fighting for a free market economy, but for a return to the comfortable existence of earlier years, when they traded political acquiescence for government protection. They negotiated with the Echeverría Administration whenever possible, completing pacts that hiked wages more than prices. They never questioned the government's right to set wages, and they supported government control over petroleum, mining, and telecommunications as mandated in the Constitution. They recoiled in horror from Echeverría's threat to allow an avalanche of imports that would compete with Mexican-produced goods and bankrupt private firms.

Because of their relatively weak position, business leaders were unable to stop the government onslaught of 1970–1982. Still, the business community became more united in opposition, and some leaders entered politics despite government admonishments against it. By the mid-1970s there were signs that the business community was beginning to conclude that they would be better off if the government got out of their way. In 1975, they created the Business Coordinating Council, CCE. The Council issued a declaration of principles that elevated the individual over the state and stated that people ought not to be arbitrarily stopped from exercising their initiative and creativity in the production of goods and services.[41]

President López Portillo's 1982 nationalization of the banks was the last straw that completely severed the traditional relationship between business and government. López Portillo sought to blame the country's crisis on private bankers and businessmen, but the strategy backfired and the public instead blamed the government. The country rallied to the side of business, leaving the private sector in a good position to influence policy once it was clear that the government-run system had failed.

Mexico in Crisis

In Mexico, the outcome of the extension of the government-controlled system to its logical limits was generalized crisis, of which the debt crisis was the most visible symptom. The moral, social, and political fabric of the country unraveled along with the economy.

In rent-seeking Mexico, only corruption and poverty thrived while real economic activity stagnated. Economic growth rates in the 1970s masked growing inefficiency and skyrocketing costs. Mainly, they reflected the growth of government and the demand generated by its expansion. As the economy became dominated by rent-seeking, the hallmarks of the blocked society manifested themselves: shortages and bottlenecks, growing budget deficits, high inflation, high interest rates, a mushrooming foreign debt, a burgeoning underground economy, capital flight, and heightened instability. Interest rates were high because inflation was high. Elites themselves had no confidence in government policies and sent an estimated $60 billion out of the country during 1974–1982.

By 1981, it was apparent that the boom would soon turn to bust. The government's expenditures were based on the assumption of a 10 percent rise in oil prices and a 75 percent increase in export volume. President López Portillo believed that $31/barrel oil prices would last forever, but oil prices instead began to decline. Oil revenues came in significantly below projections, yet the government continued to spend as if nothing had changed. Some government economists counseled expenditure cuts, but the president refused to listen.[42]

As expectations of an imminent currency devaluation spread, dollar accounts swelled and capital stampeded out of the country. President López Portillo told Mexicans that under no circumstances would he devalue the currency, vowing to "defend the peso like a dog." Notwithstanding, in February 1982 the currency was devalued by 40 percent.[43]

Shock waves roiled through the Mexican economy and panic set in. The government initiated exchange controls to try to stop capital flight and decreed that dollar-denominated deposits would only be paid in pesos at a below-market rate. In a final act of desperation, the president nationalized the banks.

Mexico was on the skids. Hecklers interrupted the Mexican president's public appearances with loud barking. They called his Mexico City mansion, symbol of profligacy, the "dog house." Still the president refused to cut the budget in an election year, when the PRI traditionally cranks up spending to buy votes.

Inflation hit 60 percent and the budget deficit reached 17 percent of GDP, while oil prices continued to fall. Meanwhile, the U.S. Federal Reserve drastically tightened credit. Mexico had contracted much of its foreign debt at fixed interest rates, and the country had bet on relatively high U.S. inflation to cheapen its repayment obligations. Inflation in the United States declined, and the greater demand for, and reduced supply of, dollars in foreign exchange markets pushed the exchange value of the dollar sharply higher, further increasing the burden of Mexico's external debt.

In August 1982, Mexico announced that it could not pay its foreign debt. The announcement sent shock waves around the world. Looking back, Mexico's failure was as stunning as the collapse of Soviet communism, and, as with communism, the failure did not occur because of a lack of resources and ideological commitment. Mexico had taken the development planning model as far as possible. Nobody could accuse Mexican presidents of not being sufficiently socialist in their outlook, nor could it be said that they did not expend sufficient resources to try to make Mexico a development-planning success story.

They embraced the entire planning model. The anticapitalist, anti-U.S. rhetoric of Mexican presidents was notorious, and they lived up to it at every opportunity, while eagerly accepting foreign loans as Mexico's due from the "oppressor nation" to the North.

When outside revenue sources dried up and the government needed money to pay the foreign debt, an economy based on subsidies could not provide it. Mexico's blocked society was in its death throes. Officials looked around, and they saw that the only part of the economy that was still standing were the assembly plants along the border, which had unique relationships with U.S. businesses and operated free of excessive interference by the Mexican government. As with Gorbachev, it dawned on Mexican officials that they needed private firms to be productive and provide a tax base, but most private firms in Mexico were dependent on government handouts. That is why Mexican officials discarded ideology and began to change the system.

Foreign advisors were the last to admit that the rent-seeking system they had helped build lay in ruins. They argued that Mexico only faced a temporary liquidity crisis. Thus, the IMF and the World Bank designed "structural adjustment" programs that aimed to facilitate debt repayment in the short run but left the bloated state sector intact. While IMF agreements between borrower countries are never made public, typically the programs have entailed cutting government spending, raising taxes, slowing monetary growth, freezing wages and prices, and devaluing the currency. This mishmash of policies is designed to curtail consumption and expand export earnings. Thus, interest payments on the debt are made by forcing down living standards.

In the 1980s, many Mexicans found themselves in the position of enforced poverty in order to pay for the mistakes of development planners. Their heavily indebted government was hard-pressed to pay salaries of the bloated bureaucracy and printed money. The high inflation, together with the IMF austerity plans, hit the poor the hardest.

Mexicans suffered through the equivalent of the U.S. Great Depression, in part thanks to IMF ministrations. The crisis hurt those who lost their livelihoods and found their living standards greatly reduced, but it did force Mexico to begin to dismantle the government-run economy and lay the foundations for capitalism.

The Rent-Seeking Experience

Rent-seeking elites mastered the rhetoric about helping poor people, but in the postwar era their development plans and projects have had very little to do with the poor. Development assistance and the billions of dollars in commercial loans that were extended in support of planning were used to grease rent-seeking wheels. Development was something that was "done" to the poor by international bureaucrats and their well-heeled counterparts in Nafinsa and the other Mexico City bureaucracies.

In Mexico, the result has been projects that serve the needs of the politically connected, while ignoring and even worsening the plight of the poor. Projects such as hydroelectric plants, urban infrastructure plans and telecommunications have more often than not displaced the poor from their homes and wrecked the environment, forcing the uprooted and impoverished to face the indignity of living beneath power transmission lines that run above their shacks to connect to the nearest cities, or above water mains and sewerage lines that skip their communities to connect to the homes of the elite.

By the 1980s, the intended recipients of foreign loans began to conclude that they did not want the aid. Mexican community activist Gustavo Esteva viewed development as a "malignant myth":

> Around us, for a long time, development has been recognised as a threat. Most peasants are aware that development has undermined their subsistence on century-old diversified crops. Slum dwellers know that it has made their skills redundant and their education inadequate for the jobs that were created. If they do succeed in installing community life in the shanties they build or in the abandoned buildings, bulldozers and the police, both at the service of development, will relocate them. . . . If you live in Mexico City today you are either rich or numb if you fail to notice that development stinks.[44]

With political elites using their control over the state for their own private gain, the government apparatus was employed to widen the chasm between the politically connected haves and the have-nots. Mexican governing elites felt justified in enriching themselves at public expense, because it had always been this way. There was no concept of public service, and a government job had been viewed for centuries as an opportunity to build a fortune. In 1979, Mexican author and statesman Octavio Paz explained that in Mexico's patrimonialist state the president considers the state to be his own personal property, as did the Spanish kings. If the state belongs to the president, then certainly it belongs to his relatives and favorites as well. Government officials form a large political family, linked together by personal ties of family, friendship, regional origin, and political favors and by their willingness to use the state to improve their personal finances.[45]

Over decades of government expansion, for Mexican elites corruption was a right of office. Two generations of uninterrupted power had allowed PRI strongmen to entrench themselves in powerful positions and carve out personal fiefdoms in the public domain. Nationalist rhetoric served up a legal fiction of public ownership, but in fact powerful PRI operatives were the real owners of state property in Mexico. Other ruling parties have worried about "rocking the boat," but in Mexico the rule was "don't rock the trough."

Like European aristocrats of former times, Mexican elites built mansions, the modern equivalent of castles, and felt few qualms about enriching themselves from public coffers. For the most part, they did not wear the look of the guilty. Indeed, they did not regard themselves as wrongdoers. Plunder has always been the job of the Mexican ruling class.

Mexican politicians live like potentates. Ex-Mexican president José López Portillo (1976–1982) reportedly grabbed a fortune estimated at $1 to $3 billion during his tenure.[46] He built a luxurious, thirty-two-acre estate overlooking Mexico City, which one Mexican magazine termed a "walled medieval fortress overlooking the capital." While many of his countrymen lived in adobe or corrugated metal shacks, López Portillo and his family have bathrooms of marble and gold. Some floors are jade, and one is transparent, with a detailed model of the Acropolis visible through it. While president, López Portillo got the public works agency Banobras to spend $33 million on the access road, sewage, and water lines for his estate.[47]

José López Portillo's administration, flush with oil revenues and foreign loans, elevated rent-seeking to an art form. A joke circulating Mexico City shortly after the December 1982 inauguration of López Portillo's successor, Miguel De la Madrid, went as follows:

> A high government official opens up the country's coffers for the first time. Finding only 70,000 pesos, or about $466, he frantically telephones his predecessor. "There are only 70,000 pesos left," the official screams into the telephone. "What happened?" "I don't know," replies the former bureaucrat. "We must have forgotten them."

Miguel De la Madrid began an anti-corruption drive in 1982, and the Mexican public began to be informed of the extent of the corruption. De la Madrid accused Jorge Díaz Serrano, a former director of Pemex under López Portillo, of diverting more than $4 billion in oil revenues during 1979 alone. Díaz Serrano was unable to account for more than 300 million barrels of oil between 1976 and 1982.

At least part of the diverted funds went to maintain thousands of "aviadores," or "fliers," ghost workers who swooped in on paydays to collect paychecks. Under Díaz Serrano's tenure, there may have been one million ghost workers who made a gilded living collecting paychecks. In all likelihood, the former Pemex director caved in to pressures from the union and the PRI political leadership to hire ghost workers as payoffs for political favors. At the time, many said Díaz Serrano was a scapegoat for other corrupt high officials, including La Quina and former Mexican president José López Portillo.[48]

Another case was that of Arturo Durazo Moreno, police chief of Mexico City from 1976 to 1982, who allegedly amassed a personal fortune of $500 million. He built a palatial house with a discotheque, race track, firing range, swimming pool, twenty-three-car garage, stables, and Roman-style sculptures nestled amid landscaped gardens, man-made lakes, and fountains. Neighbors called another of his homes, a vacation house overlooking the Pacific Ocean, "the Parthenon." Durazo fled Mexico in 1982 and was arrested by FBI agents in Puerto Rico in 1984. He was extradited to Mexico in 1986 on charges of extortion and illegally stockpiling weapons.[49]

According to the Mexican press, some of the worst offenders were López Portillo's friends and relatives. Partly at the expense of the national electric company, Refugio de Martínez Vara, the president's sister, built a luxurious house in the prosperous Mexico City suburb of Coyoacán, and a weekend estate near the resort city of Cuernavaca. Her son, Roberto Martínez Vara, head of the National Sugar Industry Commission, built a 16,000 square-meter home close to his mother's weekend estate. Before these homes were built, there was no electricity service in the area, but when they were ready, the CFE immediately arrived and connected the houses to the power grid. Another López Portillo nephew, Adolfo Martínez Vara, who managed advertising accounts for CFE and other public enterprises, also built himself a luxurious home overlooking Mexico City.

In the Mexican government, even legally sanctioned privileges were princely. For example, in 1977, the government circulated a memo that reduced automobile privileges in the ministries and state enterprises.

The following remained after the cutback:

- Secretaries (top officials) had a right to six vehicles and an unlimited supply of gasoline.
- Undersecretaries and senior managers had the right to four vehicles, also with unlimited gasoline.
- Treasurers, attorneys, and directors-in-chief enjoyed two vehicles supplied with 800 liters of gasoline per month.
- Executive assistants, advisors, directors, and deputy directors along with officials of comparable level, were given one vehicle with 400 liters of gasoline per month.[50]

Rapacious officials have been the rule rather than the exception. North Americans living in Mexico tend to gravitate to elites, because superficially they seem most like middle-class Americans. But the reality is quite different as the following typical story of one well-connected family shows.

The father was a high-ranking military official. Through his position in the PRI, he came to be the real owner of a city block of commercial shops in a prime location. His properties included jewelry shops, clothing boutiques, and supermarkets. The deeds were held by the state, though everyone knew that was a mere formality. Their home was a pleasant, though not opulent, two-story concrete dwelling in a prosperous suburb north of the capital. They had one or two servants.

His wife was a beautiful woman known far and wide for her culinary skills. There were no limits, budgetary or otherwise, on the dishes she prepared. Only the best ingredients, accompanied by the best and rarest champagnes and aged tequilas, were served at her table.

The home was relatively modest, but the family lived lavishly. There were four daughters, ages twelve to eighteen, and they had everything they could possibly want. The young women enjoyed shopping sprees in expensive boutiques in the fashionable Pink Zone where they bought Gucci bags and shoes, $1,000 dresses, and expensive makeup as if they were buying candy.

The family sometimes took guests along with friends and relatives on spur-of-the-moment trips to Acapulco, where they stayed in elegant hotels and spared no expense in having a good time. One evening's dinner bill totalled $10,000.

The eldest daughter's boyfriend owned a computer firm that enjoyed a government-protected market. It provided him, in his words, with more money than he could possibly spend in a lifetime.

Mexican elites such as these were part of a system that indulged their appetites. Even the relatively small fish lived like millionaires. An economist for the Mexico City government lived on a dirt road in the outskirts of Mexico City, where chickens kept by the neighbors roamed freely. His extensive walled-off grounds, however, contained a private zoo stocked with hundreds of birds, a lion, a tiger, and many other animals that the official had bought on his countless world travels. The house was no less extraordinary. Snakes were this official's particular passion, and a snake room was devoted to the writhing creatures, with snakeskins scattered throughout the house and incorporated into the lavish decor. Each room was decorated in the style of a country or region the owner had visited. The Asia room contained a solid gold throne perched amid silk and satin brocades.

Like the others, the economist considered it his right to use his position to enrich himself. He compared himself to his friends and colleagues in government who had equally extraordinary homes and traveled as much as he did. He competed with them in a game of one-upmanship to provision his estate with luxuries.

There was not much left for the poor after elites provisioned themselves with mansions, ski chalets in Colorado, $10,000 dinners, and legions of racing cars. In general, Mexico's working classes, like those in other Latin American countries, were impoverished.

Contrast the home of a family of four in a working-class neighborhood in Mexico City with that of Mexican elites. In a nondescript low-slung concrete building, attached to a row of similar buildings, one entered a dingy alleyway and passed a row of apartment doors. The door opened to the living room, where the eye was drawn to the cracked plaster that the family tried to hide with wall coverings. The concrete floor was softened by a few thin cotton rugs. A sofa and a couple of chairs draped with faded fabrics to hide tears furnished the living room, while a spare wooden table and four chairs completed the dining room. The only window in the whole apartment was in the galley-sized kitchen. Two small bedrooms furnished with plain-looking beds and nondescript bureaus were framed by bare white walls and more cracked plaster covered here and there with religious prints and rosary beads. A bathroom completed the picture. The mother's pride and joy was her set of matched dishware for eight purchased years earlier in the fashionable Polanco shopping district.[51]

Mexico's politicized system deeply impacted people's attitudes. Taught to hate capitalism, they viewed the private sector as the oppressor class and looked down on money-grubbing business people. The desire to succeed, to provide for one's family, was viewed as merely selfishness. There was an emphasis on couching one's own ambitions in terms of the collective good. Refined listeners would draw back in horror as a foreigner explained plans to open an import-export business and make a million dollars.

Conformity was prized and creativity, almost suspect, was quashed. Those who distinguished themselves in some individualistic way met with the envy and resentment of their neighbors. One achieved social acceptance by parroting the PRI line on Mexican politics and history. Dissenting views were not tolerated. Independent thought was dangerous to one's success.

The majority of the population felt a sense of powerlessness to change things. Their rulers had been appointed from above, and they could do nothing about oppressive local leaders. Many people accepted their poverty with fatalistic resignation, not believing that they could improve their lot through their own efforts.

There was no room in official society for economic entrepreneurs, and they were consigned to operate outside the law in the black market. Suspect individuals in a conformist society, most people thought that that was where they belonged, if not run out of the country altogether.

Name-dropping was a national obsession. Anyone who had any connections to boast of would give a resume of his or her family tree at the slightest provocation. All past and present prominent relatives, especially in government, would be mentioned, followed by any prominent friends and acquaintances. The speaker with the most contacts expected listeners to acknowledge his or her superior social status. Then the conversation would often turn to the personality quirks of ruling officials and what made them tick or how they could be influenced.

During the heyday of Mexico's blocked society, another deeply embedded view was that of Mexico as a victimized country. Mexicans thought that they could do nothing to better themselves, because the United States conspired against them. The saying went, "Poor Mexico, so far from God and so close to the United States."

At the same time, Mexicans were taught that they were somehow the morally superior nation in order to assuage their wounded pride over sharing a 2,000-mile border with the prosperous United States. This had an odd impact on people's minds. Young Mexicans would often end debates with foreigners with the words "Soy Mexicano!" (I am Mexican!), as if the mere fact of their nationality made their view automatically correct or morally superior.

Mexico's cultural milieu did not encourage the ideas conducive to success, but instead implanted a culture of poverty. A society closed to the outside world wrought a closed-minded population. There was a fear of contamination by foreign ideas and cultures, even while people eagerly snapped up foreign-made products.

Perhaps the most pernicious result of the expansion of the rent-seeking system to its logical limits was that it forced people into sleazy patterns of behavior harmful to their pride and self-esteem. Their creativity was diverted into paying bribes and avoiding shakedowns or, as the case may be, avoiding bribes and conducting shakedowns. The system attacked the soul. Honesty, integrity, and hard work were penalized in Mexico, while antisocial behavior—lying, cheating, and thievery— was rewarded. When the De la Madrid administration loosened control of the press, the picture that emerged from reports by leading Mexican news magazines such as *Proceso* and even the government's mouthpiece, the daily *Excelsior*, was of a country that had been utterly corrupted by the government and the party that ran it, the PRI.

With the PRI controlling allocation of jobs, medical care, housing, pensions, and even the acquisition of a simple driver's license, it was a matter of supreme importance to stay on the good side of political officials. With so much power in so few hands, government services were turned into commodities that were put up for sale. Not even standard permits could be obtained without bribery, extortion, or personal connections.

The corruption of life went far beyond the economic and touched virtually every Mexican institution. Most sectors of Mexican society were either coopted or coerced into the system. For example, Mexican universities were politicized, and academics were not allowed to step over boundaries set by political operatives in criticizing the government. Pseudo-students, really young thugs paid by the PRI apparatus, frequented classes to make sure that professors towed the line. Those who did not found their classes disrupted by the KGB-like "students" and sometimes were assaulted and arrested. At minimum, their careers suffered. Journalists received pay envelopes from the government in return for favorable coverage, and newspapers were kept dependent on the government for their newsprint.

Reminiscent of the KGB special section of Soviet enterprises, Mexican state enterprises and ministries had employees whose only function was to ensure that workers supported the PRI and intimidate those who did not. These PRI goons corralled workers for PRI rallies and strongarmed them to vote for PRI candidates. As in the Soviet Union, those who resisted participating in PRI activities were branded dissidents and found themselves out of a job or sometimes thrown in jail.

Even elementary and secondary education were perverted to serve the objectives of the ruling party. Like the Soviet communists, the Mexican revolutionaries rewrote history to glorify the PRI, and students were taught to confuse patriotism and even the Mexican flag with the PRI. The Mexican military, the judicial system, and the police were corrupted by the rent-seeking culture.

There were few institutions that effectively operated as a counterweight to the PRI. The Catholic Church, historically strong in Mexico, was barely allowed to exist, permitted only a tenuous position by the Mexican Constitution. The PAN, composed of independent-minded business people along the U.S. border, was the only effective opposition the PRI had prior to the appearance of the leftwing PRI breakaway faction in 1987.

Another consequence of the corruption spawned by rent-seeking was the emergence of powerful thugs who profited from the incentives. Ruthless political manipulators were best able to navigate the irrational system. It was true of the Soviet Union, and it was true of rent-seeking Mexico. Joaquín Hernandez Galicia, "La Quina," was no aberration but the very model of success, having made his fortune through political connections and bribes. The consequences for making political wheeling and dealing the most rewarding activity are severe. When administrative corruption begins at the top, it spreads its tentacles throughout all of society, resulting in moral decline and the rise of the unscrupulous. Ecuadorean vice-presidential candidate Alberto Dahik put it succinctly: "If the minister himself steals, the undersecretaries will commit assaults and the departmental directors will engage in theft, extortion, robbery, and murder. When the perception is that corruption begins at the top, everything falls into decay."[52]

When the government steals, banditry flourishes. In Mexico's politicized society, those favored with power became a law unto themselves, enjoying feudal domination over the segment of the state that they ran, whether a state company, agency, or regional or local government. Serious crimes have been committed with impunity, and some gained so much power that they surrounded themselves with private armies and could only be reined in by force. In the 1990s, diehard adherents to the old ways are known as "PRI dinosaurs."

This way of life has roots back to Spanish colonial times. The Spanish appointed native "caciques" to govern the countryside in tandem with local authorities. As long as the caciques controlled their charges, extracted tribute, and kept them subservient to colonial rule, the authorities often gave them wide leeway in their methods.

Toribio "El Toro" Gargallo was a modern-day cacique. A staunch member of the PRI, he imposed a twenty-year reign of terror on the small towns and villages that he ran in the western part of the state of Veracruz. He was a friend to the region's powerful, the mayors, the judicial police commander, and local bureaucrats and politicians. He was best man at the judicial police commander's wedding. When his friends needed him, he was there. He supplied arms to the State Judicial Police in his region and money when the mayor of Cordoba ran short.[53]

Gargallo mounted robberies and extorted money from sugar-cane growers. He forced peasants to sell their plots to him; if they refused, they disappeared and he ended up owning their plots. In a sort of feudal tribute, Gargallo extracted from each farmer in San Pablo Ojo de Agua a portion of his annual sugar-cane crop. Cane farmers were afraid to complain because it was said that he had bought off all of the local authorities.[54]

By the 1980s, Gargallo was considered one of the three legendary caciques in Veracruz state. He had accumulated 7,000 acres of sugar-cane fields and houses in Cordoba, the neighboring mountain resort of Fortin, and Omealca, the regional market town. He traveled in heavy cars with smoked windows, escorted by pickup trucks bearing bodyguards armed with rifles. He killed his opponents with impunity, slaughtering cane union organizers, peasants, and other local residents who dared to cross him.[55]

In an interview with the Mexican weekly *Proceso* a few years before his death, Gargallo openly admitted that he had killed a number of people but also declared that he never had trouble with the authorities. "On the contrary," he said, "I collaborate with the government. I am the friend of police chiefs and military leaders. A lot of times they ask me for favors."[56]

Gargallo's reign finally drew to a close when reformers rose to power in the national leadership who could no longer stomach the old order. In 1986, Governor Fernando Gutierrez, later Salinas's interior minister, declared war on the rule of the gun and the sort of extralegal authority wielded by Gargallo. Arrogantly ignoring the warnings and the changing political clime, Gargallo and his thugs murdered three cane-cutter organizers. It was the final straw. On October 10, police vehicles were deployed in ambush on either side of the main federal highway near Gargallo's estate. When he drove up in a pickup truck, he was killed by more than a dozen rounds. Four of his gunmen were also killed.[57]

This story illustrates that when government becomes too large, it effectively holds people for ransom, taking their property hostage with extorted bribes, confiscatory taxes, inflation, unpredictable regulations, and outright nationalization. With government officials shaking down individuals for payments, it is no wonder that groups outside the government get the same idea. Thuggery is the natural consequence of such a system, and when thugs run things the fundamental bonds of society are broken. Dishonesty reigns as lying, cheating, stealing, and intimidation become a way of life. The population's trust in society's institutions is destroyed, and people are forced to rely on bribes and protection money.

In Mexico, corruption and criminality eroded the government's authority. People ceased to differentiate between the government's depredations and that of bandit gangs. One Mexican explained her countrymen's indifference to drug traffickers as follows, "there is no law, the authorities have no morality."

Legal Basis of the Blocked Society

Mexico's blocked society was in part a product of the Mexican Constitution and legal system, which abrogated the rights of individuals in favor of state power. Industries and activities that were viewed as "strategic" were reserved for the state. From the outset, the 1917 Constitution specified state ownership of all exploitable minerals, including oil and all hydrocarbons, precious metals and stones, and minerals for industrial use. It made the government the original owner of all land and water and set the conditions under which the government could cede control to private parties. Telecommunications were expressly reserved for the government.

In agriculture, the Mexican Constitution established a communal landholding system known as the *ejido*. Private property was confiscated and redistributed in small holdings to the rural poor. However, the property rights of the new owners were as insecure as those of the former owners. Ownership rights to the *ejidos* were unclear, and "owners" were prohibited from selling their holdings.

From the first, the Constitution was hostile to private property and private firms, whether domestic or foreign. Private businesses are saddled with responsibilities unrelated to their operations, such as providing affordable housing for workers, schools, clinics, and other public services. At the same time, the sphere of operations of private firms is severely circumscribed, and their activities are closely monitored by the central government. The Mexican Constitution disallows individuals from owning more property than is absolutely necessary for running their legally sanctioned businesses, and, until 1992, under no circumstances could businesses own rural land, which was reserved for the communal *ejidos*.

Of all the constitutional clauses hostile to private property, business people are probably most opposed to Article 123, which regulates labor and social security in detail. They have tried unsuccessfully to have it retracted. It contains a long list of generous worker benefits that all employers must provide. The government imposed requirements on Mexico's weakened private sector akin to those of a rich European welfare state. Some of the more generous benefits include double-time pay for overtime work and a minimum of twenty days vacation per year for all workers. Profit-sharing is obligatory. The laws are enforced by tripartite commissions between labor, business, and government.

All of this is overseen by a centralized government in which the Executive is given many powers to run the economy. The Constitution grants the president the authority to run the state monopolies and allocate property to private individuals, deciding how much is to be owned by whom. Until 1974, the president had the right to appoint governors of the states, and as the 1990s began he still had wide powers to appoint and remove federal government employees.

Until 1983, successive presidents amended the Constitution to make it even more hostile to private property. Electricity generation, nuclear energy, and banking were added as state monopolies. In 1974, Article 131 was amended to give the president the power to set import-export tariffs, to tax products in transit through Mexican territory, and to regulate and prohibit the circulation of every kind of good of whatever origination. The Executive was given these vast powers for the purpose of "regulating foreign trade, the nation's economy, the stability of national production, or whatever other purpose for the benefit of the country."

The Mexican Commercial Code (1974 edition) is equally harsh on private firms. The laws mainly serve to stimulate business for bureaucratic intermediaries, a fact all but acknowledged in the Code itself. The laws governing bureaucratic intermediaries are expounded immediately after the sections outlining general business regulations. Fifteen articles of the Commercial Code deal with registering a business alone, and the code specifies that the services of a bureaucratic go-between are necessary to accomplish the transaction.[58] At the close of the Salinas Administration, major overhaul of the commercial code remained to be done.

In Mexico, with most property rights in the hands of the president, the economic system has functioned akin to a six-year rotating monarchy. Property rights have been insecure because they did not depend on law but on the whim of the president. For example, in the 1950s and 1960s, presidents delegated rights to develop resources to private firms. Firms were provided protected markets in return for sharing revenues with the government. Things changed between 1970 and 1982, when Mexican presidents undertook an ideological crusade to expand the state sector, based on the broad government powers enshrined in the Constitution.

During his tenure, President Salinas made several important changes to the Constitution to help undergird market-oriented reform. In 1992, he amended the Constitution to allow private companies to own and develop rural land for agricultural purposes. Firms were limited to owning not more than 2,500 hectares, but it was a step that introduced competition into the state-run system. Foreign investment began to be allowed in agriculture.

Salinas also eliminated banking as a strategic sector of the economy, providing the legal framework for bank privatization. A 1993 amendment gave the Central Bank independence.

Apart from these few changes, however, the antimarket bias of the Mexican Constitution survives intact. The Salinas Administration changed the system without giving the reforms a firm legal basis. With opposition often intense, it was probably the only way that thorough-going change could be implemented. Still, the danger lurks that future presidents could cite constitutional articles in order to provide a justification for rebuilding the interventionist state.

In the mid-1990s, constitutional reform is needed to bring the legal system in line with the emphasis on private sector economic development. The government still has too much power over property. The following reforms would provide the legal basis for the market economy, thereby helping to cement the transformation.

Provisions in Article 25 that give the state responsibility for overseeing national development should be eliminated. Article 26, which calls for national economic planning, should be repealed. Article 27 should be further amended to allow the privatization of the ejidos and remove the remaining restrictions on land ownership. Provisions in

Article 28 that reserve for the state the right to manage strategic areas of the economy should be revoked, and the presidential right to allocate property rights should be rescinded.

Article 123, stipulating exceedingly generous worker benefits to be provided by all employers, should be repealed or, at a minimum, amended to give flexibility to accomodate local conditions and the financial capabilities of individual companies. The provisions assigning firms public responsibilities and limiting their accumulation of property should be stricken.[59]

Finally, a clause should be inserted into the Mexican Constitution guaranteeing the presumption of innocence. A climate of judicial abuses and false denunciations has resulted from its absence.

Further economic reforms remain for President Zedillo. Salinas's economic program has transformed the basis of the Mexican economy from a rent-seeking into a profit-seeking society. Yet, while rent-seeking has been greatly reduced in Mexico, much remains.

Several huge state firms are still in government hands. Pemex, CFE, Conasupo, and Nafinsa continue to survive through government subsidies, bond issues in the international capital markets, and multilateral development bank loans. The World Bank and Inter-American Development Bank are still propping up these state firms with billions of dollars in loans. Of the four firms, only Conasupo is actively undergoing divestment, while some Pemex secondary petrochemicals firms are slated to be sold.

Corruption, though declining, is still prevalent partly because of the continued existence of Pemex and the other huge state companies. CFE is still running outrageous deficits; one subsidiary alone registered an $800 million shortfall in 1992.[60] Privatization of Pemex assets alone would bring in over $100 billion for the government.[61] Interest rates would fall dramatically as the public sector borrowing requirement was drastically reduced, thereby helping to stimulate business expansion.

Tax rates should be further reduced. Lower taxation would stimulate the economy and enable all Mexicans to enjoy the fruits of the country's new prosperity. Moreover, reducing revenues in government hands helps to change the culture by reducing the size and scope of rent-seeking activity. As long as large state-run companies continue to exist, the rent-seeking culture will retain a foothold.

Although much remains to be done, the reforms are likely to stick despite the instability injected into the system by the Chiapas rebellion, the assassination of presidential candidate Luis Donaldo Colosio, and the peso crisis. President Salinas expressed confidence that his successor would not change the economy policy, because "no one will want to go back to what we had."[62]

Brazil, Peru, and Argentina

Inspired partly by their own traditions and partly by Western insistence on development planning, Latin American countries followed a statist development approach. Four hundred fifty billion dollars in development assistance financed the growth of the unproductive rent-seeking institutions in Latin American societies. The aid did not help open markets or lower transaction costs—quite the opposite. Western loans, both government-to-government and commercial, financed the growth of bureaucracy at the expense of the market economy. With the aid contingent on the countries' adoption of a national development plan, planning ministries sprouted in the posh districts of Latin American capitals.

Over the decades, bureaucratic employment exploded as government entities competed for foreign loans. Mexico may have topped the list for the largest number of state companies, but in 1992 Brazil had over 500 state companies and Peru at least 270. In March 1992, Peruvian finance minister Carlos Boloña estimated that there were almost 1.2 million public employees in Peru, and that one out of every six workers labored for the state.[63] In Argentina, in 1988, there were almost two million bureaucrats out of a working population of 11.5 million.[64]

The World Bank, IMF, Inter-American Development Bank, and other multilateral and bilateral aid agencies contributed to the bureaucratization of Latin America. In the 1980s, the similarities between the economic bureaucracies of the different countries were striking: Peru's PescaPeru (Peruvian state fishing company) and Banpesca in Mexico (the Mexican fishing development bank); Chile's Sendos (national sewerage company) and Peru's Sedapal (the Peruvian equivalent), Brazil's Eletrobras (national electricity company), and Peru's ElectroPeru (the Peruvian national electricity company). All these state companies had one thing in common: a hunger for multilateral development bank loans. Each state company had staffs appointed as liaisons to the multilateral development institutions and departments entirely dedicated to working on projects financed by the multilateral development institutions.

This activity did not lead to sustainable economic development.

Instead, as in Mexico, the expansion of the state wreaked havoc on private property rights as governments confiscated private property to make way for state-supported ventures and loaded the productive sector with heavy burdens of high taxes, high inflation, and repressive regulation. Transaction costs rose as every transaction came to require bribes of public officials who had carved out personal fiefdoms. Entrepreneurial individuals were attracted by rent-seeking opportunities or found themselves relegated to the black market.

Economic life took on aspects of the surreal. Since bureaucrats cannot possess the information required to make informed investment decisions, bribery everywhere emerged as the most efficient way to allocate government resources. As in Mexico, channeling foreign largesse through patronage-ridden, unaccountable governments served to institutionalize corruption. It made political elites into an aristocracy similar to the communist "new class" that Milovan Djilas described in his classic book.

In Latin America, government officials, politicians, labor leaders, business people, and lawyers number among the rent-seekers who have used politics to carve a generous slice of the economy for themselves. The rent-seeking class blocked the rise of profit-seeking capitalists. The rapacity was always draped in platitudes about the "national interest," and many ghost projects, funded in the name of the poor, provided "public servants" with a luxurious lifestyle.

South American elites, like their Mexican counterparts, provisioned themselves with palatial estates, private zoos, multimillion dollar collections of classic cars, and fat Swiss-bank accounts. Not since those ancient, heady days when the officers of the Spanish monarchy plundered the treasure at Potosí and the mines of New Spain had government officials so freely converted vast public resources to their own use.

Brazil is still dominated by the interventionist state. Echoing Mexico's Octavio Paz, Brazilian diplomat José Osvaldo de Meira Penna observed that in his country the government "is owned by a 'New Class' or a *Nomenklatura*, which is incapable of differentiating what is public and what is strictly their private patrimony." The *Nomenklatura* are the politicians and bureaucrats who rule the country, some seven or eight million officials and their families who have their hooks into the economy.[65]

Brazilians rage against these governing "maharajahs," who carve out kingly privileges for themselves and enjoy phenomenal incomes at the expense of society. While many working-class Brazilians cannot even afford to rent a cardboard and tin shack in the slums known as "favelas," members of the government class enjoy mansions with marble flooring and heated pools.

With numerous perks and privileges known as "mordomias," Brazil's political elites have no reason to envy their Mexican counterparts. Functionaries receive their regular salary plus bonuses and additional compensation, which can bring their total compensation to over $5,000 per month, a vast sum in a country where the per capita annual income is $2,100. State-run country clubs cater to their every whim, and luxurious cars are at their disposal.

As in Mexico, "phantom" government employees show up only on pay days to collect their checks. In April 1991, the news magazine *Veja* reported that maharajah Antonio Rogerio Magri, minister of labor and social welfare, received a regular monthly salary of $4,000, plus another $4,000 monthly from the São Paulo state electric company Eletropaulo. Although he had left Eletropaulo fourteen years earlier, he not only continued on the payroll, but his career at the electric company had advanced five grades![66]

With everyone intent on carving out a piece of the state for themselves, in present-day Brazil the layers of bureaucracy and the in-bred network of go-betweens are so dense and impenetrable that legally appropriated government funds do not reach their destination unless the designated recipients, including government departments, pay bribes. Seplan, the Brazilian Ministry of Planning, has received substantial funding from the multilateral development banks, including a $29 million World Bank loan approved in 1986 for the purpose of "institutional strengthening." Yet, in 1988, Luiz Magnabosco, mayor of Sacramento in Minas Gerais state, told the newspaper *O Estado de São Paulo* that only those who hired consulting firms to "assist" in the process received their appropriated funds from Seplan.[67] Similarly, Gumercindo Domingos, mayor of a city in the São Paulo area, said that in order to obtain 900,000 cruzeiros legally approved for the expansion of a school by the Ministry of Education and Culture, the city had to pay a "middleman" a 20 percent commission to pry loose the appropriated funds.[68] In February 1988, former Brazilian finance minister Francisco Dornelles said that the disbursement of federal funds "facilitates influence peddling and corruption."

Brazilian senators and representatives treat the federal budget like their own bank account, using federal funds to pay for exclusive private schooling for their children. The *Jornal da Tarde* reported in March 1991 that almost a fifth of the budget of the National Social

Service Council, a welfare agency created to aid the poor, is spent for tuition of the legislators' children and children of their friends and relatives. The rest of the welfare budget supports a plethora of nonprofit organizations run by members of congress themselves or their relatives and friends. For example, the *Jornal da Tarde* reported that the Eva Candido Institute for Political and Social Development, named for the daughter of Delegate Raquel Candido of Rondonia state, functions as the congresswoman's campaign headquarters.

In October 1993, a vast corruption scheme came to light involving congressional deputies, six ministers and three governors. The scheme worked as follows: congressional deputies would propose appropriations for ghost public works projects and ghost agencies. The ghost proposals would be coordinated within the Congress and presented to the budget director, who would prepare them for approval by the Ministry of Education or the Ministry of Social Action. On approval, the representatives, their campaigns, and supporters would be issued the money, and the budget director and ministers would receive a kickback.

In Peru, where the rent-seeking society is beginning to retreat, public officials likewise have treated the national budget like their own bank account. Critics on the left and right decry the "immorality" of government spending. In June 1991, the Peruvian newspaper *El Comercio* reported that over the past two decades, tens of billions of dollars in public monies have disappeared without a trace.[69] Former Peruvian president Alan Garcia (1985–1990) himself was accused of spiriting $50 million out of the country through the scandal-ridden Bank of Credit and Commerce International.

In June 1991, Peruvian Senator Daniel Bocanegra, president of the Joint Review Committee of General Accounts, told *El Comercio* that it was impossible to audit public agencies. Half do not prepare financial statements, and others produce incomplete or unreliable documents. The National Customs Superintendency, for example, prepared only a statement of expenditures, but not of revenues.

The Review Committee faced an enormous task in attempting to bring the state sector to account, because of the "resistance on the part of state entities to the fiscalization of their accounts" and "the powerful tendency to spend taxpayer funds without controls."[70] The Committee had its work cut out for it—its staff of nine was investigating the case of 10,564 fraudulent checks written by the Peruvian National Bank (Banco de la Nación) in 1986 alone, defrauding taxpayers to the tune of $1.3 billion.[71]

Like other Latin elites, Peruvian officials, who view the national budget as their personal property, can hardly be expected to spend foreign loans in a manner benefiting the entire population. Instead, Peruvian officials have treated foreign loans as a source of "commissions" that fatten their individual pockets. Through their behavior, they have earned their popular nickname: "ladrones"—thieves.

Venezuela is the same story. In 1983, the Venezuelan government set up a system to subsidize exchange rates for importers of goods deemed critical to the economy. This crackpot scheme was a prime example of how to institutionalize corruption by making over-invoicing the most profitable business activity. Everyone with any political connections reaped handsome profits. By the fall of 1989, 20,000 importers were under judicial investigation for using the system to speculate in dollars. Even officials from other South American countries got in on the deal.[72]

Prior to President Menem's successful reforms, Argentina was rife with rent-seeking. In December 1990, one prominent Argentine was very candid about the source of his personal fortune. Luis Barrionuevo, head of the Argentine national health administration and leader of the restaurant workers' union, told the *Washington Post* that he did not make his millions working in the food industry. In fact, he pointed out, "I didn't make it working because it's very difficult to make money working." Instead, he celebrated the unique financial opportunity inherent in holding office in a union or an insurance plan. Barrionuevo said that he made a lot of money "from law firms and accounting firms. Take a union like the restaurant workers, so large, with so many outlets. You give an accounting firm 50 or 100 clients, and you're working." The kickbacks, Barrionuevo maintained, were enough to give "all the compañeros" in the union leadership their share. Such an admission put Barrionuevo in the headlines for a week, but soon prominent defenders lined up in support, arguing that he shouldn't be punished for saying what everybody already knows. In the end he received a mild rebuke from President Menem, who said, "It would be good if he talked a little less."[73]

As for the privileges of Argentine functionaries, they rivaled those of any other socialist aristocracy. Argentine jurist Jorge Bustamante reported in 1989 that most employees within Argentina's state companies received "additionals" and "supplements" to their incomes, at times totaling thousands of dollars per month.[74] Apparently, every excuse has been used in order to entrench bureaucratic privileges into law. For example, officials who advanced in their careers obtained extra pay for the "hierarchical responsibility," while those who stagnated got bonuses for their "permanency in position." Those who simply worked satisfactorily received bonuses for "dedication" or for "effective performance of their responsibilities."[75]

The privileges of Argentine officials were not limited to extra monetary compensation. Typical perks included the right to import cars duty-free at a time when auto imports were entirely prohibited for the population at large, and free vacations at luxurious state resorts at the expense of the average Argentine taxpayer, to whom the system was off-limits.[76]

The attitude of Latin America's aid-financed aristocracy was perhaps best summed up by Luiz Gonzaga Mendes de Barros, an official of the Brazilian state of Alagoas. In 1990, he told the Brazilian news magazine *Veja*: "There is nothing wrong with a public official who wants to live well . . . to be a maharajah is a way of life."[77] It cannot be surprising that placing large sums in unaccountable government hands enriched the few and did not produce the revenues to repay the loans.

From the Rio Grande to Patagonia, people's economic opportunities were blocked by the rent-seeking society that grew out of the statist approach to development. Leading Latin American authors call the incentive-sapping system by different names, but they unanimously agree that theirs were blocked societies. Argentine Jorge Bustamante prefers the term "corporativism," while Brazilian José Penna uses the term "patrimonialism," Peruvian Hernando De Soto says "mercantilism," and Colombian Edgar Revéiz describes Colombia as the "co-opted society." Whatever we call it, it is a common condition of state-controlled and regulated economies.

In Latin American countries, with government tentacles reaching into every activity, a web of controls ensured that nothing got done without a bribe. From cradle to grave, our Latin American neighbors have operated in a jungle of conflicting regulations, and the simplest transactions that North Americans take for granted have been extremely difficult to accomplish. Businesses throughout the region succeeded by lobbying the government for protection and special privileges. A rent-seeking culture predominated over capitalism.

Peruvian entrepreneur Hernando De Soto was the first to demonstrate the real barriers to economic development in his now classic book, *The Other Path*, first published in 1986. De Soto's Institute for Liberty and Democracy undertook the legal establishment of a small garment factory in Lima, Peru. To register the company required 289 days of full-time effort and an expenditure in bribes and lost earnings of $1,231, equal to thirty-two times the monthly minimum wage.

At the time, setting up the same type of business would have taken four hours in Florida. Next, De Soto examined the problem of access to housing for the popular classes. The Peruvian entrepreneur found that families who petitioned the Peruvian state for a piece of vacant land on which to build were faced with seven years of red tape and a per capita expenditure equal to fifty-six times the monthly minimum wage. De Soto found that even obtaining a license to open a small shop required forty-three days and an expenditure equal to fifteen times the monthly minimum wage. Faced with such insurmountable obstacles to joining the legal economy, it is no wonder that 60 percent of Peruvians made their living beyond the reach of the law in the informal economy.

Transaction costs were high in Peru, because organized interests comprising political parties, the mass media, the informal sector, business corporations, and influential families competed to obtain privileges and protection from the state.[78] In Peru, as elsewhere, the system worked to move redress away from less regulation to more in an effort to gain favorable regulations to offset unfavorable regulations. For example, in March 1990, the Association of Exporters (ADEX) complained that they were being hurt by government policies of prohibitive exchange rates for exporters and a delayed adjustment for inflation. They said that these costs were being imposed on top of already high costs inflicted on them by the government.[79] They successfully lobbied the state for the creation of a state agency, Cértex, which functioned to return a portion of the taxes to exporters in order to partly compensate for the unfavorable exchange-rate policies. Association members received $100 million in 1989. Rather than pushing for deregulation of the export sector, ADEX president Gastón Benza lobbied for the maintenance of Cértex and increased government compensatory payments.[80]

The deluge of arbitrary, personalized legislation created high costs for businesses. For example, on April 29, 1990, the Ministry of Industry, Domestic Commerce, Tourism and Integration issued a resolution that overturned the right of Moto Vespa del Perú S.A., a motorcycle manufacturer, to produce two specific motorcycle models. The profusion of laws enabled the Peruvian government to legally back up any decision, and the Ministry cited a Supreme Decree that it contended did not permit the extension of the company's right to produce the motorcycles.[81] Therefore, rather than serving consumers and expanding production of the Vespa Elestart and Vespa "S" motorcycles, the management of the Moto Vespa company then had to devote extensive lobbying efforts to reversing the unfavorable ruling.

For the Peruvian government it seemed that few human activities were too trivial to merit intervention. For example, on June 22, 1988, the Executive branch issued a Supreme Decree, signed by President Alan Garcia, authorizing a religious congregation to receive the donation of exactly one Toyota truck that was held up in Customs. Officials felt the need to cite Article 86 of the Peruvian Constitution to legalize this minuscule transaction: "the State recognizes the Catholic Church as an important element in the historic, cultural and moral formation of Peru."[82] On the same day, the Minister of Education issued a resolution authorizing a Doctor Daniel Conche Zuta to attend a seminar on "Participation, Plurality and Development" to be held in Quito, Ecuador, the following week.[83]

In Peru, with everyone forced to go to ridiculous lengths to influence the government, very little productive activity occurred until President Fujimori began to free the private sector to produce. People tired of fighting to obtain rights that citizens from other countries take for granted. Between the 1970s and 1990s, there was a massive exodus of able-bodied young people who took their talents and their capital elsewhere.

De Soto concluded:

> In a country where the law can be bought, where both left- and right-wing political parties agree that it is the state's prerogative to regulate and legislate in detail, and where the false ethic of redistributive justice has evaded and consigned to oblivion the ethic of productive justice, there are no secure property rights and no legal incentives for creating wealth. The inevitable hallmarks of the resulting system are instability and anarchy.[84]

Argentina was equally afflicted with disincentives to work, invest, and save prior to President Menem's comprehensive reforms. In 1988, Argentine jurist Jorge Bustamante described his country as "blocked by a web of controls that has submerged us into collective paralysis."[85] In his book, *La república corporativa* (The Corporatist Republic), he detailed the breakup of a once successful country into separate territories of privilege.[86]

Interest blocs in Argentina have competed for state favors in various ways. Practitioners in all occupations have sought to achieve "professional" status, while businesses have worked to have their line of business classified as a national priority. Such classifications enabled groups to press for a series of regulations, such as complicated licensing requirements or production restrictions, that served to limit entrants to the field and restrict competition in their areas of activity.

Such machinations reached an extremely high level. For example, photographers pushed regulation of their field to such an extent that in the provinces of Chaco and Santa Fe the public was prohibited from taking pictures in the central plazas. Only persons possessing cards identifying themselves as members of the photography council were allowed to carry out such a mundane activity.[87]

The Argentine government even granted bureaucratic go-betweens their own status as professionals, recognizing their cartel as the Administrative Procedures Agents. These were the slippery operators who guided Argentine businesses and individuals through the labyrinthine bureaucracy for a fee.

Argentine officials responded to complaints by proclaiming, "the State cannot remain indifferent," as if the government had a moral obligation to generate income for all occupations in the country. As a result, by 1988 "virtually all conceivable privileges [had] already been awarded and it [was] practically impossible to start new productive activities not only due to bureaucratic regulations but to the obstacles created by the privileges granted to everyone else."[88]

Since protected industries and professions managed to suppress competition in their fields, the high costs of lobbying the government (including bribery) have been passed on to consumers. In Argentina this is known as the "costo argentino," or the Argentine cost.

Nothing escaped the Argentine cost. For example, in December 1990, a nonprofit research institute in the United States shipped 5,000 copies of an economic study to a Buenos Aires think tank for distribution in Argentina. The shipment was a nonprofit donation to the Argentine research institute, but it was held up in Argentine customs for months, pending payment of over $2,200 in "fees" to various cartels in Argentina. The Argentine think tank finally paid a bureaucratic go-between $1,200 to persuade Customs to free the shipment.

In other countries the story is much the same. In Colombia's "co-opted society," competition for government favors is cutthroat. According to Colombian economist Edgar Revéiz, interest groups in regional blocs compete for privileges and broker lobbied contracts as the government parcels out the pieces.[89]

Public and private sector distinctions became blurred, as everyone from bureaucrats to politicians to private firms sought favors from the redistributive state. As in other rent-seeking societies, the most powerful cartels or producer associations became quasi-governmental institutions.

In Colombia, the powerful cartel of the National Federation of Coffee Growers (FEDERACAFE), although legally private, carries out many public functions. In 1940, the government created the National Coffee Fund and put the Federation in charge of its administration. Since then the coffee fund has expanded investments into the areas of finance, insurance, construction, shipping, and other agricultural endeavors, as it receives income from a variety of coffee taxes, coffee exports, and sales of coffee for domestic consumption. In addition, the Federation has represented Colombia in international negotiations and maintains tight control over information on the country's largest legal export.

In order to achieve such prestige and power, the Federation long ago obtained representation in organizations within the Executive Branch of the government. In this cozy relationship between coffee growers and the state, the Federation influences general economic policy behind closed doors, and all major elements of coffee policy—domestic price supports, marketing strategies, taxes, credits to coffee growers, and so on—are determined either within the Federation or within the Executive Branch by organizations in which the Federation is represented.[90]

The Colombian state has been weak, because a state that functions to redistribute wealth among competing interest groups cannot effectively carry out the traditional functions of government. Private firms have been likewise distracted from carrying out their traditional functions of innovating and serving consumers. Instead, they operate virtually as a branch of the government. In such a system, as one Brazilian wit put it, private companies are companies controlled by the government, while state companies are companies controlled by no one.

In Colombia, the Constitution and legal system did not function to safeguard individual rights, and the network of impenetrable pacts among the privileged elites has served to exclude the majority of Colombians from participation in the system. Revéiz blames the rising level of violence in Colombia on the blocked society.[91]

In Brazil's patrimonialist system, official bribery, theft, illicit favoritism, nepotism, "commissions," and kickbacks are a way of life—tribute collected by elites for their position as owners of the state. As in all societies where the state dominates economic activity, the governing elites constitute a form of mafia. Indeed, even that word downplays their power, as they milk every type of legitimate activity for their own gain. Penna observed that in the United States, public officials are quickly investigated for even the appearance of conflicts of interest, while in Latin America's rent-seeking societies, officials abuse their positions with impunity.[92] They have turned government into a centralizing behemoth that obstructs the growth of a modern nation. A dinosaur, says Penna.

In Brazil, the fight to shrink the state and limit its interventions is opposed by the governing elite and privileged private business executives, who run to the state for bailouts whenever they suffer losses. The socialization of business losses is characteristic of blocked societies.

Latin Americans spent the twentieth century building the blocked society. They never managed to develop the institutions conducive to progress, such as efficient capital markets, legal systems that protect private property rights, or banking institutions that serve the public. Theirs was a poverty of policy, not of people or natural resources.

Ultimately, the system became unworkable and ungovernable, and its failure forced politicians to give up their statist ideology. Argentine economist Martín Krause put it well when he said that former statists became privatizers because the "state went bankrupt and crumbled, and I mean every part of it."[93]

The West is partly to blame for the economic, social, and political backwardness of Latin America—but not for the reasons usually given by leftists. The West is culpable for squandering a historic opportunity in the post-World War II period to transmit the ideas of free markets and free enterprise conducive to economic success. Latin Americans anxious for progress were deterred by the extraordinary resources that the developed countries committed to the imposition of socialist development planning. A skeptical observer could come to the conclusion that development planning was a Machiavellian strategy by which the West shielded itself from competition from less developed countries.

Notes

1. José López Portillo, "Sexto Informe de Gobierno," presented to the Mexican Congress on September 1, 1982, in *El Ejecutivo Ante el Congreso 1976–1982* (Mexico City: Secretaría de Programación y Presupuesto, 1982), 223.
2. CIA estimate cited in Jack Anderson, "Mexican Wheels Are Lubricated by Official Oil," *Washington Post*, 14 May 1984.

3. Inter-American Development Bank, *External Debt and Economic Development in Latin America* (Washington, D.C.: IDB, 1984), 176.
4. Luis Pazos, *Hacia donde va Salinas* (Mexico City: Editorial Diana, 1989), 168.
5. Peter Smith, *Labyrinths of Power: Political Recruitment in Twentieth-Century Mexico* (Princeton: Princeton University Press, 1979), 249–71.
6. Ibid.
7. Juan Miguel de Mora, *!No!, Señor Presidente: La Realidad Nacional del Actual Sexenio sin Maquillaje Oficial* (Mexico City: Anaya Editores S.A., 1983), 291–96.
8. Youssef Ibrahim, "Mexico Suffers Greatly as Oil Prices Decline But Debts Linger On," *Wall Street Journal*, 9 October 1985.
9. Francisco Gil Díaz, "Mexico's Experience with Foreign Aid," in Uma Lele and Ijaz Nabi, eds., *Transitions in Development: The Role of Aid and Commercial Flows* (San Francisco: ICS Press, 1991), 246.
10. World Bank and Inter-American Development bank loans.
11. René Villareal, *Mitos y Realidades de la Empresa Pública* (Mexico City: Editorial Diana, 1988), 163–67.
12. World Bank Annual Report 1972, 44.
13. Luis Pazos, *El Gobierno y la Inflación* (Mexico City: Editorial Diana, 1980), 134–35.
14. Ricardo Medina Macías, *Crónica del Desengaño* (Mexico City: Editores Asociados Mexicanos, S.A., 1983), 87.
15. de Mora, *!No! Señor Presidente*, 96–98.
16. Government intervention in the market for basic foodstuffs has been institutionalized in modern Mexico since 1934, when the first regulatory agency was created during the administration of Lázaro Cárdenas.
17. Oscar Vera Ferrer, *El Caso Conasupo: Una Evaluación* (Mexico City: Centro de Estudios en Economía y Educación, 1987).
18. Ibid., 102, and Table 3.10, 111.
19. Ibid. 94, 252.
20. Ibid., 94.
21. Ibid., Table 3.12, 112.
22. Alejandro Junco, "Mexico's Private Sector Reels Under Government Control," *Wall Street Journal*, 29 June 1984.
23. Vera Ferrer, *El Caso Conasupo*, 253.
24. Richard Meislin, "Mexico's War on Corruption Is Taking Prisoners," *New York Times*, 27 August 1983.
25. World Bank and Inter-American Development Bank Annual Reports, 1970–1984.
26. Inter-American Development Bank, *Economic and Social Progress in Latin America*, External Debt: Crisis and Adjustment (Washington, D.C.: IDB, 1985), Table 57, 424.

27. Rainer Godau Schucking and Viviane B. de Márquez, *Burocracia Pública y Empresa Privada: El Caso de la Industrialización Mexicana* (Austin: University of Texas, 1982), 13; *Código de Comercio y Leyes Complementarias* (Mexico City: Editorial Porrua, S.A., 1974), Primera Parte, Libro Quinto, Apéndice núm. 4, Capítulo IV.

28. See Robert Aubey, *Nacional Financiera and Mexican Industry: A Study of the Financial Relationship Between the Government and the Private Sector of Mexico* (Los Angeles: University of California, 1966).

29. Ibid., 102–109.

30. Smith, *Labyrinths of Power*, 206–209.

31. Ibid. 207.

32. Ibid., 206–209, 267.

33. "Bribery Inquiry Leads to Arrest of 4 in Mexico," *Wall Street Journal*, 5 May 1982; and Robert Taylor, "Ruston Gas Accused by U.S. of Bribery of Mexican Officials," *Wall Street Journal*, 23 September 1982.

34. Carlos Arriola, *Las Organizaciones Empresariales y el Estado* (Mexico City: Conafe, 1981), 12–13.

35. Ibid.

36. *Mexico's In-Bond Industry Is . . .* , study sponsored by the Bank of America, Mexico Representative Office, Mexico City, 1985.

37. Khosrow Fatemi, ed., *The Maquiladora Industry: Economic Solution or Problem?* (New York: Praeger, 1990), 3.

38. Arriola, *Las Organizaciones Empresariales y el Estado*, 76.

39. Ibid., 98–99.

40. Ibid., 87–88.

41. Ibid., 108–109, 168–69.

42. Jorge Hierro and Allen Sanginés, "Public Sector Behavior in Mexico," in Felipe Larraín and Marcelo Selowsky, eds., *The Public Sector and the Latin American Crisis* (San Francisco: ICS Press, 1991), 137–81.

43. Ibid.

44. Gustavo Esteva, "Development: Metaphor, Myth, Threat," in *Development: Seeds of Change*, Vol. 3, 1985.

45. Octavio Paz, *El Ogro Filantrópico* (Mexico City: Editorial Joaquín Mortiz, S.A., 1979), 91–94.

46. Jack Anderson, "Mexican Wheels Are Lubricated by Official Oil," *Washington Post*, 14 May 1984.

47. Jack Anderson, "Mexico Makes Its Presidents Millionaires," *Washington Post*, 15 May 1984.

48. Articles by Jack Anderson, "Politics Dilute Anti-Corruption Effort in Mexico," *Washington Post*, 24 August 1984; and "Mexican Wheels Are Lubricated by Official Oil," *Washington Post*, 14 May 1984.

49. Edward Cody, "Ex-President of Mexico Denies Corruption Charges,"

Washington Post, 24 April 1986; and William Branigin, "Pace Slow in Mexico's Drive Against Corruption," *Washington Post*, 16 September 1987.

50. Medina Macías, *Crónica del Desengaño*, 77.
51. Karen LaFollette, trip to Mexico City, September to December 1981.
52. Interview with Sixto Duran-Ballen, Republican Unity Party presidential candidate and vice presidential candidate Alberto Dahik, leader of Conservative Party of Ecuador, in Quito *El Universo*, 25 January 1992.
53. Edward Cody, "Mexico Modernizes, but 'El Toro' Died by the Old Rules," *Washington Post*, 25 October 1991.
54. Ibid.
55. Ibid.
56. Ibid.
57. Ibid.
58. *Codigo de Comercio y Leyes Complementarias* (Mexico City: Editorial Porrua, S.A., 1974), Primera Parte, Libro Primero, Título Segundo, Capítulo II, Art. 18–32; Título Tercero; and Libro Quinto, Apéndice núm. 2 and 3.
59. *Constitución Política de los Estados Unidos Mexicanos*, Art. 123.
60. Roberto Salinas, "Mexico, Markets, and Multilateral Aid," in Doug Bandow and Ian Vásquez, eds., *Perpetuating Poverty: The World Bank, the IMF, and the Developing World* (Washington, D.C.: Cato Institute, 1994), 172.
61. Pemex's proven oil and gas reserves alone are worth at least $100 billion.
62. Caspar Weinberger, "Commentary," *Forbes*, 11 April 1994, 37.
63. Interview with Economy Minister Carlos Boloña Behr by Vidal Silva Navarrete, Lima *La República*, 16 February 1992.
64. Instituto de la Economía Social de Mercado study published in Buenos Aires *La Prensa*, 19 March 1989.
65. See José Osvaldo de Meira Penna, *O Dinossauro* (São Paulo: T. A. Queiroz, 1988), 139–63; and "Patrimonialism in Latin America: In a Brazilian Perspective," unpublished paper, April 1991.
66. "Ha Marajá na Previdencia," *Veja* (São Paulo), 24 April 1991, 25.
67. "Prefeitos Dizem que Verbas não Chegaram," *O Estado de São Paulo*, 24 February 1988; and "Brazil de Hoje e o 'Pais da cleptocracia," *O Estado de São Paulo*, 14 February 1988.
68. "'Contrato de risco' na Intermediação," *O Estado de Sao Paulo*, 26 February 1988.
69. "Entrevista: Urge que administración pública incorpore modernos sistemas de control de gasto," interview with Senator Daniel Bocanegra Barreto, Lima *El Comercio*, 2 June 1991.
70. Ibid.
71. Ibid.

72. María Yolanda García, "Fiscal Consignió Ayer Otro Expediente sobre Recadi," *El Diario de Caracas*, 8 April 1989; "Intereses de sus Miembros Harán Retorcer a la Subcomisión Recadi," *El Diario de Caracas*, 8 April 1989; Merrill Collette, "Executives Fleeing Venezuela," *Washington Post*, 25 July 1989; and Jose de Cordoba, "Many Executives Flee Venezuela in Scandal over Dollar Reserves," *Wall Street Journal*, 24 August 1989.
73. Eugene Robinson, "The South American Way of Graft," *Washington Post*, 2 December 1990.
74. Jorge Bustamante, *La República Corporativa* (Buenos Aires: Emecé Editores, 1988), 99–100.
75. Ibid., 100.
76. Ibid., 102–104.
77. "Salario Doce," (Editorial), *Veja*, (São Paulo) 22 August 1990.
78. Hernando De Soto, *The Other Path: The Invisible Revolution in the Third World* (New York: Harper & Row, 1989, originally published in Spanish in 1986), 190.
79. "Exportadores Piden Reglas Estables," Lima *El Comercio*, 25 March 1990; "Hay que Estabilizar Primero la Economía, Sostiene Gastón Benza Pflucker," *El Comercio* (Lima), 25 March 1990.
80. "Hay que Estabilizar Primero la Economía, Sostiene Gastón Benza Pflucker," *El Comercio* (Lima), 25 March 1990.
81. "Declaran improcedente solicitud de Moto Vespa de Perú S.A.," *El Peruano* (Lima), 29 April 1990.
82. "Autorizan donación de un vehículo a favor de una congregación religiosa," *El Peruano* (Lima), 22 June 1988.
83. Ibid.
84. De Soto, *The Other Path*, 199.
85. Bustamante, *La República Corporativa*, dust jacket.
86. Ibid., 11.
87. Ibid., 129.
88. Ibid., 13.
89. Edgar Revéiz, *Democratizar para Sobrevivir* (Bogotá: Producción Editorial: Poligrupo Comunicación, 1989), XII.
90. Jonathan Hartlyn, "Producer Associations, the Political Regime and Policy Processes in Contemporary Colombia," *Latin American Research Review*, Vol. 20, No. 3, 1985, 111–38.
91. See Revéiz, *Democratizar para Sobrevivir*.
92. de Meira Penna, *O Dinossauro*, 146–47; see also Mario Barros Junior, *A Fantástica Corrupção no Brazil* (São Paulo: published by author, 1982).
93. Personal correspondence with Martín Krause, 11 September 1990.

4

Development Planners in Their Heyday

Five-year plans are the invention of, and were once the exclusive possession of, the Soviet Union. Now Americans and Western Europeans assemble without thought to consider how they may help finance the five-year plans of India or Pakistan. The country which does not have goals, and a program for reaching these goals, is commonly assumed to be going nowhere.

JOHN KENNETH GALBRAITH,
Economic Development in Perspective

Future historians are sure to wonder about the countries composing the Western Alliance in the second half of the twentieth century—the most economically successful countries in history—that had so little confidence in capitalism that they recommended socialism to poor countries already burdened with too much government. Historians will certainly notice the irony of the economically developed West recommending institutions that were the antithesis of the ones undergirding their own economic success. Radicals among them will interpret development planning as a form of neocolonial exploitation through which rich countries maintained hegemony over poor ones.

In the postwar period, "development economics," a discipline that found inspiration in Soviet central planning, stepped onto the international scene promising to make things better for the poor of the Third World. Planners armed with "shadow prices" and "input-output analysis" were believed capable of outperforming markets with real prices. Development economists were confident of the powers of their conceits.

Input-output analysis was foremost among the conceits. Economic planners undertook to inventory a country's resources and relate these in a matrix to a desired product mix. This impossible task was then wedded to statistics that had been concocted to attract foreign aid.

These activities employed many economists and cast a sheen of science over institutionalized corruption.

Development experts believed that knowledge and science would rescue poor people from their miserable lives without having to empower the poor themselves with private property rights and good incentives. What was left out of the development plans was the necessary requirement that people be responsible for themselves. The centralized schemes cooked up in Washington offices and Third World capitals left opportunity in the hands of government. Much like the U.S. approach to the inner cities, "development" became something that was done to the poor. The international welfare approach led to the development of bureaucracies and the shriveling of the people.

In the post-World War II period there was a feeling of desperation that poor countries could not afford to take the capitalist route to development that Britain and the United States had taken. Part of the urgency was Cold War-related: during the 1950s and 1960s faith in Soviet economic success was so high that most economists believed that the Soviet planned economy posed a real challenge to the West. Policy experts thought that only rapid development could keep poor countries from falling like dominoes to communism, and experts recommended planning as the fastest and surest path. In addition, there was a humanitarian concern for poor countries and a feeling that they should take the quickest path to development in order to rapidly alleviate suffering. Finally, there was also a heavy dose of guilt involved. Leading development thinkers had convinced the West that its development was purchased at the expense of the Third World and that, therefore, sending them advice and aid was required to help atone for past transgressions.

By 1956, the extent of the faith in planning was so great that Gunnar Myrdal was able to claim that "all special advisors to underdeveloped countries who have taken the time and trouble to acquaint themselves with the problems, no matter who they are . . . all recommend central planning as a first condition of progress."[1]

There was no successful experience anywhere with central economic planning institutions, yet the experts pushed these institutions on developing countries with incompetent governments. Marxist and Keynesian economics, British and French socialism, the New Deal in the United States, and the postwar Marshall Plan for Europe all played a role in convincing the West to impose development planning on the Third World. Above all else, however, academic claims for planning were buttressed by the alleged success of the Soviet planned economy—one of history's great frauds. A leader was Gunnar Myrdal, who viewed the Soviet model *"as fundamentally a system for the development of underdeveloped countries.* This particular point cannot be stressed too much."[2]

Other thinkers, including Ragnar Nurkse and J.K. Galbraith, joined Myrdal in accepting highly exaggerated Soviet economic statistics as evidence that rapid growth could be achieved by comprehensive economic planning.[3] Stanford University Professor Paul Baran marshaled dubious East Bloc statistics to attest that growth rates in the socialist countries averaged 10 percent per year, in contrast with rates in capitalist countries that rarely exceeded 3 percent per annum.[4]

Similarly, Robert Heilbroner observed that "communism has a *functional* attractiveness to the underdeveloped lands ... it may be the political and economic system best adapted to the tasks of the backward areas."[5] Heilbroner believed that Soviet drabness was "more psychologically appealing, to the common man of the backward areas than the gaudy and fantastically removed way of life of the West."[6]

Ragnar Nurkse even contended that the Soviet system of collectivization of agriculture offered advantages for the Third World. Fourteen million people died in the forced collectivization of Soviet agriculture, but what mattered to Nurkse was that the "crucial problem of collecting the food seems to be solved in Soviet Russia by the system of collective farms."[7] He also opined that "it may be that the iron curtain is necessary for the maintenance of a high rate of saving and investment in the Soviet Union."[8]

The illusion that economies could be planned also came from a new field of economics—econometrics. This new approach combined statistics with mathematical models of economies. The equations and numbers gave planners a false sense of precision and resulted in tremendous mistakes. Econometrics was the field of Jan Tinbergen, a Dutch socialist and pacifist, who had a naive faith in the capacity and benevolence of government to do good. Tinbergen died in 1994 after seeing his hopes come to nothing, but those hopes were high in 1963 when Tinbergen wrote that "it should be recognized and expressly stated that the Soviet Union was the pioneer of central economic planning and has taught the world some of the possibilities in this field."[9]

While they extolled Soviet communism, development experts could not see a role model in Western capitalism. A kind of hypocrisy prevailed in which influential economic thinkers in developed nations argued that the strong private business sectors found in their own countries were somehow unsuitable engines for growth in the developing countries. People who themselves relied on the market every day somehow believed that it would not work for anyone else. Paul Baran asserted in his influential 1957 book *The Political Economy of Growth* that capitalist development was outdated because "the dominant fact of our time is that the institution of private property in the means of production—once a powerful engine of progress—has now come into irreconcilable contradiction with the economic and social advancement of the people in the underdeveloped countries."[10] Likewise, Ragnar Nurkse argued that "the contemporary emphasis on government planning for economic development is to a great extent an outcome of the failure of nations under laissez-faire conditions to accumulate capital rapidly enough for the desired rate of growth."[11]

Development planners set themselves up as oracles proclaiming the gospel of planning and spread their theories throughout the developing world. There was little if any thought given to the rent-seeking character of the patrimonial economy or to the real barriers to development.

In pushing planning, the development economists took for granted that capital and labor are as productive in government hands as in private hands. Today, no one believes that government can use resources as efficiently as the private sector, but in those days prestigious economists and economic theories gave government a role that was beyond its capability. Among the culprits were the following theories.

Import Substitution and Dependency Theory

Leading development thinkers accepted the Soviet Communist Party's view of imperialism, modified in 1928, which stated that colonialism was economically regressive for the colonies. In fact, the evidence shows that the Marxist view was the reverse of the truth, as former colonies and those countries with the most contacts with the West progressed the fastest.[12] Economic development is in itself a Western concept, and it is inseparable from private property and market pricing. After World War II, when most former colonies had achieved their independence, the Marxists were loath to give up the term "imperialism," which had worked so well for them in advancing the cause of international communism. They redefined imperialism to mean that the rich countries were economically exploiting the poor countries through trade. The Marxist view of free trade as a form of imperialism permeates the development literature.

Academics took different routes to arrive at the conclusion that the West was to blame for the "backwardness" of the Third World and that, therefore, "colonized" countries should withdraw from the world trade system. In the 1950s, Ragnar Nurkse and Gunnar Myrdal were leaders in promoting the conclusion that foreign trade had not done much to improve the prospects of Third World countries and that contacts with the West had further impoverished poor countries.

Myrdal decried the international inequalities between the rich and poor countries and believed that without appropriate action, these would continue to grow. The Swedish socialist alleged that development in rich countries sucked resources from the poor and impoverished them. He called this process "Cumulative Causation." The multinational corporations were the main culprits in cumulative causation, since Myrdal saw them as stripping countries of resources, sending profits back home, and contributing very little to the development of the Third World.

Terms of trade for primary goods produced by most poor countries were said to be deteriorating, and their prospects were judged to be dim. Myrdal blamed the worsening situation on the market: "Market forces will tend cumulatively to accentuate international inequalities."[13]

Contact with capitalist countries was also perceived to be polluting their cultures with crass money-making. Myrdal observed that "in most underdeveloped countries the trading contacts with the outside world have actually impoverished them culturally."[14] He said the harmful process would continue until the world economic system was changed to take into account the interests of the poor countries.[15]

Unable to recognize the real barriers to development, Myrdal and others of his persuasion believed that poor countries owed their poverty to exploitation by rich countries. Myrdal's solution was for poor countries to take a strongly nationalist approach in order to push their way into the international spoils system that the Swedish economist saw as the world economy. First, they should build up their economies through the implementation of a comprehensive national plan. Then they should integrate with other poor countries to form a powerful negotiating block to wrest power from rich countries and break their stranglehold on the world international order. Myrdal encouraged poor countries to make shrill demands for a New International Economic Order within the UN system.

In the interim, Myrdal argued that the Third World should withdraw as much as possible from the world trade system and focus on developing self-sufficient economies. Since Myrdal believed that rich countries were guilty of obstructing the development of poor countries, he regarded foreign aid as reparations extracted through a system of international taxation administered by the multilateral aid institutions.

Myrdal's "cumulative causation" theory convinced people in poor countries that they had no control over their own fate. He helped persuade Third World countries that all agents of change were external to them and that their economic development depended on foreign advice, foreign aid, and economic planning that would give their governments more power over their lives.

Compatible with Myrdal's vision was "dependency theory." Initially promoted by Marxists, the argument wended its way into the mainstream and was used to support calls for a new international order and the implementation of protectionist policies. Basically, the theory held that the so-called center composed of capitalist countries has been exploiting the underdeveloped countries on the "periphery" for hundreds of years, first through "colonialism" and "imperialism" and later, after colonial independence, through an insidious neocolonial form of "dependent capitalism."[16]

Proponents of the theory argued that exploitation consists of appropriating the "surplus value" of the Third World. Many development economists were obsessed with the Marxist concept of surplus value, defined to be the output produced by labor beyond what was required to sustain a minimum living standard. Economists believed that governments of poor countries should somehow get hold of that surplus and spend it on industrial development programs. In their view, industrial countries, such as the United States and Britain, were keeping Third World countries down by buying their raw materials and siphoning off the surplus value through trade.

Many development economists blamed multinational corporations and the market system for a growing gap between low prices for Third World raw materials exports and high prices for manufactured goods exported by the developed countries. The "unequal exchange" was alleged to intensify the exploitation. Foreign aid was seen as a way for poor countries to recapture some of their expropriated surplus value.[17]

Myrdal's UN colleague, Argentine economist Raul Prebisch, was the strongest proponent of dependency theory and import substitution. Prebisch urged countries to adopt protectionist trade policies in order to build up domestic industries and reduce their dependence on foreign imports. The rationale for walling off Latin America from international trade was contained in the Prebisch Thesis, which held that the classical theory of international trade was incorrect, because the benefits of trade did not flow evenly to all parties to the trade. The capitalist countries of the "center" of the international economic system bene- fited much more than the producers of primary commodities of the "periphery," of which Latin America was a part.

Prebisch predicted worsening terms of trade for producers of pri- mary commodities, because in his view the capitalist countries kept all the benefits of technological progress for themselves. He wrote that "the centres kept the whole benefit of the technical development of their industries," and "the peripheral countries transferred to them a share of the fruits of their own technical progress."[18]

The "worsening terms of trade" argument has been proven false, and there is no need to debate it here. Even if it were the case that a country was continually faced with falling prices for its exports and earning declining amounts of foreign exchange from their sale, the culprit would be inflexible domestic economic policies that did not allow the country to adapt to changing international markets.

In his position as Executive Secretary of the Economic Commission for Latin America, based in Santiago, Chile, Prebisch successfully propounded his ideas throughout Latin America. Throughout the region, Latin American countries adopted protectionist policies in accordance with comprehensive development plans. Tariff and quota barriers were raised, repressive investment laws were drawn up to keep out foreigners, and domestic companies, both state-owned and privately held, were chartered to sell to the domestic market with little or no competition. Paradoxically, amid the nationalist fervor, nobody seemed to care that Marx was no Latin American, or that Prebisch owed his prominence to his acceptance among Western development economists.

Raul Prebisch's status and impact in Latin America can hardly be exaggerated. The term "Prebischiana" was coined to refer to details of the economist's life. Indeed, even in the 1990s, although discredited in Latin America, the Argentine economist is still lionized among inter- national bureaucrats. In November 1991, the Inter-American Devel- opment Bank organized a conference in honor of Prebisch on "Latin American Thought: Past, Present, and Future." Out of sync with free- market thinking in Latin America today, conference presenters waxed nostalgic about the good old days when their antimarket ideas wrecked economies. Prebisch biographers Edgar Dosman and David Pollock told conference attendees that "the magnitude of Prebisch's achievement can scarcely be exaggerated."[19] They attributed the failure of Prebisch's ideas to misapplication by his disciples.[20]

Stages of Economic Growth

Economist W. W. Rostow was the most prominent proponent of the Stages of Economic Growth theory used in the 1950s and early 1960s to justify planning and the disbursement of large amounts of foreign aid to developing countries. Rostow had found Marx's explanations of economic history unsatisfying and proposed an alternative in his 1960 book *The Stages of Economic Growth: A Non-Communist Manifesto*.

Rostow concluded that the process of development was a series of five stages through which all countries had to pass, without exception. The stages comprised the traditional society, a society with the pre-conditions for takeoff into sustained economic growth, takeoff, the drive to economic maturity, and maturity or the age of high mass consumption.

The traditional society, as described by Rostow, was one without access to modern science and technology and dependent on subsistence agriculture. While economic growth was possible, for instance, by putting more hectares under cultivation or from improvements in farming methods, there was a ceiling on the growth in output per head.[21]

The second stage of the theory, the preconditions stage, was characterized by a gradual change in values of the population at large—people becoming convinced that economic growth is good and necessary for some larger purpose such as national dignity or a better life for the children. In this stage, education broadens the outlook of some and prepares them for modern society. "New types of enterprising men come forward—in the private economy, in government, or both—willing to mobilize savings and to take risks in pursuit of profit or modernization." Banks appear, some modern manufacturing begins to take place, investment increases, and the scope of foreign and domestic trade widens. But the society is still characterized mainly by the old values and social system and regional political structures.[22]

The takeoff stage into sustained economic growth, according to Rostow, is the one in which "the old blocks and resistances to steady growth are finally overcome." The forces for economic progress expand and gradually take over the entire economy leading to a spiraling circle of growth, or "compound interest." Rostow's thesis was that the building of the centralized nation-state was the precondition for takeoff into sustained growth for the industrialized countries. He believed that the national state-building process shook up the traditional landed regional interests or the colonial power or both and set free forces for economic growth.[23]

The drive to maturity stage is characterized by a long interval of "sustained if fluctuating progress, as the now regularly growing economy drives to extend modern technology over the whole front of its economic activity."[24] Investment of 10 to 20 percent of the national income regularly occurs, and the makeup of the economy changes rapidly as new industries proliferate and older industries decline.

Finally, countries would reach the stage of maturity and the age of high-mass consumption after about sixty years of steady progress toward that goal. This was defined as the stage in which modern technology has been applied over virtually the entire breadth of the economy, and the leading sectors shift to production of durable consumer goods. A broad range of goods and services becomes available to the population at large.[25]

As did most development economists, Rostow misidentified the forces of economic growth. He believed that the generic application of capital and modern technology produced development, rather than entrepreneurs free to use capital and new ideas to create wealth. Rostow believed that to accelerate Third World economies through the stages of growth to maturity, the right mixture and quantity of foreign aid, investment, and technology were all that were required. Rostow concluded that government had to take a central role in the development process in order to guide the economy through the stages. As the expertise to design and implement a development plan did not exist in the "backward" countries, outside experts would have to be involved.

Enamored of his stage theory, Rostow lost sight of reality. He believed that Stalin had completed the modernization of the Soviet Union, which he thought was about to enter the age of mass consumption—and this in a country where you could not even buy a roll of toilet paper or a ballpoint pen! He was convinced that China and India were entering the "takeoff" stage in 1960, because "the plans of both countries, in their overall investment goals and sectoral composition, are consistent with the takeoff requirements."[26]

With the benefit of hindsight, we can wonder at the low level of intellectual acuity prevailing in those years that permitted such silliness to become the conventional wisdom of that time, adversely impacting the lives of hundreds of millions of people. The more government failed in Russia, China, and India, the more planning was seen to be a success. The greater the postwar recovery of Europe and the more Japan prospered from trade, the more inappropriate the market model was thought to be and the more refuge was sought in import-substitution policies and trade protectionism. Economic development was believed to be independent of private property, open markets, entrepreneurs, incentives, or any input from the population. It was enough for planners to guide the economy through the stages of growth.

The Harrod–Domar Growth Model

This model underpinned the idea that planned investment could ensure progress through the stages of growth. The model contended that economic growth was a function of national saving and the national capital/output ratio. If countries were able to save a sizeable portion of their national income and channel it into investment, countries would experience economic growth. By leaving incentives and the human element out of the equation, the model encouraged the view that government and private sector investments were equally productive. If countries were too poor to save, injections of foreign aid could propel the development process.[27]

W. Arthur Lewis

Princeton University professor W. Arthur Lewis, was, like Rostow, an influential mainstream economist who recommended planning and the channeling of large amounts of foreign aid into "backward" countries. While Lewis made some positive contributions to development economics, he, too, was mesmerized by planning.

To his credit, Lewis did not go along with Prebisch's theory that countries needed to protect themselves from free trade in order to develop. In *Aspects of Tropical Trade 1883–1965*, he said that the engine of growth was trade and exports. Using admittedly sketchy statistics, Lewis conducted a survey of international trade for the years 1883, 1899, 1913, 1929, 1937, 1955, and 1965. He concluded that during the late 1800s and before World War I the less-developed countries did not suffer when more industrialized countries grew.

In his *Report on Industrialization and the Gold Coast*, Lewis stressed the importance of foreign investment, as opposed to foreign aid. However, his pro-market stance was clouded by the heavy pro-regulatory views of the time. In the end, Lewis sidled up to the import-substitution theory when he concluded that some companies needed a regulatory climate that would protect them from competition from imports. He even softened his views toward nationalization of foreign firms as long as the foreign owners were compensated and governments had valid reasons for running industries, which were "most economically conducted as a monopoly, or at any rate on a scale of production so large that the producer would have the power to exploit the consumer."[28]

Despite a mainly positive view of private enterprise, Lewis was ensconced in the planning camp. He believed that in "backward" countries the efforts of private business should be channeled to fulfill the goals of the national development plan. Lewis said that "planning is at the same time much more necessary and much more difficult to execute in backward than in advanced countries."[29] He complained that civil servants in "backward" countries were not up to snuff, but contended that since Lenin had managed to turn the Communist administrative apparatus into "a highly trained and disciplined priestly order," other "backward" countries could "create an administrative machine that can do the work of planning."[30]

Lewis argued that a continuous increase in foreign aid was needed to help tropical countries close the "trade gap," which he defined as the difference between planned growth targets and the growth in demand for traditional agricultural products. For example, income growth targets of 6 percent a year exceeded the forecast of 4 percent growth in demand. Lewis called the difference of 2 percent the "trade gap," and said that rising levels of foreign assistance would help countries meet their goals for economic growth.

Theory of Balanced Growth

Columbia University professor Ragnar Nurkse's theory of balanced growth dovetailed with Rostow's stages of growth approach. Nurkse's 1953 book *Problems of Capital Formation in Underdeveloped Countries* became a cornerstone of development doctrine. Nurkse ascribed to the notion of the vicious circle of poverty—people were poor because they were poor. Nurkse joined Rostow in believing that the accumulation of capital was the critical determinant of economic growth, and that what determined the rate of capital accumulation was the rate of saving. The Columbia University economist illustrated the vicious circle of poverty as follows. In developing countries, the small capacity to save results from the low level of real income, while the low real income is a reflection of low productivity, which in turn is due largely to the lack of capital. As he put it, "the inducement to invest may be low because of the small buying power of the people, which is due to their small real income, which again is due to low productivity."[31]

In order to break the underdevelopment stalemate, Nurkse believed that capital must be introduced into many economic sectors at once, to induce "balanced growth." He believed that any single enterprise could easily be doomed by the small market existing under conditions of poverty, but

> a wide range of projects in different industries may succeed because they will all support each other, in the sense that the people engaged in each project, now working with more real capital per head and with greater efficiency in terms of output per man-hour, will provide an enlarged market for the products of the new enterprises in the other industries.[32]

Since the problem with poor countries was believed to be a lack of capital and not the lack of property rights, incentives, and a predictable legal system, the introduction of large amounts of foreign aid was seen as the solution. Associated with this approach was an inexplicable confidence that those in the government who controlled the funds would invest them wisely in the general interest of society as a whole. Wherever expertise was lacking, foreign experts could fill the role. Faith in government was so overpowering that development economists never considered the impact on the societies of placing large sums in untried and untested government hands with little tradition of accountability. The temptations and corruptions that the aid introduced overwhelmed fragile societies, many of which in Africa were artificial constructs composed of competing tribes with no national consciousness. As Peter Bauer was to note, by concentrating economic power in the hands of the state, development planning made control of the government a life-or-death matter for millions of people.

Like the others, Nurkse saw only advantage in placing huge sums in the political arena where, in fact, they would be stolen, expended in political patronage, used to suppress the tribes that did not control the government, provoke civil wars, finance genocide and the relocation of populations, and politicize every strand of society by spreading a rent-seeking culture. The experts were blind to every practical reality. Instead, they pontificated that "foreign loans for capital expenditure by public authorities have the advantage that they can be used for domestic economic development in accordance with a coherent over-all programme."[33] As with Rostow's stages, the details of Nurkse's Balanced Growth approach were endlessly debated, but the total reliance on government was not questioned.

The Theory of Unbalanced Growth

Yale professor Albert Hirschman[34] was dissatisfied with Nurkse's balanced growth approach and decided that what would really precipitate development in poor countries was "unbalanced growth." Hirschman believed that Nurkse took a flight of fancy in recommending that planners should focus on remaking the economy as a whole, an impossible task according to the Yale economist. Of course, Hirschman did not challenge the planning approach itself, but instead recommended that planners funnel foreign assistance and government funds into certain key industries deemed to have "complementarity" effects on other, related industries in order to start a chain reaction of development. Planners would use input-output analysis to carefully study the economy to determine which industries had the highest complementarity effects on each other,[35] and the results would determine the flow of investments.

The "Big Push"

MIT Professor and director of the Center for International Studies Paul Rosenstein-Rodan believed that the existing planning approaches had not stimulated sustained economic growth in developing countries because "the whole of industry to be created" should be "treated and planned like one huge firm or trust."[36] He claimed that the market economy never worked properly, because "it is not profitable for a private entrepreneur to invest in training labor."[37] The learned professor was apparently unaware of this common practice. He recommended the creation of state-run "industrial trusts" that would realize extensive external economies and have the resources to train workers to be industrial workers.

In his view, unemployed farm workers should be removed from the land to work in manufacturing industries that would produce goods in demand by the workers, such as shoes. An entire related set of industries would then be created, which would produce most of the goods on which workers would spend their wages. According to Rosenstein-Rodan, it was preferable to put government in charge of planning the industries, because it would reduce the risk of not being able to sell. Rosenstein-Rodan believed that planners could foresee the needs of the workers in poor countries, where they could not do so in rich countries, because it would not be difficult to predict what formerly unemployed workers in low income countries would spend their wages on.[38]

Rosenstein-Rodan's ideas epitomized the arrogance and condescension that was so typical of development planners. He believed that multi-degreed experts, particularly from the advanced countries, should dictate to the mass of simpletons residing in the Third World what their needs were. The MIT economist assumed that planners would automatically make far superior decisions than individual producers and consumers.

Rosenstein-Rodan concluded that the private sector should not undertake industrial development because there could be insufficient demand for the products produced, involving excessive risk for the entrepreneur. Moreover, private firms were concerned only with private profits and would not undertake investments with wider social benefit, such as job training or the construction of infrastructure systems such as power and communications.

The "Big Push" vision was expensive, as the government would have to come up with all the resources to develop the industries as well as pay for the expensive foreign consultants who would help train and equip all the bureaucrats and planners needed to oversee the scheme. But like other development visionaries, Rosenstein-Rodan did not believe that cost was a problem. The initial outlay for the "Big Push" would be provided by foreign aid. Once under way, it would finance itself.

Structural School

The structural school gained prominence in the 1970s and was essentially a rationale for why development planning had not succeeded. The theory posited that societies stagnated because there were structural rigidities, both domestic and international, that had to be removed before planning could take root and societies could progress. Obstacles included the "international capitalist order,"[39] existing land tenure arrangements in developing countries, dominant local oligarchies, unresponsive bureaucrats, and multinational corporations operating in developing countries. The imported system of development planning clashed with both the indigenous socioeconomic system and "international capitalism." Dual systems working at cross purposes reduced the efficiency of the aid resources. The solution, said Myrdal, was more aid and more planning in order to prevail over the resisting economic structures.

Myrdal concluded that "international inequality" contributed to the development impasse. He saw the economic inequalities between industrialized countries and poor countries as chronic and growing over time, and he also attacked the unequal income distribution within poor countries. These income inequalities were said to be the main cause of the persistence of widespread poverty.

The solution was to use foreign aid to create the welfare state. Mahbub Ul Haq, a Pakistani planner who became a World Bank senior vice president during the 1970s, was influential in changing the focus of planning from GNP growth to the relief of poverty. Instead of the "hot pursuit of GNP growth," planners were to focus on "fixing national consumption and production targets on the basis of minimum human needs." [40]

Professors became so involved with speculative theories that they ceased to observe the real world. One, Michael Todaro at New York University, forgot all about the massive flows of aid and commercial bank lending to government entities and concluded that the economies of poor countries were being dominated by investments by multinational companies that were minuscule in comparison to the aid flows. [41] In 1981, when capital inflow to Latin America was at a high, the net inflow of public and publicly guaranteed long-term loans totaled $20.6 billion, while the net inflow of private foreign direct investment was $7.3 billion. [42] At no time did this ratio reverse. During the era of development planning, aid flows dwarfed private foreign investment.

If Todaro were right that, despite the small size of their investments, multinational corporations were dominating economies, then the conclusion follows that aid inflows in support of planning were misdirected, and, therefore, should have been curtailed or reallocated to private direct investment. Unfortunately, the government investments dominated economies and perpetuated rent-seeking cultures.

The structural school was a bonanza for development economists. With the entire range of human activities now fair game for government intervention, reams of studies were needed on everything from education development, urban development, and regional development, to population control, women in development, environmental problems, and preserving Indian languages. The studies virtually always recommended more government intervention to solve social problems and more foreign aid to pay for it.

It is one of the many curious inconsistencies of the economic development literature that the same experts who concluded that the solution to poverty was the international redistribution of income to support Third World welfare states also thought that the indigenous populations should be ruthlessly squeezed in order to restrict consumption and free up resources for investment. Myrdal, who wanted to boost Third World living standards with the international redistribution of income, also argued that "there is no other road to economic development than a forceful rise in the share of the national income which is withheld from consumption and devoted to investment. This implies a policy of the utmost austerity."[43]

The belief was strong that governments should use "forced saving" to appropriate "surplus value" from the economy (especially agriculture) and divert it into a multisectoral program of development. The experts made no bones about it. The poor were to suffer most from this austerity "for the simple reason," as Myrdal put it, "that they are the many."[44]

The experts were often more heartless than the international capitalists were assumed to be. For instance, Nurkse recommended that underemployed peasants be diverted from farming into working on capital projects, while their cousins still living at subsistence levels on the farms should be taxed more heavily to prevent them from eating more and draining the agricultural surplus.[45] Heilbroner concurred, recommending that planners establish "measures that will transfer the food surplus from the peasant cultivator to workers on capital projects."[46]

W. Arthur Lewis concluded that if "backward" countries are to industrialize "they have either to cut severely into the consumption of necessaries, or else to borrow abroad. A ruthless dictatorship can cut consumption to the desired extent, but a democracy will always have to rely largely on foreign capital in its early stages of development."[47]

Development economists admired the ability of dictators to impose their theories on recalcitrant populations. Julius Nyerere received much laudatory ink for his forced resettlement "villagization" plan in Tanzania. Nyerere sent army troops to drive the peasants off their land, burn their huts, load them onto trucks, and take them to where the government thought they should live. People were resettled in government villages far from the lands that they were supposed to work, with the result that hunger greatly increased in Tanzania. Yet Nyerere became the darling of World Bank President Robert McNamara, whose institution sent the Tanzanian dictator more bank aid per capita than any other country.[48]

Academics supported Indonesia's brutal resettlement plan as well. The Indonesian government sent tribal groups to barren islands. Nothing awaited people at the new locations, but when they tried to return to Java, they were jailed to prevent them from spreading negative reports.[49]

When mild planning failed, experts called for more thoroughgoing efforts. When this failed in turn, experts supported brutal coercion reminiscent of Stalin's treatment of the kulaks. For most development economists, planning was a religion reflecting their faith that government was the means for improving the lot of humanity. As various permutations of development planning failed, they invented another. They could not admit that their approach was wrong, because it would mean unraveling the belief system on which they had based their careers. Only a strong man can say, "My God! Look at the devastation that I have wrought!"

There was one man, a burr under their saddle, so to speak, who kept pointing out to them the consequences of their ideas. Peter Bauer, now a life peer, was a Hungarian émigré who became a Cambridge don and professor at the London School of Economics. Bauer was the voice of dissent.

Bauer exposed the main tenets of the development creed as products of slipshod analysis. For example, in 1965 Bauer pointed out that the most elementary analysis refutes the notion of the vicious circle of poverty. The very existence of the rich industrialized nations flies in the face of the thesis. All began poor and developed without foreign aid. If the vicious circle of poverty were true, then innumerable individuals and groups as well as countries could not have risen to riches from poverty as they have done throughout the world.

Bauer dismissed as dangerous nonsense the belief that development required the redistribution of income. Such a policy would strike at the heart of private property and incentives that are essential to motivation and progress. Moreover, he noted that there are groups of rich people and poor people in every country no matter what its state of development. There was nothing fair about taxing workers in rich countries in order to subsidize the rich lifestyles of political elites in poor countries. Filtered through layers of bureaucracy and political manipulation, very little of the aid would ever reach the poor. Even if it did, their motivation could slacken, making them worse off in the end.

Bauer argued that development planning was based on misplaced Western guilt. He denied that successful countries had advanced at the expense of poor ones. They advanced because they built institutions that facilitated economic progress. In markets, incomes are not stolen. They are earned as a reward for providing society with needed goods and services. The problem lies in economies that have been politicized by planning. There political elites prosper from their control over resources. They have no interest in the development of markets that would undermine their power and control. The persistence of poverty, Bauer concluded, was the direct result of blocking the development of the institutions that foster individual success.

Bauer took a commonsense view of economic achievement, which was politically incorrect for his time. He said that economic advancement relied first on human aptitudes and attitudes, on social and political institutions, on historical experience, and external contacts. He stressed the importance of the individual. The largest single determinant of economic achievement in his view was the personal and cultural characteristics held by individuals—the spirit of the people. His views enraged the collectivists, who saw the human race as automatons to be molded by the government.

Bauer early concluded that central planning was much more likely to retard economic progress than to promote it. He saw planning for what it was: a concentration of power in the hands of a political elite. He observed, "It is certainly not clear why overriding the decisions of private persons should increase the flow of income, since the resources used by the planners must have been diverted from other productive public or private uses."[50] He wrote that the close economic controls involved in planning "restrict the movement of resources to directions where they would be most productive" and "inhibit the establishment of new enterprises and the expansion of efficient producers."[51] He rejected the notion that development could be fostered by shielding poor but pristine economies from external influences: "in poor countries enforced restriction of external contacts is often extremely damaging to material progress."[52]

Bauer foresaw the violence that would result from the expansion of state power. He wrote: "When state control over social and economic life is extensive and close the achievement and the exercise of political power become all-important. . . . The stakes in the fight for political power increase and the struggle for it intensifies."[53]

He also predicted the growth of the rent-seeking society: "When political action is all-important, the energies of able and ambitious men are diverted from economic activity to political life."[54]

Bauer's facts cut no weight because they provided no role for development economists, advisors, and planners. Development is something that people achieve by their efforts; it is not something that is done for them or to them. Allowing people to get on with their lives would have cut out all the fat consulting fees that the development experts collected from governments and multilateral aid organizations. Many a development economist and international bureaucrat enjoyed a luxurious lifestyle and frequent travel to exotic places—all in the name of rescuing poor lands from poverty. Development economists were able to combine a high living with a high opinion of their calling. A Mercedes, fine restaurants, luxury apartments, and first-class air travel became the normal accoutrements of good deeds. Moreover, they were the rewards for good works and not spoils captured from outcompeting one's fellows in capitalist markets.

Planning and the International Development Institutions

To live the good life one had only to hook up with one of the international development institutions. These included the World Bank, the International Monetary Fund, the UN system, the regional multilateral development banks, the U.S. Agency for International Development (USAID), and, until its demise, the Alliance for Progress. All of them reflected the postwar bias in favor of government-run economies.

Academics oversaw the creation and expansion of these institutions, nonexistent before World War II. From his post at the helm of the United Nations Conference on Trade and Development (UNCTAD), Myrdal promoted acceptance of his elitist theories throughout the international organizations.

Founded in 1945, the World Bank, the largest development lender with $22.5 billion in loans in 1995, was envisioned by its founders as a lender of last resort to economically sound projects in the so-called backward countries at a time when private capital flows were scarce because of the postwar reconstruction of Europe and Japan. Almost at once, however, influential academics, World Bank employees, and interest groups lobbied for more aid on easier terms, and lending standards fell as the World Bank expanded its loan portfolio. By 1950, the World Bank was advocating the adoption of national development plans as a way of increasing the number of projects available for financing.

The International Monetary Fund was established in 1945 with the aim of helping countries to maintain fixed exchange rates under the Bretton Woods system. The IMF's Articles of Agreement authorized the institution to collect a pool of currencies that would be used to support any currency that came under pressure caused by temporary balance of payments deficits. When the Bretton Woods system collapsed in 1971, the IMF found a new mission in lending to developing countries.

The Inter-American Development Bank, the U.S. Agency for International Development, and the Alliance for Progress were all created in the early 1960s at the height of the planning craze. President Eisenhower lent his authority to the establishment of special lending institutions for Latin America in 1959, five months after Castro marched into Havana. Many feared the spread of communism throughout Latin America, where it was said to be "one minute to midnight."[55]

The Inter-American Development Bank (IDB) officially began operations in October 1960 with original authorized capital of $850 million and made its first loan in February 1961. Between 1961 and 1994, the IDB had lent a cumulative $70 billion to Latin American governments. Planning figures prominently in the IDB Charter, which provides that the "loans made or guaranteed by the Bank shall be principally for financing specific projects, including those forming part of a national or regional development program."[56]

In 1960, the Act of Bogotá set forth the outlines of "a cooperative program of economic and social progress" for the hemisphere. It prompted President Kennedy in March 1961 to call for an Alliance for Progress among the American states.[57] The Alliance for Progress was essentially a cooperative effort between the Organization of American States, USAID, the Inter-American Development Bank, the World Bank, and the UN system to foist planning on Latin America.[58] Its creation was a landmark event that marked the acceptance in capitalist America of socialism for developing countries. With the United States pledging to provide the bulk of $20 billion in aid, over a ten-year period,[59] countries scurried to open planning ministries and to undertake the writing of plans that would attract the aid.

In 1961, President Kennedy created the U.S. Agency for International Development (USAID) by an Executive Order to implement the Foreign Assistance Act of 1961. In Latin America, USAID became the U.S. arm of the Alliance for Progress.[60]

Experts hailed the founding and expansion of the international development institutions as the greatest hope for progress for the peoples of the Third World. They concluded that the industrialized countries would have to move over to make room for the economic powerhouses that would emerge. Heilbroner enthused about the "Great Ascent" of Third World peoples that would have no parallel in history.

The only ascent was that of the international bureaucrats. Under the influence of planners such as Gunnar Myrdal, Ragnar Nurkse, and Raul Prebisch, thousands of international bureaucrats churned out development plans. Complex planning models using matrix equations and requiring vast quantities of statistics were employed. Even if the models had been realistic, the statistics were not. Economists were well aware that the poor countries had no reliable statistics. In 1970, Myrdal stressed *"the urgent need to improve statistics* in underdeveloped countries."[61] He chided the international organizations for uncritically accepting whatever statistics came their way. But by then most participants understood that statistics were a requisite for aid and that their worth had nothing to do with their validity.

A country that decided to take seriously the formulation of a comprehensive development plan was faced with an endeavor of impossible proportions. The World Bank's 1950–1951 Annual Report described the planning technique as nothing less than making an inventory of all resources in an economy and then "deciding the order in which various development projects should be undertaken within the limits of available resources." A government deemed capable of planning the development of its economy would be instructed to begin setting policy objectives and mapping out a strategy to reach those goals. Three basic steps were involved.

First, an economic growth target was set, and economists would calculate the amount of savings needed to produce it. For this, economists needed the capital/output ratio for the economy. Next economists would calculate the investment requirements of individual industries and industrial sectors necessary for achieving the growth objective.

This step required input-output analysis to determine the investment requirements for each industry to produce a specified level of output. The final step was the use of "project analysis" to allocate resources to the various projects. To get some idea of the relative merits of the competing projects, planners devised "shadow prices" to try to rank the social usefulness of the projects.

The reliance on shadow prices was an indirect way of admitting that a price system was necessary to ascertain the most efficient use of resources. Rather than attempting to approximate a market system, it would have been far better simply to rely on one. The assumptions and statistics undergirding the planning process bore only the most tenuous relationship to reality. The result was to accumulate investments that were not economically justified and would not repay the loans.

As the poor countries lacked indigenous planning capability, the multilateral development banks rushed to open training programs and send consultants to imbue bureaucrats with the techniques of planning. This led to a form of insider trading on the part of consultants. First they helped the lending agencies design the conditions borrowers would have to meet to qualify for aid. Then they advised the borrowers how to meet those conditions. It was a lucrative business, because a World Bank or IDB consultant's approval of a country's development plan meant large inflows of aid. These consultants were "rainmakers" on a vast scale.

Planning succeeded in making consultants and political elites rich while loading poor countries with unserviceable debts, but it did not succeed in its formal goals. In 1965 World Bank economist Albert Waterston lamented:

> The record is so poor—it has been worsening in fact—that it has sometimes led to disillusionment with planning and the abandonment of plans. . . . The record is not one in which planners can take pride. It can hardly be a source of complacency for planners when they reflect how few are the less developed countries which succeed in achieving even modest plan targets.[62]

In country after country the plan turned out to be no more than a wish list that was constantly subject to revision as its irrationality became apparent. Among others, Aart van de Laar, a World Bank employee during the 1970s, decried the high costs of planning that failed to improve the quality of projects. Laar contended that economists would have been more productively employed in other work.[63]

By the early 1970s, there was a "crisis in planning." The high hopes had been dashed. Economic growth had not kept pace with population growth, and living standards stagnated. The development agencies sponsored numerous meetings to try to resolve the problems. International bureaucrats were forced to confront the question, "To what degree is planning responsible for the insufficient dynamism of Latin American economies?"[64] Analysts observed that the planning bureaucracy in Latin American countries contrived to grow despite the lack of results. Planning was criticized for creating a "parallel government" that spewed forth tons of useless paper and a flood of contradictory directives.[65]

The very officials who had set up the system were called on to fix it. Not surprisingly, the preferred solution was more planning and more aid. In order to make planning effective, participants in a 1972 seminar on planning co-sponsored by the Santiago-based Latin American

Institute for Economic and Social Planning, the Organization of American States, and the Inter-American Development Bank proposed the creation of "superministries" linked to the political nerve centers of governments, and the opening of planning offices in the state ministries.[66]

The plans were never meant to be operational in the sense that Western academics intended. Rather, they were elaborate documents designed to attract large sums of foreign money that was then divvied up in ways that served the ruling elite's interests. It could not have been any other way considering the poor quality of the statistics and the unrealistic economic assumptions.

In 1974, after surveying over 200 planners in the Third World, University of California, Berkeley, professors Naomi Caiden and Aaron Wildavsky concluded that development plans had little connection to reality. Planning officials in Peru told them that their medium-term plan suffered from statistics that "were not always designed to reflect reality and are completely unsatisfactory for our purposes."[67] In Argentina, planners described the national plan as "rough estimates on the basis of rough estimates," with one planner admitting that his predecessors "had to make up all the statistics they used since their availability at the time was so poor."[68] Mexican political scientist Federico Reyes Heroles put it even more bluntly: "we don't have a tradition of fact in Mexico, even in economics."[69]

Third World bureaucrats quickly realized the futility of planning, but the international organizations required a plan as a prerequisite for aid. All was not lost, however. Planners took their cue from one of the chief European administrators of the postwar Marshall Plan, who resolved: "We shall produce any statistic that we think will help us to get as much money out of the United States as we possibly can. Statistics which we do not have, but which we need to justify our demands, we will simply fabricate."[70] In the final analysis, the international organizations only wanted the plans to obtain lists of projects to finance. Caiden and Wildavsky concluded:

> It didn't matter whether the plan worked; what did count was the ability to produce a document which looked like a plan, and that meant using economists and other technical personnel. If these skills were not available within the country, they had to be imported in the form of planners and foreign-aid advisors. A demand existed and an entirely new industry was created to fill the need. Thus national planning may be justified on a strict cash basis; planners may bring in more money from abroad than it costs to support them at home.[71]

Financing Development Planning

The ideas of the development planners translated into large financial flows to developing country governments. In the postwar period, Latin America's massive government expansion was financed mainly by government-to-government and government-guaranteed loans. Between 1945 and 1992, Western governments had allocated some $400 billion to Latin American governments.[72] In addition to this, private banks made loans to "sovereign" Third World governments. By 1982, private creditors had lent some $136 billion to Latin American government agencies, with about 80 percent of the private financing from commercial banks.[73] In 1982, the public sector in Latin America absorbed 76 percent of total long-term capital inflows.[74]

Private creditors followed the advice of the World Bank and IMF to channel loans to Third World governments so that they could be used to build up state enterprises in accordance with a development plan. It did not make sense for the leading institutions of capitalism, such as Citibank and Chase Manhattan Bank, to be fostering the growth of socialism south of the border, but the World Bank was successful in convincing public opinion that government was the engine of growth in developing countries.

Commercial banks piggybacked on some World Bank loans and lent massively to developing country governments that had received the World Bank-IMF seal of approval. World Bank president Robert McNamara observed in October 1979 that

> The Bank has sought to support flows of private capital on reasonable terms through its own direct lending, through co-financing operations with commercial banks and—perhaps most importantly—through its efforts to promote in individual countries strategies of development which are realistic and sustainable.[75]

Commercial bank funding was a relatively smaller portion of total funding for development planning because it did not get under way until 1973 and screeched to a halt in 1982, while international development assistance began with the establishment of the Bretton Woods institutions in 1945 and continues in the 1990s.

The government-to-government loans were termed foreign aid or development assistance. Calling these transfers foreign aid was a misnomer. As Peter Bauer has observed, the resources were mainly in the form of loans that had to be repaid. Only the loans made to the least creditworthy countries by the International Development Association, the World Bank's soft loan window, have been long-term loans at very low interest rates. Outright grants comprised a small percentage of the total.

Multilateral development bank loans have an element of subsidy to the interest rates charged, but the rates have not been lower than what successful countries can obtain in international markets. The development institutions have not been allowed to discriminate among borrowers in order to set interest rates according to creditworthiness; therefore poorer, less creditworthy countries receive a higher level of subsidy than more successful countries.

Throughout the postwar period, bilateral lending to Latin American governments has been sizeable as well. This lending comprises bilateral development agency lending and loans for political and military purposes. The USAID is the largest bilateral development institution, but all the industrialized countries have development agencies that funnel credits to the Third World. European Community lending is also included in this category.

World Bank and Inter-American Development Bank officials have boasted that for every dollar of their lending, $2 of commercial bank lending flowed to developing countries. In the heyday of government expansion in Latin America, this claim seems too modest. Our comparison of the stocks of Latin American countries' public commercial bank debt to multilateral development bank (MDB) debt during the years 1973 to 1981 shows that in 1973 commercial banks lent $1.8 for every $1 of MDB loans. In 1974, commercial banks lent $2.4 to the region for every dollar of multilateral lending and the ratio rose steadily until 1981, when every dollar of lending by the multilateral institutions generated $5.1 in commercial bank loans to governments.[76] This is not to say that commercial banks were massively cofinancing MDB projects, but rather that they followed World Bank and IMF advice to forego market lending standards and funneled large loans to government entities under sovereign guarantee.

In retrospect, after the beating that the commercial banks took when the irrational government-run systems collapsed in 1982, the commercial bank loans would be better termed foreign aid. Commercial bank loans have been written down, rescheduled, and forgiven to the extent that Latin America's foreign commercial bank debt was reduced by more than 60 percent between 1987 and 1993.[77] Meanwhile, the multilateral development banks still hold their portfolios at face value.

During the years that the massive growth in government occurred, private lending to private companies in the region was a declining percentage of the total. In 1972, private, non-guaranteed loans to private firms amounted to 40 percent of total long-term debt in the region. In 1977, while all lending had risen in absolute terms, the private sector's relative share of long-term debt fell to 27 percent. By 1980, it had declined to 25 percent.[78] According to an IDB finance official, the loans to private firms were used mainly for the import of consumer goods.

There were inflows of private direct investment to the region in those years, but they constituted a relatively small portion of total long-term capital inflows. In 1980, private direct foreign investment in Latin American countries totaled $5.7 billion, about 20 percent of total capital inflows for that year.[79]

As blocked societies emerged, development economists ever more stridently blamed the system's flaws on the market, when a quick perusal of the financial flows would have told them that the market economy had been eclipsed by government.

The Role of Development Planning in Building Up State Sectors

Throughout the decades of debt-financed development, the aid institutions continued to play an important role in the creation of state companies, thereby strengthening the position of the governing elites vis-à-vis society. United Nations agencies, such as the Economic Commission for Latin America (ECLA) and the UNCTAD, promoted Third World nationalism and propagated the view that it was in the interest of developing country governments to nationalize foreign-owned firms. The World Bank and Inter-American Development Bank also condoned nationalization. Nationalization accorded with the emphasis on planning, since planners believed that control over investment was the key to success. The World Bank and the Inter-American Development Bank were quick to provide large loans to newly nationalized companies, once the furor died down.

Self-serving elites seized on nationalism, long a potent force in Latin American countries, as a convenient banner to hide behind in their quest for control of national resources. After all, who could be against national pride, the *Patria*? Still, as Mexican jurist Luis Pazos pointed out, it was a myth that nationalized companies were run in the public interest. From Mexico to Argentina, traditional elites took over companies and doled out jobs as patronage to their friends, relatives, and supporters. Often, the most fervent nationalists were also the most outspoken in demanding higher aid levels.

The development of dense layers of bureaucracy in Latin American countries is partly attributable to the fact that each aid agency has different rules and procedures, which the countries had to follow in order to receive aid. An OECD-sponsored study found that "local officials have to deal with at least ten and sometimes twenty or thirty different procedures. Unless the government machine is well equipped to cope, departments become clogged with project documents."[80] The result, according to the 1986 study, is that large segments of developing country governments have been reoriented to serving the international aid bureaucracy, diminishing what little accountability they had to local populations. The study observes that "little by little the agencies' rules and regulations have taken such hold in government services that most local officials regard them as the tablets of the law, or at very least as non-negotiable conditions."[81]

In truth, threats from the World Bank and Inter-American Development Bank to cut off funding due to non-compliance with rules are not credible, because developing country officials know that the international institutions are money-moving bureaucracies faced with tremendous pressures to lend. Moreover, beset with regulations raining down from both their own governments and the lending agencies, officials in recipient countries chose the regulations that best serve their interests.

For example, a component in a development project calling for the creation of a state company was heeded, as the additional jobs and patronage increased the power of the governing elites, while the universal call of the international institutions for standardized accounting systems has been routinely ignored for forty-five years. Functionaries simply have no incentive to overhaul ad hoc accounting procedures that allow them to plunder state property for their own personal use.

The flow of international aid channeled productive resources into the expansion of bureaucratic fiefdoms. In the 1990s, World Bank economists themselves recognize that building up governments led to unproductive rent-seeking and large-scale waste of resources. In 1988, World Bank researchers Alan Gelb, John Knight, and Richard Sabot reported that the increased concentration of resources in the public sector that aid made possible stimulated a disproportionately rapid increase in public sector employment: "The greater the size of the public sector the greater the scope for lobbying for more jobs."[82] They concluded that economies with "powerful bureaucracies and little public accountability are fertile grounds for rent-seeking behaviour and patronage."[83]

The World Bank economists observed that governments perceive the creation of jobs to be a relatively painless method of rewarding political supporters. The patronage creates a push for more influence-peddling, however, as more groups coalesce to obtain the benefits won by earlier petitioners. Soon, the wage rate in the public sector rises relative to jobs in the private sector, attracting still more job seekers. An unproductive "sink" of surplus labor in the public sector forms. Unemployment in the private sector rises, as more resources are pulled from the productive sector to maintain the unproductive public workers.

According to the World Bank researchers, the government's response to unemployment often takes the form of creating still more public employment, which in turn generates more excess labor in the public sector, along with further migration to the capital city where the majority of public sector jobs are located.[84]

In short, development planning combined with the pre-existing institutions to stimulate rent-seeking coalitions that excluded the mass of the population from economic opportunities. The planning system brought by the international development institutions served to consolidate and strengthen the existing system of government overregulation of the economy. The result was the emergence of a technocracy or "transnational elite" that substituted its decisions for the market's, thus foreclosing real economic development.

The technocrats and political elites who incrusted themselves in the newly created government agencies, ministries, and state companies outmaneuvered traditional regional interests to gain an increasing concentration of power at the national level.[85] This had the effect of diminishing local participation in the development process. The poor and those who lacked political connections were marginalized and impoverished by the rent-seeking activities of those with access to government.

Edgar Revéiz found this to be the case in Colombia, and the result was the same in every Latin American country that adopted the planning model. Whether a particular government was democratic or military-led, whether the reigning ideology was more socialist or less socialist, the experience throughout the region has been similar. The creation of planning authorities at the behest of foreign aid-dispensing institutions accelerated the growth of government.

The advent of the debt crisis in 1982 and the sea change of thinking within Latin American countries forced the experts in the West to water down their statist advice with more market-oriented policies. In 1980, Mexican economist Luis Pazos decried the "keynesian-marxist policies" that had created the interventionist state in Mexico. Pazos concluded that "reality has shown that social tensions, higher unemployment and a growing underclass" resulted from the approach.[86] Guatemala's Francisco Marroquín University president Manuel Ayau concurred:

> It is very sad to observe that in once prosperous countries with tremendous potential such as Argentina, Brazil, Mexico and Venezuela . . . the prevalence of the interventionist economic thesis expounded by Keynes, Prebisch, et al., caused shameful poverty that demands handouts from charitable countries that have permitted their citizens to create wealth, such as the United States.[87]

Aid-dependent governments could not prevent the "transnational elite" from taking control over their economic policies. The Third World became a vast playground where American and European development experts conducted their experiments. The legacy of these experiments was unserviceable debts and rent-seeking institutions that blocked true economic development.

The development planners were the shamans of the postwar era. If they had been knowledgeable of the countries they advised, they would have known that economic development required that the rent-seeking tradition be replaced with a new ethic of profit-making. Relying instead on abstract theorizing and faith in planning, Western experts strengthened the rent-seeking institutions and ultimately brought the countries to a crisis that forced a change in approach. The era of development planning is an object lesson of the dangers of applying abstract knowledge without regard to a country's history and institutions.

Notes

1. Gunnar Myrdal, *An International Economy: Problems and Prospects* (New York: Harper, 1956), 201.
2. Ibid., 144. Emphasis in the original.
3. See, for example, John Kenneth Galbraith, "Reflections: A Visit to Russia," *The New Yorker*, 3 September 1984, 54–65; Ragnar Nurkse, *Problems of Capital Formation in Underdeveloped Countries* (New York: Oxford University Press, 1953; reprinted 1962), 63–64, 76, 150;

and League of Nations *International Currency Experience: Lessons of the Inter-War Period* (New York: League of Nations, 1944; reprinted by the United Nations in 1947), whose preface notes that most of the book, except 143–61, was the work of Ragnar Nurkse.

4. Paul Baran, *The Political Economy of Growth* (New York: Monthly Review, Inc., 1957), xxix.
5. Robert Heilbroner, "The Struggle for Economic Development in Our Time," in Harry G. Shaffer and Jan S. Prybyla, eds., *From Underdevelopment to Affluence: Western, Soviet and Chinese Views* (New York: Appleton-Century-Crofts, 1968), 42.
6. Ibid., 43.
7. Nurkse, *Problems of Capital Formation*, 43.
8. Ibid., 76.
9. Jan Tinbergen, *Lessons from the Past* (Amsterdam: Elsevier, 1963), 24.
10. Baran, *The Political Economy of Growth*, xl.
11. Nurkse, *Problems of Capital Formation*, 144.
12. See Peter Bauer, *Dissent on Development* (Cambridge: Harvard University Press, 1972), and *Reality and Rhetoric: Studies in the Economics of Development* (Cambridge: Harvard University Press, 1984).
13. Gunnar Myrdal, *Rich Lands and Poor: The Road to World Prosperity* (New York and Evanston: Harper & Row, 1957), 55.
14. Gunnar Myrdal, "International Inequalities," in Gerald Meier, ed., *Leading Issues in Development Economics* (New York: Oxford University Press, 1964), 344–48.
15. Myrdal, *Rich Lands and Poor*.
16. Deepak Lal, *The Poverty of 'Development Economics'* (Cambridge: Harvard University Press, 1985), 43–45.
17. Ibid.
18. Raul Prebisch, "The Economic Development of Latin America and Its Principal Problems," *Economic Bulletin for Latin America*, February 1962, 5.
19. Edgar Dosman and David Pollock, "Raul Prebisch, 1901–1971: The Continuing Quest," prepared for a conference in honor of Raul Prebisch, "Latin American Economic Thought: Past, Present and Future," organized by the Inter-American Development Bank, Washington, D.C., 14–15 November 1991.
20. Ibid.
21. W. Rostow, *The Stages of Economic Growth: A Non-Communist Manifesto* (Cambridge: Cambridge University Press, 1960), 2–6.
22. Ibid., 6–7.
23. Ibid.
24. Ibid., 9.
25. Ibid., 59–64, 67–74.
26. Ibid., 45–46.

27. Michael Todaro, *Economic Development in the Third World* (New York: Longman Inc., 1977), 52–54.
28. Arthur Lewis, *Report on Industrialization and the Gold Coast* (Accra: Government Printing Department, 1953), 8, 9–11.
29. Arthur Lewis, *The Principles of Economic Planning* (London: George Allen and Unwin Ltd, 1965; first printing 1949), 121.
30. Ibid., 121–22.
31. Nurkse, *Problems of Capital Formation*, 5.
32. Ibid., 13.
33. Ibid., 89.
34. Albert Hirschman was based at Yale University when he wrote his treatise on unbalanced growth, published in 1958. He went on to professorships at Columbia University, Harvard University, and Princeton University from which he retired emeritus in 1985.
35. Albert Hirschman, *The Strategy of Economic Development* (New Haven: Yale University Press, 1958), 51–55, 62–63, 65–70, 73, 205–208.
36. Paul Rosenstein-Rodan, "Problems of Industrialization of Eastern and South-Eastern Europe," *Economic Journal*, June–September 1943, 204.
37. Ibid., 205.
38. Ibid., 205–206.
39. The "international capitalist order" consisted of the United States, Canada, Japan, and West Germany, since literally every other country was extensively socialized.
40. Mahbub Ul Haq, *The Poverty Curtain: Choices for the Third World* (New York: Columbia University Press, 1976), 33, 43.
41. Todaro, *Economic Development in the Third World*.
42. Calculated from Latin America external debt data provided by the Inter-American Development Bank; and Inter-American Development Bank *Economic and Social Progress in Latin America*, 1983, Table 50, 376.
43. Myrdal, *Rich Lands and Poor*, 84.
44. Ibid., 85.
45. Nurkse, *Problems of Capital Formation*, 43.
46. Robert Heilbroner, *The Economic Problem* (Englewood Cliffs, N.J.: Prentice-Hall, 1968), 621.
47. Lewis, *The Principles of Economic Planning*, 126.
48. James Bovard, "The World Bank vs. the World's Poor," Cato Institute Policy Analysis paper, 28 September 1987.
49. Ibid.
50. Bauer, *Dissent on Development*, 73.
51. Ibid., 84.
52. Ibid., 85.

53. Ibid., 86–87.
54. Ibid., 87.
55. Abraham Lowenthal, "Alliance Rhetoric Versus Latin American Reality," *Foreign Affairs*, April 1970, 495–96.
56. IDB, *Agreement Establishing the Inter-American Development Bank*, (1988 reprint) Art. III, sec. 7 (a) (vi).
57. Richard Stebbings, ed., *Documents on American Foreign Relations 1961* (New York: Harper & Row, for the Council on Foreign Relations, 1962), 396–97.
58. See Inter-American Economic and Social Council, *The Alliance for Progress: Its First Year: 1961–1962*, ser. (Washington, D.C.: Pan American Union, General Secretariat, OAS, 1963).
59. Ibid., 57.
60. Organization of American States, *External Financing for Latin American Development* (Baltimore: Johns Hopkins Press, 1971, published for the Organization of American States).
61. Gunnar Myrdal, *The Challenge of World Poverty: A World Anti-Poverty Program in Outline* (New York: Pantheon Books, 1970), 448. Emphasis in the original.
62. Albert Waterston, *Development Planning: Lessons of Experience* (Baltimore: The Johns Hopkins Press, 1965), 4.
63. Aart van de Laar, *The World Bank and the Poor* (Boston: Kluwer-Nijhoff Publishing, 1980), 235.
64. Ricardo Cibotti, Arturo Núñez del Prado y Pedro Sáinz, "Evolución y Perspectivas de los Procesos de Planificación en América Latina," conference paper presented at the Planning Seminar, Santiago, Chile, 1972, in *Experiencias y Problemas de la Planificación en América Latina* (Mexico City: Siglo Veintiuno Editores, S.A., 1974), 29.
65. Conference papers presented at the Planning Seminar, Santiago, Chile, 1972 in *Experiencias y Problemas de la Planificación en América Latina*.
66. Ibid., 12–16.
67. Naomi Caiden and Aaron Wildavsky, *Planning and Budgeting in Poor Countries* (New York: Wiley-Interscience, 1974), 176.
68. Ibid.
69. Mark Uhlig, "A Daring Magazine and Its Awkward Questions," *New York Times*, 21 March 1991.
70. Oskar Morgenstern, *On the Accuracy of Economic Observations* (Princeton: Princeton University Press, 1963, Second Edition, First Edition 1950), 21.
71. Caiden and Wildavsky, *Planning and Budgeting in Poor Countries*, 286.
72. Includes loans and grants from all sources, multilateral and bilateral.
73. Total stock of disbursed external publicly guaranteed debt owed to

private creditors. Calculated from external debt data provided by the Inter-American Development Bank.

74. Calculated from external debt data provided by the Inter-American Development Bank, and Table 51 in the Inter-American Development Bank, *Economic and Social Progress in Latin America*, 1987.

75. *The McNamara Years at the World Bank*, Major Policy Addresses of Robert S. McNamara 1968–1981 (Baltimore and London: Johns Hopkins University Press, 1981), 604.

76. Calculated from external debt data provided by the Inter-American Development Bank.

77. Ibid.

78. Calculated from external debt data provided by the Inter-American Development Bank, and Table 51 in the Inter-American Development Bank, *Economic and Social Progress in Latin America*, 1987.

79. Ibid.

80. Bernard Lecomte, *Project Aid: Limitations and Alternatives* (Paris: Organization for Economic Cooperation and Development, 1986), 61.

81. Ibid., 62.

82. Alan Gelb, John Knight, and Richard Sabot, "Lewis Through a Looking Glass: Public Sector Employment, Rent-Seeking, and Economic Growth," Working Paper, World Bank, Washington, D.C., November 1988, 4.

83. Ibid., 9–10.

84. Ibid., 12–23.

85. Revéiz, *Democratizar para Sobrevivir*, 44–45.

86. Luis Pazos, *El Gobierno y La Inflación* (Mexico City: Editorial Diana, 1989, first printing 1980), 138.

87. Manuel Ayau, *La Década Perdida* (Guatemala City: Manuel Ayau, 1989), 74.

5

Latin America's
Statist Tradition

In making the transition to capitalism, Latin Americans are escaping from their history as well as from development planning. Things went wrong in the very beginning when public offices were privatized and the private economy was brought under the government's sway through heavy regulation.

Imagine the United States without a stock market in which to buy and sell companies but with an organized market in which mayoralties, the state treasurer's job, government procurement positions, and the like could be bought and sold and you have a picture of colonial Latin America. A person could buy and sell government jobs, and heirs could inherit them. On the other hand, a person who wanted to sell sugarcane had to do it in the Caribbean. If he wanted to produce cacao, Venezuela was the permissible site. Planters in Chile could cultivate wheat but were denied the right to produce tobacco.

Such a system developed perverse property rights. Markets were created for public offices, but were stifled for commodities and manufactures. A system that encouraged people to compete to buy the equivalent of the New York mayor's office, but did not allow free enterprise, could not develop the capital markets and other institutions of a free society.

Instead, they developed institutions that placed economic decisions in the hands of those who purchased government offices. In a market economy, the stock exchange is the single most important economic institution, but in the Spanish colonial empire the Seville-based royal House of Trade (also known as the India House) was all-important.[1] Created in 1503, the House of Trade was given a monopoly over trade with the Spanish colonies, and its jurisdiction stretched from Spain to the Caribbean to Patagonia. By 1579, the House of Trade had comprehensive legal jurisdiction over economic affairs throughout the Spanish empire. In addition, India House received all revenues from duties, tolls, customs, salt-pits and playing cards in the realm, while it simultaneously issued laws regulating economic activity. India House had not only administrative but also judicial functions. The same institution that received vast revenues also enforced economic laws and investigated wrongdoing.[2]

The House of Trade regulated every aspect of trade in the Spanish colonies. No ship set sail without its permission. A horde of officials inspected the papers of every ship that arrived from, or set sail to, America, with the authority to approve all passengers and cargo. Bureaucrats specified even such nitty-gritty details as instructions for the baking of biscuits to be consumed aboard ship and the packaging of mercury, essential to mining operations in Spanish America, "into a Sheep's Skin well bound with hempen Cords."[3] Its regulatory authority even extended to the fixing of prices, parceling out rights to own fishing boats, and setting the ferry charge on the river at Santo Domingo in what is today the Dominican Republic.

In contrast to the U.S. stock market, where power is dispersed among millions of stockholders, the House of Trade was highly centralized, which placed great responsibility in the hands of a few. The duties of the president of the House commingled administrative, legislative, and judicial functions, leading to severe conflicts of interest. The president managed all revenues and distributed justice, enforcing all laws and ordinances throughout the realm pertaining to trade and commerce. In addition, he was expected to outfit the Spanish Armada and the Spanish fleet, which comprised merchant ships, naval galleons, and ships carrying mail and royal representatives to the New World. He oversaw the assembling of crews and the licensing of passengers aboard ship in order to prevent travel by unauthorized persons. As if that were not enough, he also supervised the buying of guns, cannons, and ammunition out of the revenues accumulated through a convoy duty known as the *avería*. Finally, the president had a seat in the Chamber of Justice of the House, where civil and criminal cases were decided. He had a voice in the outcome of civil cases involving sub-stantial sums of money and could decide the outcome of both criminal and civil cases where judges were stalemated.[4]

Conflicts of interest were worsened by the fact that officials could hold more than one position. The Treasurer, Comptroller, and Com-missioner, all important persons in the management of the King's rev-enues, could also be judges in the Chamber of Justice with the authority to decide civil and criminal cases. They could appoint deputies as they saw fit to carry out their various responsibilities.

The concentration of power had many adverse consequences. The numerous conflicts of interest encouraged wealth transfers to govern-ing elites, as the very persons with the easiest access to the king's rev-enues were given the power to prosecute wrongdoing. The king's officers, entrusted with so much, soon convinced themselves that with-out their interference the kingdom would collapse. Soon no area was too inconsequential to merit their interference.

The main focus of India House bureaucrats, as well as that of their colonial counterparts, was on lining their pockets and elevating their status. The highest pomp and ceremony ruled in the House of Trade, and courtiers enjoyed privileges according to their place in the hierar-chy. On entering the court, the initiated knew whom he was dealing with by scanning seating arrangements and assessing the comparative finery of the chairs. Officials spent much time pontificating on trivial matters, such as the proper greetings to be used in official correspon-dence. This weighty issue required attention from the king himself, who promulgated a 1786 regulation intended to solve "the frequent disputes about the proper form of address in official correspondence."[5]

The House of Trade did not foster open markets or provide a frame-work that enabled private persons to easily transact business. On the contrary, rather than transmitting prices and market signals, as the U.S. stock market does, the House of Trade sought to stamp out market forces and impose economic rule by government fiat.

The Spanish monarchy transplanted centralized institutions to run its colonies. The colonial viceroys, the king's representatives, were given extensive powers. The viceroy was the chief civil and military officer, supervising justice as well as the colonial Treasury and the secular aspects of the Catholic Church. The *audiencias,* judicial and administrative tribunals that served simultaneously as advisory coun-cil to the viceroy, were also imbued with extensive powers, in mimicry of the relationship between the king and the House of Trade. The *audi-encias* were headed by an *oidor,* or judge of appeal who also had administrative and advisory duties. The viceroys and *audiencias* had some authority to write legislation, but their primary function was to enforce legislation promulgated by India House.

The colonial treasuries, repositories of the king's wealth, were naturally of prime importance. Much regulation was directed to their organization and management in an effort to eliminate theft and waste. Ever distrustful of his royal servants, the king placed responsibility for the iron safes that held Crown revenues in the hands of at most two or three officials in each colony, all of whose keys were needed to open the safes. Nothing stopped officials from colluding to divert revenues to their own uses, however, before they ever reached the safes.

Colonial government mirrored the flaws of Spain's leading institution. Top comptrollers had wide civil and judicial powers, and the viceroy was able to influence the outcome of cases. Top financial officials, although hired directly by the king, in reality often served at the pleasure of the viceroy. Moreover, the privilege-ridden royal administration created animosities that encouraged officials to use power to obtain what others were granted as privilege.

Municipal government was more of the same. In the main, the municipal councils were little aristocracies, consisting primarily of permanent officials who had purchased or inherited their posts, and who became deadwood in the system, with little concern for their public role. They used their ability to issue economic regulations for self-enrichment. They collected some taxes for the king, administered price controls and, in tandem with the viceroy, enforced Crown regulations pertaining to property. Throughout the colonies, corruption in municipal administration was universal, with no accounts kept at all in many towns.

The opportunities defined by the framework of bureaucratic institutions shaped the outlook of the people who emerged as economic leaders. These people looked to the state as the source of economic opportunity. Markets were not allowed to perform their function of providing information feedback to economic actors. The primacy of politics over markets meant that economic failures were subsidized and success was penalized.

The strongest property rights were in government offices and the Catholic Church. There were two ways to acquire government jobs, either by purchase or by privilege. Royal office both in Spain and in the colonies was granted to members of the Spanish aristocracy and to those who had served the king in some way, such as military service or lending the Crown large sums of ducats. Beginning in 1503, people could purchase their jobs. Government salaries and compensation throughout the realm varied widely according to no objective standards but at the whim of the king and his courtiers. The common thread throughout the royal administration was that royal officeholders were allowed to treat their positions as private property.

In an environment in which the government was regarded as the ultimate owner of all wealth, the sale of public offices was viewed as a means of generating revenue. In 1559, King Philip II established the sale of offices as an important revenue-raiser for the Crown. Inheriting a bankrupt treasury, he perceived a pressing need for a new revenue source in the colonies. The office of notary was put up for sale, followed by numerous positions in the royal mints, the treasury, and the courts of law. Most municipal offices, both in Spain and the colonies, were sold. Some important colonial offices were sold by the Crown, such as positions within the treasury and courts, while the viceroy sold minor colonial posts.[6] In the seventeenth century, the sale of offices even extended to the House of Trade, where from 1604 the office of notary of the Chamber of Justice was vendable, along with other minor offices. Under the reign of Charles II (1665–1700), even the position of Councilor was occasionally sold (on one occasion for a sum of 145,000 ducats).

The sale of offices openly turned public jobs into the private property of the purchasers. Prices rose and fell on a job's income-generating possibilities. If the salary plus opportunities to garner additional income was greater than the sum of the amount invested plus interest, then the job was a good buy. The highest-priced jobs were those that gave the purchaser access to the most government resources, such as positions within the royal treasury, procurement positions and the office of viceroy, the king's representative in the colonies (sold in some minor posts), and offices that gave the holder power to regulate some aspect of economic life. In hard times, prices fell and in wealthier areas, such as Lima and Mexico City, prices were higher. Anxious to raise revenues, the kings tended to sell the positions that would fetch the highest prices, which were the very jobs with the easiest access to the king's wealth.

There was a full-fledged market in government jobs, complete with public auction of positions, speculation in jobs, and property titles for the buyers. Buyers could even purchase their jobs on the installment plan.

This was in stark contrast to the determined repression of markets in the private sector. Citizens often witnessed the public auction of government jobs, but public auctions of goods were obstructed by myriad regulations and the imposition of punitive taxation. The auction of the position of *regidor,* or councilman, was conducted in the following way. A messenger of the tribunal with the vacancy would stand in a public square and announce the sale in a loud voice thirty times, usually every day for a month. At any time during the thirty days and for a limited time afterwards, an applicant could submit his bid in writing to treasury officials. Successful applicants usually bought their jobs on the installment plan—their bids included the total price, down payment, and number and dates of installments to be made. Persons of substance were found to vouch for the applicant's ability to pay and fulfill the duties of office.[7]

If officials received a better offer, the first applicant was informed and given the chance to increase his bid. All applicants were provided similar opportunities.

Finally, officials accepted the highest offer and then the messenger announced the winning bid at a final public auction and invited any higher offers. If none were forthcoming, the vacant position was declared to be sold. The buyer then received from the *audiencia* a written title and took the oath of office. Something is seriously amiss when one can acquire a property title to a government job. When private interests reign supreme in government, public service becomes a private activity.

The purchaser had bequeathing rights and the right of resale. Some jobs were passed down from father to son for centuries, like a treasured family heirloom. Often the positions were resold. When a first-time officeholder sold his position, he was supposed to deliver one-half of the sale price to the king. On subsequent sale of the position, only one-third of the sale price was payable to the king.[8] This amounted to a tax on the right to divert public resources to one's own use.

The buyer of a government job could not escape red tape requiring further payments. The buyer was required to send a petition for confirmation of his position to Spain. A 1606 decree stipulated that he be able to produce royal confirmation of his title within four years, otherwise the position had to be resold. The buyer usually resorted to hiring a lawyer in Spain to handle the complicated transaction of registering his position, which required, like everything else, an avalanche of paperwork and payments to the king and his courtiers.

Many records exist documenting the sale of offices. Historical records tell us that the post of treasurer of the mint in Mexico was sold in 1584 for 130,000 pesos, 60,000 down and two equal annual installments of 35,000. The same post at Potosí, location of the rich silver mines in what is now Bolivia, was sold in 1656 for 124,000 pesos, one-half cash on the spot and the rest in three annual installments. In Lima, the post of treasurer of the mint was sold for 20,000 pesos in 1581 and for 80,000 pesos in 1702.[9]

The market in government jobs gave rise to absurdities. An example was the Crown employment of officials who acted as job appraisers. Their function was to evaluate the value of vendable offices in order to ensure that the king received a fair price. One can just picture a haughty official decked in knee breeches dryly interviewing the existing holder of a job in the royal mint, for instance, about the job's prospects for personal enrichment. With the official wanting to record the highest value possible for the job, the seller would glowingly describe the vast amount of minted coins that passed through his hands, and his opportunity to shave a percentage of the gold and silver from the coins for himself.

Instead of speculating in commodities, people speculated in jobs. Peruvian jurist Gaspar de Escalona Aguero complained that positions were sold and resold and very often the king was never notified of the sales.[10] Bribes were paid to colonial officials to neglect the necessary paperwork. Men often tendered other positions in partial payment for a job whose value seemed likely to rise.

The consequences of privatizing governmental functions were severe. There was a massive diversion of effort from productive economic activities into government. The population aspired to government employment as a way to build a personal fortune, or at minimum have a steady income. It was difficult to make money by producing something of value, with legions of bureaucrats arbitrarily taxing and regulating economic activity. It was far easier and more socially acceptable to make money by skimming revenues from the government. Buyers faced strong incentives to personally profit from their positions, not only to recoup their investment, but also raise the resale value of their jobs. It was understood, for example, that officials of the India House had a right to a share of the revenues they passed on to the king. Similarly, colonial Treasury officials were expected to take a cut of the tax revenues raised. Regulators were given a free hand to enact regulations that would benefit them personally.

What we would call corruption was simply the way the system operated. The bureaucratic class became entrenched and viewed the monarchy's property as its own. The Spanish bureaucracy became a "new class," independent of the state, not unlike the later communist bureaucracy that Milovan Djilas said "instinctively feels that national goods are, in fact, its property."[11] The difference was that for those Spanish royal officials who had purchased their jobs, there was no need to feel "instinctively" that national property was theirs. They had bought it outright.

Everyone wanted to administer taxes and regulations, which were gold mines for personal profit. Under the colonial system taxes proliferated and were haphazardly administered. The complicated procedures for collection and accounting ensured that numerous officials were required. For revenues to flow through so many hands to the king required what Pedro Muchada decried as a "tyrannical and destructive tax system."[12]

The system did not make sense if one assumes that officials were trying to serve the public interest. However, if officials were acting in their own self-interest, the chaotic tax system was ideally suited to allow them to extract the maximum personal benefit. The system's fragmentation made it impossible for the government to calculate the real value of tax collections, creating cover for massive fraud and abuse. Muchada reports that officials were able to tax at will, and taxpayers would pay bribes to avoid even heavier levies. The king was defrauded of the greater part of the revenues.[13]

Officials were only investigated and punished when they took too much and threatened the system. A notorious case was that of Francisco Gómez de la Rocha, provincial mayor of the rich silver mining center of Potosí, in what is now Bolivia, who was found to have defrauded the royal mint of 472,000 pesos and was executed together with the assayer of the mint in 1654.[14]

The monarchy relied on centralization to protect its revenues, but overlapping responsibilities created confusion that allowed officials more freedom to act independently. With each official out for his own gain, the royal administration was fragmented. The profusion of contradictory laws, designed to benefit bureaucrats and favored interest groups, spawned chaos. The monarchs lost power to an unwieldy bureaucracy that operated according to its own priorities.

Reformers denigrated the "absurd and unsupportable" system. One high-ranking fiscal official in the Peruvian colony complained that privileged ministers of the court had "the ability to derogate the most fundamental laws simply by saying 'The King wishes—The King orders—' . . . when in all probability the king neither wishes nor orders." The official further decried the resulting situation of "despotism, turmoil, and a chaos of decrees, orders and declarations, which far from prescribing the limits of the rulers and the obligations of the ruled, serves to enable each to do as he pleases."[15]

Since the position of the king's self-serving officers was strengthened by the confusion, all attempts to reform the system resulted in more regulation and closer control of the economy.

The property rights of the bureaucrats made it difficult and costly for economic agents to transact. Real private property was almost unobtainable, except by privilege. Goods and services often could not be bought and sold easily. Officials could grant a monopoly, and it was much easier to obtain a successful business that way than by producing and marketing a good product.

From the first, the monarchy possessed all rights, both sovereign and property rights, in the American colonies. The Crown granted every privilege and position, whether economic, political, or religious. With the most profitable opportunities to be gained by petitioning the government to obtain protected profits, rent-seeking was the order of the day. Property rights were acquired as privileges and not as rewards for productive work.

Real entrepreneurs were considered a threat to the entire system. They wanted strong property rights in order to develop resources and contract in markets—rights that were at odds with the regulatory rights of the privatized public offices. Consequently, entrepreneurs were relegated to the black market, smuggling, and piracy.

The Spanish monarchy was ideologically opposed to much productive enterprise, believing in the bullionist theory of wealth that was popular in the fifteenth century. According to that theory, the wealth of a country is based on precious metals such as gold and silver. The monarchy viewed the colonies as a supplier of mineral riches and exotic tropical products and as a market for Spanish goods.

The consequences for property rights of the Crown's erratically applied aversion to productive enterprise were profound. Potential economic entrepreneurs in Spanish America confronted an institutional framework that made it very costly to transact. There was no impartial contract law to help ensure that parties would comply with agreements. Moreover, Spanish law was hostile to economic activity not expressly permitted by the Crown. Property rights were status-based privileges, not something acquired through economic success in markets.

The Spanish Crown tried to abolish competition. The king's officers saw the realm as a single economic organism and allocated production to protected areas where neither competition nor change was supposed to upset the balance regulators were trying to achieve. The state itself ran some monopolies. In other cases, monopoly rights were sold or granted through royal dispensations to those who had rendered services or who were deemed capable of developing the specific resources the king wished to promote. Monopolies included gold and silver mining, sugarcane production, mercury for use in the silver mines, production of cacao, tobacco, salt, and wheat and snow gathering for drinking water.

Favored individuals and groups who obtained royally sanctioned monopolies benefited at the expense of the rest who were denied such opportunities. Privileges were granted sometimes for fixed periods to be extended at the whim of officials, at other times for life, and at still other times were made hereditary. Beneficiaries often negotiated hereditary privileges out of what were supposed to be short-term rights. Conversely, privileges were sometimes withdrawn, and property was confiscated and reallocated to others.

Regions were allocated different monopolies. Throughout the Caribbean, sugarcane production enjoyed the protection and financial support of the Crown. In 1600, seventeen plantation owners in Cuba received a loan from the Crown along with special legal protection against seizure for debt payment and facility in importing slaves and equipment.[16] The special privileges enabled growers to expand production to such an extent that twenty years later there were fifty sugar mills in Cuba. Cuban growers enjoyed these special privileges for three centuries. Santo Domingo (capital of what is today the Dominican Republic) received similar treatment, but Mexico was denied the right to expand the production of sugarcane. Peru had the legal right to expand production of sugarcane, but production was limited to certain areas of the colony and growers were denied the right to import iron tools to update production methods.[17]

The province of Caracas (Venezuela) wrangled the privilege of cacao cultivation and was guaranteed a huge protected market that extended throughout Mexico and north to California and Texas, at the expense of other provinces such as Guayaquil (Ecuador) and Maracaibo (Venezuela), where production of cacao was repressed. In compensation, Guayaquil was awarded the protected rights to exploit wood and create a shipbuilding industry.[18] Planters in Chile received the right to cultivate wheat, but were denied the right to produce tobacco.

Spanish industries, strategically positioned to lobby the Crown, received the highest level of protection. No one was allowed to compete with Spain's olive growers and textile producers. Playing cards, shoes, wine, and hardware were other goods that only Spain enjoyed the legal right to produce and market. Peru and Chile were granted dispensations to grow wine and olives because they were too far away for Spain's growers to be able to serve their markets.

In the all-important case of mineral wealth, Peruvian jurist Gaspar de Escalona Aguero recommended that mines be sold or leased at the discretion of the viceroy to a good administrator.[19] Since mineral wealth was fraught with risk for those who undertook its development, the royal administrators did provide incentives by taxing mines lightly during the early years of development.[20] Indians were distributed to work the mines, at first as slaves, but later in the sixteenth century as paid laborers.

Officials treated their subjects heavy-handedly, convinced of their superior knowledge of economic conditions. Typically, high-ranking colonial royal officials would recommend the development of certain industries. For example, Viceroy Manuel Guirior of the New Granada colony recommended encouraging the development of cotton and wool, even to the point of expropriating land from those who refused to comply.[21]

With monopolies at their foundation, the Spanish American colonial economies evolved along a different path than the North American colonies, where relative economic freedom had spawned competitive industries and thriving agriculture. One royal official neatly summed up the results obtained by the monopoly system. He said that a monopoly in government hands meant that costs would exceed revenues, while a private sector monopoly would produce limited output of low quality at high prices. This is exactly what occurred. Consumers suffered from high prices for goods as monopolistic producers, shielded from competition, passed on their high costs. Private property became quasi-public with the imposition of taxes and regulations that limited the use and transfer of resources.

With government interference as the main feature of economic life, one had to adapt or perish. The monarchy's tax system was designed to garner maximum revenues in complete disregard of the impact on economic activity. The heavy, haphazard taxation and regulation, though never scrupulously obeyed in the colonies, forced people to spend time negotiating deals with government officials rather than in productive activity. Different taxes and regulations fell on different occupations, and well-connected individuals were able to wrangle exemptions. No two individuals were taxed alike, but in general poorer members of society, bereft of connections and money to bribe officials, paid more.

Consider the case of an owner of an agricultural estate in Peru that produced wine. His attention was consumed by the numerous taxes and regulations affecting his business. First, he was subject to the sales and turnover tax on all transactions. This tax, known as the *alcabala,* began at a rate of 2 percent and by the end of the colonial era was assessed at 10 percent. Plantation owners were required to report three times a year to the tax collector the details of every transaction that took place, down to barter transactions, and pay the tax due.[22] If the owner exported the wine to other colonies, which was alternately allowed and prohibited, an import-export duty of 2.5 percent was assessed.[23]

Next came a tax on one-third of the value of the production on his estate and a 10 percent tithe to the Catholic Church. In Spanish America, the tithe was an income tax collected at the source on agricultural and pastoral industries.

There were other taxes as well to which the plantation owner could be subject. He probably would have paid a strange tax, called the *cruzada,* or "bulls of the crusade," which was essentially a head tax collected by the Catholic Church but administered by the monarchy. Leftover from the medieval crusades, the purpose of the tax was allegedly to extend the Catholic faith. The amount assessed varied with the means and social position of the subject and ranged from two to four pesos every other year for landowners between about 1550 and 1700.[24]

The vintner also had to contend with the monarchy's habit of tapping the subjects whom it had privileged for forced loans and surtaxes whenever it ran short of funds, as it perpetually did during its expensive wars. Groups of subjects were expected to cough up "gifts" or at best loans at 3 to 5 percent interest amounting to hundreds of thousands of pesos. Even more insidious, the Crown often seized merchant ships on the high seas when it ran short of cash, expropriating hundreds of thousands of pesos in private gold and silver. Those confiscated were often compensated with additional privileges.[25]

Beyond the conglomeration of taxes, the vintner had to deal with the fact that the official tax rates were often meaningless. Until the late colonial era, administration and collection of taxes was often farmed out to the highest bidder. Tax farmers worked on a percentage basis or paid an annual lump sum for their franchise, keeping for themselves whatever they could collect above that sum. They had wide leeway in their methods of collection—beatings were common. As the Crown demanded ever higher payments, tax farmers compensated themselves however they could and "changed the lightest tax into an insupportable burden."[26] Throughout the realm, the population saw royal tax collectors as no different from bandits.

To further complicate the life of the vintner, there was a host of regulations regarding landholding to which he was subject. One of the most rigorously enforced was the entailment of property. Land was to be passed down to the firstborn of a family and numerous regulations limited the resale of properties.[27] This, combined with the extensive property holdings of the Catholic Church, served to create and maintain a system of large estates, or *latifundios*.

Another regulation specified that landholding was conditioned on the occupation and use of the property by the owner; title alone was insufficient. Unused land was subject to Crown confiscation.[28] Land-use restrictions stipulated that land be employed in the specific use set out by the Crown, and was subject to Crown confiscation if changed to another use.[29] Much evidence exists that such restrictions were actively enforced, with disputes dragging on for long periods, even centuries.

Even when years of growing a single crop had depleted the soil, plantation owners could not freely change crops without bureaucratic permission. A landowner had to allow fields to lie fallow until he got permission from municipal authorities and the viceroy to change its use, often a lengthy process. Meanwhile, the land was subject to confiscation because it wasn't being worked.

Subsoil and topsoil rights to land were separated and only topsoil rights could be held by individuals. Subsoil rights belonged to the Crown, which could grant exploration and development rights to develop mineral wealth therein. Even minerals found in the topsoil, or cultivable layer, belonged to the Crown.[30] Any mineral wealth found on the vintner's property could upset his title to the land and it was not at all certain that he would be given the right to develop mineral resources found on his property.

The vintner also most likely faced the problem of defective title to his land. Landholdings granted by the Crown were often extensive, with the size and dimensions of properties varying according to the degree of certified noble lineage and service to the Crown, but surveying methods were primitive. By 1560, according to Spanish historian Jaime Vicens, it was doubtful whether anyone knew the exact boundaries of his land. The situation never really improved. Property holdings in many countries are still uncertain to the present day.[31] The vintner most likely was embroiled in disputes with neighboring property holders over the boundaries of his land. He had no incentive to improve lands within disputed property boundaries, as a governmental decision against his interest would result in confiscation of the land with its improvements.

The plantation owner could not pay all the duties required of him and survive, nor could he follow all the regulations. Clearly, the property owner had a great stake in cultivating contacts in the royal administration to help him obtain exemptions to the onerous taxes and regulations and protect himself from the tax farmer. His Crown dispensation to hold land shows that he was already a favored subject, but still he could be stripped of his property if the plantation was found to be remiss in its obligations to the Crown. It behooved him to join forces with other vintners and meet regularly with Crown officials to maintain his favored position. The vintner bribed the king's officers to document wine production at his dictation and carried out unrecorded barter transactions. He could better serve his interests by lobbying in the colonial capital than by investing his time in improving cultivation—hence the reputation that Spanish American plantation owners earned for being absentee landlords.

This example illustrates the fact that even privileges were a mixed blessing. They loaded the beneficiary with a host of responsibilities that were impossible to meet unless the beneficiary spent considerable resources to maintain the favor of bureaucrats and win special exemptions. Property rights in the private sector, even to favored subjects, were devalued by numerous restrictions that did not apply to public sector employees.

The colonies created little wealth. High tariffs protected industries from competition, allowing inefficient producers to charge high prices for inferior goods, while heavy excise taxes and extensive regulation tended to stifle colonial industry.[32] Restricted property rights in few hands meant that resources were not exploited. The owner of a vast plantation could earn a living working only a small portion of the land. Of course, he needed to stay on the good side of the authorities to avoid possible confiscation of the unworked land.

Small proprietary farmers, who greatly stimulated agricultural production in the British colonies, could not buy land. Instead, people ended up forced to labor for others on the large plantations for low wages with little hope of ownership or advancement. There was little incentive for innovation, and productivity was low.

With individual initiative circumvented, the Spanish colonies lost the creative energy that is unleashed when producers compete to serve consumers. When markets did form, it was in spite of the efforts of officials. Creativity was directed into overcoming government obstacles, and aspirations were quashed or diverted into avenues that were unproductive for society as a whole. Innovations that catapulted England into the Industrial Revolution did not occur in Spain or the Spanish colonies because the conditions did not foster an entrepreneurial climate. In Spanish America, potential innovators were comfortably ensconced in the government or the church.

The bureaucratic hordes at all levels wreaked havoc on production. They minutely regulated each industry. Municipal councils, in conjunction with the viceregal authority, regulated prices of consumer goods. Officials promulgated ordinances concerning the price of bread and other foodstuffs, the supply of meat, and the regulation of wine shops.

Royal officials believed that the colonists' access to goods at reasonable prices depended on the thoroughness of their administration. Thus, in the retail trade of every colonial city, almost every article was carefully controlled as to price, weight, and quality. A member of the town council, the *fiel ejecutor*, inspected the markets, held hearings on the price of items, and fixed a scale that was set up in a public place where all could see.[33] Producers had to allocate time and effort defending themselves from the bureaucratic onslaught, to the detriment of the quality and quantity of goods produced.

In Mexico, even the production of bread was politicized. Eighteenth-century Mexican viceroy Count Revillagigedo observed that every aspect of bread-making and retailing, down to minute production details, had to be negotiated with the municipal governments. In an attempt to control arbitrary swings in the price of bread, every four months public inspectors set prices by decree, according to the cost of wheat purchases. This led to bakers being forced to declare under oath the quantities purchased and their prices. Sellers of wheat also had to give statements of sales under oath, and with these declarations the inspectors derived a price in terms of the number of ounces of bread that could be purchased with a half-crown. The official price was then transmitted to the bakers' attorneys and submitted to the attorney general for approval. If the price was approved, it was published. The transaction costs of supplying a loaf of bread were, thus, extremely high.[34]

The outcome was that the Spanish-American colonies suffered from shortages of basic goods. In times of shortage, prices were even more closely regulated, which only served to make the shortages even more acute by making production and trade unprofitable.

The solution was always more government interference. Internal customs zones were set up to try to control intra-colony trade and prevent goods from crossing into other areas. This worsened the situation, and state-run granaries were established to ease the endless shortages but failed to achieve their goal.[35] While colonial officials believed that unstable markets necessitated their intervention to protect consumers' interests, the real culprit in causing the shortages was the lack of competition, excessive regulation of existing producers, blocked entry of new producers, and the proliferating monopolies in each sector. Periodically, severe crises spawned riots and rebellions.

The guild system of production was another natural outgrowth of the state-directed economy. Producers needed to organize to protect themselves from arbitrary government-imposed costs and seek favors from the monarchy, while the monarchy favored guilds because they constituted large, easy targets to tax.[36]

The earliest craft guilds (*gremios de artes y oficios*) were established in Mexico City. Many guilds were established in the sixteenth and seventeenth centuries, until in Mexico City there were about 100, with more in the major provincial cities. Some of the more important guilds were the silversmiths, merchant consulates, goldbeaters, harness and saddle makers, potters, weavers, hatters, and candle makers. Also, bakers, butchers, wheat farmers, sheepherders, and other livestock growers were organized into guilds. Some guilds achieved great wealth and prestige, such as the silversmiths in Mexico City, with seventy-one shops in 1685, and in Lima, Peru, where there were eighty silver shops in the early 1600s.[37]

In Latin America, as in Spain, petitioners' claims for redress against the "unfair" privileges of others, combined with the belief of the king's officers that the private economy was not self-regulating, led to ever-higher regulation of economic activity. Thus, the organization and activities of the guilds came to be minutely regulated by elaborate ordinances issued by the municipal *cabildos* or councils, with the confirmation of the viceroy or the king. The regulations primarily worked to preserve protected spheres of operation for the guilds and exclude upstart entrepreneurs, for which in return the royal administration demanded ever-rising levels of taxation.

As in mercantilist Europe, regulations stipulated a graduated system of instruction from the rank of apprentice through that of journeyman to the rank of master craftsman, with admittance to the highest grade jealously limited in order to stifle competition. In the case of Spanish America, regulations worked to reserve the rank of master craftsman for colonists of pure Spanish descent, and bar from entry Indians, mulattoes, Negroes, and, in some guilds, mestizos, although they included most of the journeymen.[38]

The regulations governing the guilds illustrate the extent to which government crowded out private decision-making. Juan Francisco del Barrio Lorenzot, an official in the royal administration, compiled a work on guild regulations. Del Barrio's collection of guild ordinances details how both the regulators and the regulated strived to throttle all competition with regulation.[39]

For example, regulations governing the hatmakers' guild prevented the emergence of labor markets and wholesale trade in millinery. Numerous regulations were designed to limit the number of shop owners or master craftsmen. Aspiring hatmakers were required to present their credentials to two inspectors elected from guild ranks, pay two pesos, and pass an exam conducted by those officials. Using their own materials, novices had to produce a "a good satin hat, a white hat, a brown hat and a black hat" and "each hat should be all of a piece, without seams."[40] Those unable to produce hats to satisfy the inspectors were prohibited from being master craftsmen,[41] were relegated to working as apprentices and laborers, and fined 10 pesos.

In keeping with the objective of reducing the supply of hats so that shop owners could charge higher prices, there were many other requirements. For example, only master hatmakers could sell hats and no one could buy hats for resale; those doing so faced a maximum penalty of thirty days in jail. Hats of different hues could be made only by using specific types of wool, not by using dyes, subject to 10 pesos penalty; those shops that put their trademark on hats made by others were to be fined 6 pesos and the offending merchandise confiscated. Also, no master craftsman was allowed to undertake the repair of an old hat for resale purposes, or even to have such a hat in his shop, under penalty of shop closure. Finally, those who brought hats in from other places were to be hauled before the authorities and their hats judged according to the high standards of the guild inspectors. If they met with approval, the hats could be sold, otherwise they would be burned and their owners fined.[42]

Labor costs were kept down by preventing master craftsmen from bidding for labor. No master craftsman could accept workers who had been working in another shop without the knowledge and consent of the other craftsman, under penalty of 10 pesos. The rule barring entry of Negroes from owning their own shops also helped to ensure a larger supply of workers relative to shop owners.

The close collusion between the guilds and the government muddled the distinction between the government and the private sector. The powerful merchant consulates or guilds in New Spain and Peru became quasi-governmental institutions, as they were given the responsibility of assessing and administering the various taxes among their members.

Similar rules applied to all officially sanctioned industries, with disastrous results. Labor markets were prevented from forming, and markets in goods were very rudimentary. The financial system was undeveloped. The Catholic Church served as banker to elites, and the merchant consulates undertook some financing. Opportunities for investment afforded by the system were limited to landholding, government jobs, and the mines. Capital and labor were trapped in uneconomic ventures. Small wonder, then, that elites were known for lavish luxury expenditures and magnificent celebrations. There were few alternatives to consumption.

Mancur Olson's analysis of how organized groups pursuing self-interest create economic, social, and political rigidities that lead to decline explains the fate of Spain and its colonies. Each interest group used government to increase their own gains. Consequently, policies that were inefficient for the society as a whole were advantageous for the organized groups, because the costs of the policies fell disproportionately on the unorganized.[43] In this way, privileged elites created a blocked society.

Entrepreneurs fleeing from the ponderous royal administration and the privileged guild monopolists found opportunity in the Catholic Church and the black market. Accorded a privileged position, the Catholic Church received vast resources and was largely exempt from taxation. Everybody had to tithe to the Catholic Church (with exceptions, as always the case under Spanish rule), and from the first the laws of mortmain reserved large estates in perpetual entailment to the church. The Catholic Church ending up acquiring much of the most productive agricultural land by means of benefactions, purchase, or mortgage. By the eighteenth century, reformers complained that too much wealth had been amassed into the "dead hands" of the Catholic Church. Laws were decreed to try to limit ecclesiastical privilege but to little avail.[44]

The clergy could run businesses with little interference on church-owned land to support its schools and missions, hospitals, and charitable institutions. Church privileges provided cover for secular entrepreneurs to transact illegally. Church exemption to taxation was supposed to apply only to transactions necessary to ecclesiastical functions, such as the purchase of chalices, robes, and objects for ceremonial use, and the direct sale for the local market of such products as agricultural goods and *aguardiente,* a liquor, produced on church-owned plantations.[45] The practice, however, was different. Royal functionaries complained that the clergy transported both their own and the agricultural products of others to distant markets where scarcity dictated higher prices, and insisted, apparently to little avail, that such transactions required the imposition of the sales and turnover tax and the customs duty.[46]

With the church viewed as a career for the ambitious, and all entrants at minimum ensured a stable income, there were powerful economic incentives for young men and women to join the church. Many people with an aptitude for business were diverted into the church, where their prospects for managing large properties and businesses were great. Throughout the colonial period observers complained that too many people were entering the church and that many entrants did not have a true vocation for the spiritual life.

The entrepreneur could also find opportunity in the black market. If the regulations governing economic activity had been scrupulously followed, monopolistic guilds would have limited production of consumer goods to a trickle and charged consumers extremely high prices. However, the worst effects were mitigated by black markets. From Mexico to Argentina, black market factories, home-based businesses, and contraband traders competed with the ossified guilds. The extensive regulation served to create a repressive economic climate in which entrepreneurs survived by bribing officialdom.

Contraband trading brought the highest profits. Throughout most of the colonial period, Spain forbade the colonies from trading with each other or with foreign powers. This ill-considered policy was alternately strengthened and relaxed and unevenly enforced. In general, it meant that a wider variety of consumer goods was available in black markets than in the official economy. Thus, the scope of contraband trading was much broader than merely running guns and whiskey. It included all manner of consumer goods such as clothing, food, toilet articles, shoes, and so on, as well as capital goods such as tools and implements.

Contraband trading also benefited from the bureaucratic hindrances in the way of Spain's trade with her own colonies. The Spanish fleet set sail twice yearly to provision the colonies. Prospective Spanish traders had a difficult time getting a ship included in the fleet. The privileges claimed by the House of Trade bureaucrats were nearly insurmountable obstacles. All traders had to first obtain permission through the House of Trade, a lengthy process involving large payments to the king and sizeable presents to the king's officers, "from the greatest to the least."[47] Such a process easily took longer than a year. Meanwhile, the prospective trader could not order goods from Spanish factories, mainly textiles, until permission was obtained.

Such delays and political intervention greatly increased the cost of doing business and helped make Spanish goods sold in the New World extremely expensive and out of easy reach of all but elites. Also adding cost was the long and perilous journey with pirates lying in wait for the ships, along with a host of tariffs, beginning with an export tax of 2.5 percent applied to goods sold at each port.

Tariff rates were complicated and encouraged noncompliance. At first, the tariff rate on goods entering the colonies was 5 percent. Later, it was raised to 10 percent. Duties were paid at some transit ports and again at the final destination, based on the price of the goods at each port. With high price markups on imported goods, tariff rates could reach 35 to 40 percent of the cost of the boarded goods in Spain.[48] This, of course, encouraged under-invoicing and smuggling.

Contraband traders took advantage of the opportunities. The closed system with its high costs, along with Spain's disincentives to produce and the unsatisfied demand in the colonies for consumer goods, meant profitable business for privateers from England, France, Holland, and the North American colonies. Frustrated Spanish merchant traders often joined forces with privateers to circumvent formal procedures. The King's officers seized advantage of the chaos created by their own decrees and ran contraband empires themselves. The literature of the era, while condemning foreign pirates and privateers, reserves the strongest condemnation for the Spanish officials and merchants who violated the system for their personal gain.

Royal functionaries everywhere facilitated contraband trading. They took bribes to under-invoice, and approve false documentation. Typically, traders would register a trading vessel as containing under 300 tons of merchandise, when actually it held over 600 tons. The high tariff levied on exports was therefore only paid on half the cargo, with shippers often making profits of 200 to 300 percent on the rest. Ships returning to Europe with 600 to 700 tons of cargo flashed authentic certificates from all the officers of the king of Spain that they carried under 300, with a bill of lading to the same effect.[49] The ruse was widely used because cargo inspections were infrequent. Moreover, the penalties for contraband trading were light as they were promulgated by officials who were themselves engaged in the practice, and regulations provided cover for black market trading.

Privileges held by the viceroy and his ministers to import an unspecified amount of goods free of duties for use in their residences and in the discharge of their duties provided cover for contraband trading. Another regulation stipulated that ships (including foreign ships) that were deemed to have washed ashore in the ports were not subject to confiscation and their owners were allowed to sell their cargo, subject to the prevailing 5 percent import duty.[50] Spanish historian Jaime Vicens observed that

> under the pretext of repairing some damage, a ship would get permission to tie up in a port; then it would proceed to unload the merchandise it carried "to lighten the cargo." The cargo was apparently guarded by a party of soldiers, but in fact it was being sold under the complaisant gaze of everyone.[51]

Also, merchandise that was pronounced by royal officials to have been lost at sea could be written off and was not subject to duties. By the year 1686, contraband trading represented two-thirds of colonial commerce.[52]

Black-market factories sprang up in the Spanish colonies. At first, even production and trading of such basic goods as woolen and cotton textiles were conducted in the black market. This outcome was by no means an optimal solution, as the lack of legal contract and shaky property rights led to high costs for consumers. Later, in the seventeenth century the Crown gave official sanction to basic industries that were already widely operating in the colonies.

Poor people, meanwhile, opened home-based businesses or peddled trinkets because the monopoly system generated few jobs. Their alternatives under the system were limited to laboring for low wages on the plantations, in the mines, or as domestic servants and gofers for elites. With luck, they could learn a trade and find employment with one of the craft guilds. Opportunities were very limited there, however, with the guilds' severe restrictions on entry. With economic opportunity sewed up by elites, upward mobility was limited. Those of the poorer classes who were not willing to live a life of penury turned their backs on government and operated illegally.

Others of the poor found jobs in black-market factories, of which the most numerous were the textile factories. Known as *obrajes,* these were notorious sweatshops, but many found the jobs they provided better than the alternatives.

Rich elites—comprising government officials and bureaucrats, privileged monopolists, clergy, and landowners—were best positioned in the black market because their connections and capital, derived from legally sanctioned activities, allowed them to exploit the opportunities created by the shortages resulting from the government's policies.

Due to the emergence of thriving black markets and contraband trade, there was more economic activity in the Spanish colonies than many scholars reported. Nevertheless, the rent-seeking system drained the talents, resources, and energies of the population away from economic development. The system maximized inefficiency and waste, both of resources and human potential.

From the eighteenth century onward, the economic history of Latin America has been one of alternately strengthening and weakening the old statist institutions without ever breaking away from them. At times when economic controls were decreased, production and trade increased, the power of political elites declined, and a middle class of merchants, artisans, and professionals emerged. At other times, during periods of widespread confiscation of private property, production collapsed, the middle class disappeared, and economic opportunities became concentrated again in privileged sectors.

As early as 1743, enlightened reformers of the Spanish monarchy, such as Joseph del Campillo,[53] called for the strengthening of private property rights throughout the realm in order to revive the moribund empire. During the nineteenth century, classical liberal ideas penetrated many countries to varying degree. Francisco Pimentel of Mexico and Juan Alberdi of Argentina were forthright in urging an economic overhaul that would make possible a system of free enterprise.[54]

Spain, burdened by rent-seeking, never built the institutions conducive to economic success and neither did most of its colonies. The colonies eventually broke free of Spanish rule but not from the rent-seeking culture. Consequently, they remained economic backwaters until the last two decades of the twentieth century.

The development-planning approach sponsored by the World Bank and the United Nations in the second half of the twentieth century strengthened the rent-seeking culture that had hindered Latin American economic progress for 400 years. Western "experts," ignorant both of the region's history and of the rent-seeking implications of their aid schemes, squandered their opportunity to help Latin America break away from a mercantilist tradition that stimulated the growth of anti-market institutions. By pouring huge sums into government coffers, Western development assistance strengthened the barriers to economic progress.

Today Latin American countries are privatizing their economies and replacing rent-seeking institutions with profit-seeking ones. The development banks are relics of a failed approach. The Western commercial banks that followed the World Bank's lead in lending to sovereign governments instead of capitalists have adjusted to their mistake and written off their loans. Now it is time for the World Bank, the International Monetary Fund, and the Inter-American Development Bank to adjust to the emergence of capitalism in Latin America.

Notes

1. Brazil endured a similar system of government control over the economy under Portuguese rule.
2. Joseph de Veitia Linage, *The Spanish Rule of Trade to the West Indies*, translated by Capt. John Stevens (London: Printed for Samuel Crouch, at the Corner of Pope's-Head-Alley in Cornbil, 1702).
3. Ibid., 68.
4. Ibid., 13–25.
5. Eusebio Bentura Beleña, *Copias a la Letra Ofrecidas en el Primer Tomo de la Recopilación Sumaria de todos los autos acordados de la Real Audiencia y Sala de Crimen de esta N.E.* (Mexico City: D. Felipe de Zuñiga y Ontiveros, 1787), 122–23.
6. C. H. Haring, *The Spanish Empire in America* (New York: Oxford University Press, 1947), 165–71, 289–92.
7. Ibid., footnote on p. 291.
8. Gaspar de Escalona Aguero, *Gazofilacio Real del Peru*, (La Paz, Bolivia: Editorial El Estado, 1941), 198. Fourth edition, originally published in 1647.
9. Haring, *The Spanish Empire in America*, 290–91.
10. de Escalona Aguero, *Gazofilacio Real del Peru*, 191–208. Decries corruption in the sale of offices, 203: "Y lo peor es que algunas veces se han hecho remates con las tales condiciones y en virtud de ellas han sido recibidas los compradores a los dichos oficios, y gozarlos mucho tiempo sin que se les confirmen ni puedan confirmar semejantes contratos."
11. Milovan Djilas, *The New Class: An Analysis of the Communist System* (New York: Praeger, 1957), 65.
12. Francisco Pimentel, *La Economía Política Aplicada a la Propiedad Territorial en México* (Mexico City: Ignacio Cumplido, 1866), 17–19.

13. Ibid., 18–19.
14. Manuel Moreyra Paz-Soldán, "La Tesorería y la Estadística de acuñación colonial en la Casa de Moneda en Lima," *Cuadernos de Estudios* (Lima), September 1942, tomo II, no. 4, 13–23.
15. de Escalona Aguero, *Gazofilacio Real del Peru*, prologue by Leon Loza, XI.
16. Joseph del Campillo, *Nuevo sistema de gobierno económico para la América* (Merida: Universidad de los Andes, 1971; first edition published 1789), introductory study by Eduardo Arcila Farias, 42–45.
17. Ibid., introductory study by Eduardo Arcila Farias, 42–45.
18. Ibid.
19. de Escalona Aguero, *Gazofilacio Real del Peru*, 138–39.
20. Ibid., 132–33.
21. Luis Ospina Vasquez, *Industria y Protección en Colombia: 1810–1930* (Medellín: Biblioteca Colombiana de Ciencias Sociales FAES, 1979, second edition), 84–85.
22. de Escalona Aguero, *Gazofilacio Real del Peru*, 180–85.
23. Ibid., 165–67.
24. Haring, *The Spanish Empire in America*, 286–87.
25. See J. H. Elliott, *Past and Present*, No. 20, 1961, 52–75; Douglass North and Robert Thomas, *The Rise of the Western World: A New Economic History* (Cambridge: Cambridge University Press, 1973), 129–30; and de Escalona Aguero, *Gazofilacio Real del Peru*, 38.
26. Jaime Vicens Vives, *An Economic History of Spain* (Princeton: Princeton University Press, 1969), 454.
27. Ibid., 296.
28. del Campillo, *Nuevo Sistema de gobierno económico*, introductory study by Eduardo Arcila Farias, 50–53.
29. Miguel Cruchaga, *Estudio Sobre la Organización Económica y la Hacienda Pública de Chile* (Madrid: Editorial Reus, S.A., 1929), Tomo II.
30. del Campillo, *Nuevo Sistema de gobierno económico*, introductory study by Eduardo Arcila Farias, 50–53.
31. Vicens Vives, *An Economic History of Spain*, 318–20.
32. See Cruchaga, *Estudio Sobre la Organización Económica*, Tomo I; and Ospina Vasquez, *Industria y Protección en Colombia*, 82.
33. Haring, *The Spanish Empire in America*, 168.
34. Pimentel, *La Economía Política Aplicada a la Propiedad Territorial en México*, 16.
35. Ibid., 17.
36. Vicens Vives, *An Economic History of Spain*, 429–31.
37. Haring, *The Spanish Empire in America*, 269–70; and Juan Francisco del Barrio Lorenzot, *Ordenanzas de Gremios de la Nueva España* (Mexico City: Secretaría de Industria, Comercio y Trabajo, 1920), Introduction by Genaro Estrada.

38. del Barrio Lorenzot, *Ordenanzas de Gremios de la Nueva España.*
39. Ibid.
40. Ibid., 99.
41. Note: there were master craftswomen in the Spanish colonies, but they were generally widows of master craftsmen, who, on payment of a fee, were allowed to open their own shop.
42. del Barrio Lorenzot, *Ordenanzas de Gremios de la Nueva España,* 99–103.
43. Mancur Olson, *The Rise and Decline of Nations: Economic Growth, Stagflation, and Social Rigidities,* (New Haven: Yale University Press, 1982), 37.
44. del Campillo, *Nuevo Sistema de Gobierno Económico,* 87.
45. de Escalona Aguero, *Gazofilacio Real del Peru,* 173; and Bentura Beleña, *Copias a la Letra ofrecidas en el Primer Tomo de la Recopilación Sumaria,* Otra No. 37, 152.
46. Bentura Beleña, *Copias a la Letra ofrecidas en el Primer Tomo de la Recopilación Sumaria,* 152.
47. John Campbell, *A Concise History of the Spanish America* (New York: Barnes & Noble, 1972; reprint of 1741 edition published in London), 285.
48. C. H. Haring, *Trade and Navigation Between Spain and the Indies* (Cambridge: Harvard University Press, 1918), 84–85.
49. Campbell, *A Concise History of the Spanish America,* 284–86.
50. de Escalona Aguero, *Gazofilacio Real del Peru,* 165, 219.
51. Vicens Vives, *An Economic History of Spain,* 406.
52. Ibid.
53. del Campillo, *Nuevo Sistema de gobierno económico.*
54. See Pimentel, *La Economía Política Aplicada a la Propiedad Territorial en Mexico*; and Juan Alberdi, *Bases y Puntos de Partida para la organización Política de la República Argentina* (Buenos Aires: Editorial Universitaria de Buenos Aires, 1966; first published 1858).

6

Outdated International
Development Institutions

The World Bank, International Monetary Fund (IMF), and Inter-American Development Bank (IDB) own or lease space in some twenty-five buildings in downtown Washington, D.C. Their principal buildings reflect an opulence that only public money can afford. The IMF headquarters is located at 700 19th Street. Inside, an imposing lobby is crowned with a twelve-story atrium. Marble and fountains abound. Stairs rise to a second-level dining room where international bureaucrats and their guests dine under chandeliers among flowers and tropical trees.

Across the street on a site two blocks from the White House, a new World Bank headquarters is under construction. The complex, with gleaming glass towers, will occupy a city block. According to the *Financial Times,* the construction costs were $83.5 million over budget as of July 16, 1993. Still unfinished in 1996, the overruns alone may exceed the original estimate of $200 million for the building.

The Inter-American Development Bank is a spectacular twelve-story building that fills a city block along New York Avenue at 13th Street. A central atrium of beige, black, and white marble sports a seven-story stone fountain in an Aztec reminiscent design from which a waterfall cascades to the lobby below.

These extraordinary palaces reflect the high moral intentions of development planning or the arrogance of international bureaucrats, depending on one's point of view. The fact remains that the opulence of the headquarters stands in stark contrast to the failure of their aims.

At the joint World Bank–IMF annual meeting held in Madrid in October 1994, international bureaucrats supped on fine Spanish cuisine leavened with the usual rhetoric about helping the poor. However, their message no longer resonated outside the five-star hotels and elegant cocktail parties. The fall in prestige of the international institutions was captured by a photo in the *Financial Times* of protesters hoisting a placard demanding "Defund World Bank!"

It is one of the ironies of history that in the postwar period pre-Adam Smithian ideas monopolized Western thinking about economic development. Hundreds of billions of dollars of counterproductive aid were poured into strengthening the very rent-seeking behavior and institutions that had prevented Latin American progress for centuries. In the 1990s, the perpetrators of development planning still churn out billions of dollars in loans yearly to build up state sectors, even while countries privatize previous development bank projects. Paradoxically, part of the government-to-government lending now goes to assist countries in downsizing governments that were built up by previous loans.

It is not the World Bank's fault that its approach to economic development reflected the antimarket ideas prevailing in government and academic circles in the West after World War II. The Bank's operation today reflects the incentives originally established in its charter and the response of top officials over the years to their interaction with the elites in donor and recipient countries. However, even if the development banks had been pro-market in their approach, they may have been unable to foster economic development because they themselves are politicized institutions enveloped in many layers of rent-seeking.

From the start, the development banks were burdened with the interests of the politicians who gave them powers and funding. Roland Vaubel argues that national political leaders use international organizations both to appease certain interest groups and take the heat for unpopular policies. With the costs of funding the agencies dispersed among many governments, national representatives find it advantageous to push politically unpopular programs, such as foreign aid, to the International Monetary Fund, the World Bank, and the other multilateral agencies, in order to reduce the appearance of such programs in national budgets.[1]

At the same time, however, the nature of an international organization makes it less publicly accountable than national bureaucracies. In a 1991 study, Swiss economist Bruno Frey concluded that "international bureaucracies have greater room for discretionary action because neither the opportunity nor the incentive to control these bureaucracies exists."[2] Control is difficult because the "output" of an international organization is undefined and usually cannot be measured. Moreover, national governments have no incentive to closely monitor them, because they would risk conflict with other national governments if they tried to interfere with the internal workings of such institutions. The lack of effective controls means that "no member in the hierarchy has any real incentive to work toward the 'official product.'"[3]

Such expanded freedom of action makes international agencies more susceptible to the maneuvers of interest groups and, therefore, the agencies tend to supply more favors to pressure groups than national bureaucracies would have done.[4] There are many examples. Women's groups and environmental groups have successfully lobbied for the inclusion of their agendas in World Bank programs and have won fat consulting contracts from the World Bank and other agencies. None of the organizations is accountable for what actually happens during project implementation, and the interest groups use the money to further expand their pro-government regulatory activities and agendas.

For their part, private firms in donor countries, attracted to the opportunities represented by $60 billion in annual development assistance, have obtained a large share of the aid resources. World Bank and regional development bank contracts are open to international competitive bidding, and companies large and small jockey for the opportunity to sell consulting services and equipment to project managers in developing countries. However, since neither the donors nor the recipients are accountable for how development projects are actually carried out, private contractors on development bank projects have had little incentive to do their best work. Companies with sterling reputations at home have often provided shoddy goods and services at high prices to projects funded by development banks.

Staffing creates conflicts of interest that further deflect the banks from their official function. Positions are filled by political patronage operating along a national quota system.[5] Thus, the appointed officials have a personal stake in lobbying their employer on behalf of the interests of the political elites in their native countries to whom they owe their jobs.

Additional conflicts of interest arise from the incentives that international agencies have to please political elites in the developing countries, the end users of their loans. If developing country governments were to cease borrowing, the agencies' raison d' être would disappear. Since all bureaucracies benefit from larger budgets and a greater number of employees, international agencies face strong pressures to lend. Political sovereignty issues further complicate accountability as lending agencies are reluctant to meddle in the internal affairs of borrowers.

This combination of incentives leads to all sorts of self-dealing that is independent of the bureaucracy's official goal. Putting international bureaucrats in charge of managing so many billions of dollars without a real owner has meant that a considerable share of the budget has been diverted for internal purposes and to provide side benefits for the bureaucrats themselves.[6] Operations are characterized by a low degree of efficiency and a profusion of red tape. Much time is spent negotiating internal rules, yet, according to one IDB official, this time is wasted since there are so many exceptions made to every rule, depending on who is involved, so that effectively the rules do not apply and the institution functions according to personalities. For instance, an IDB official who was a Finance Minister in his country is accorded very different treatment than a less well-connected person holding the same position without such a background.

There is little evidence that the operations of the World Bank, IMF, IDB, and other lending institutions have actually helped to improve living standards in developing countries, but there can be no doubt that international bureaucrats have amply benefited personally from their employment. The most effective lobbyists for privileges and perks from the international agencies have been the staff associations of those institutions. Their success can be measured by the large portion of budgets of the World Bank, IMF, and other multilateral institutions that pays for high salaries and handsome staff benefits. British journalist Graham Hancock aptly terms the aid bureaucrats the "Lords of Poverty."

Michael Irwin, a director of the Health Services Department of the World Bank in 1989–1990, decried the exceedingly generous, tax-free salaries and benefits funded by Western taxpayers. He noted that in 1990 the World Bank president earned $154,000 a year; while the fifteen vice presidents earned, on average, $123,000, and the fifty-eight directors $105,000. Just below the level of director, hundreds of "technical advisers" earned between $80,000 and $105,000.[7]

Perks and privileges that make employment at the World Bank a gilded life include a salary supplement of up to $3,000 a year to make up for a spouse's "inadequate income" and $420 per year for each dependent child. Subsidized meals, a good medical insurance plan, excellent insurance benefits, and an exceedingly generous pension plan help ease the cares of World Bank staff. In addition, expatriate staff can receive up to $5,480 in education benefits per child between the ages of five and twenty-four, and they are also entitled to home-leave travel for themselves and their families every two years flying business class. Staff get pocket money of $1,070 and a spouse and dependent children each get $534 for each home-leave trip. Washington-based staff reassigned to positions in the bank's overseas offices receive tens of thousands of dollars in additional compensation in salary adjustments, moving expenses, and "settling-in" expenses, not to mention a "grant on return" when staff come back to Washington.[8] Terms of employment at the IMF are even more generous, with compensation levels averaging 5 percent higher than the World Bank.

The IDB has similar levels of compensation, perks, and privileges as the World Bank. At the IDB, much staff time is spent in Staff Association meetings lobbying for higher salaries and perks and on negotiating the rules of the internal workings of the organization.

Arbitrary privileges and stifling bureaucracy cause a high level of dissatisfaction among staff at the international organizations, but most stay put because, as a computer programmer at the IDB put it, "Here I make $75,000 a year and have all these perks and benefits. For the same job in the private sector I wouldn't be paid more than $25,000 a year. It's a golden cage."

Individuals, attracted by the generous terms, flood the World Bank personnel office with applications for employment. With few restraints on the taxpayer-funded budget, the size of the World Bank's staff is rapidly rising. In 1990 there were 6,100 full-time staff and 500 long-term consultants, plus another 500 temporary staff.[9] In 1996, the Bank's personnel office reported that there were 6,629 full-time employees, 1,366 long-term consultants, and 802 temporary workers and short-term contractual employees.[10] Salary increases have been well above the U.S. inflation rate.

Another outcome of the incentives faced by international agencies is irrational lending policies. The development banks as taxpayer-funded organizations face few restraints on their budgets and do not adhere to the discipline of the market in their own operations. International organizations, by definition, operate in the political arena, and the resources they channel to Third World governments tend to finance projects that have little to do with supply and demand and everything to do with enriching favored political groups.

Some examples illustrate these tendencies. In 1992 the World Bank approved a $266 million loan for a Third National Roads Sector project in Colombia. Yet no one—Colombian car owners, Colombian truckers, or the World Bank economists who worked on preparing the project—had any confidence that the loan would be of lasting benefit to Colombia. Since 1951, World Bank lending to the transport sector in Colombia has totaled $1 billion. Yet, the World Bank is the first to admit that the country does not have much to show for past lending. The project report, one of the widely circulated documents that the World Bank deemed confidential until the mid-1990s, reveals that bank loans to the railway sector, for instance, "were unsuccessful in bringing about the hoped-for improvement in railway operations." As for roads, the sector has received $558 million in the past, but according to the report, "the results of Bank involvement to date have been mixed."[11]

Much of the money approved for Colombia apparently never made it to the intended projects. The World Bank complains that the borrower, the Colombian Ministry of Public Works and Transport, makes "low budget allocations" to the road projects. Moreover, once the meager project funds run out, the government does not maintain whatever physical plant was built. This is because the Ministry, according to the World Bank, has tended to "start work on more projects than the number which its financial resources could sustain."[12]

A large portion of the funds managed by the Colombian Ministry of Public Works ends up enriching bureaucrats and paying off political favors. Providing services for the public is a low priority. This was no secret to the World Bank, which in 1991 concluded in a confidential review of the entire Colombian public sector that there is a "lack of control over the size and composition of public expenditures in Colombia."[13] The report was utterly frank in its depiction of a country divided into rent-seeking coalitions seeking goodies from the state, leading any analyst to conclude that lending more money to the Colombian government is throwing money down a rathole.

Notwithstanding the record of failure, the World Bank approved another $266 million for the Colombian transport ministry. The rationale for the commitment of additional Western taxpayer dollars was truly breathtaking: in 1992 after the collapse of the Soviet planned economy and the implosion of the Soviet state, the World Bank argued that performance would be different this time, because the Colombian transport ministry was required to submit for the Bank's approval a five-year official investment plan.[14]

Another example of gargantuan failure is the case of Sudene, Brazil's Superintendency of Development of the Northeast, formed in 1959 to plan the development of Brazil's impoverished Northeast region. By 1972, it was apparent that USAID loans channeled through Brazil's Sudene had failed to achieve their intended purpose of stimulating the industrialization of the Brazilian Northeast region.[15] Indeed, very little of the monies was actually spent on the intended projects. Analysts concluded that Sudene quickly became coopted by local elites who ran the agency as their own private fiefdom.

Beginning in the 1970s, the multilateral development banks channeled over $1 billion through Sudene for the so-called Polonordeste program. Comprising forty-three projects by 1982, Polonordeste was a rural development program for the impoverished Brazilian northeast. After ten years of operation, the Brazilian government concluded that Polonordeste did not benefit more than 3 percent of the rural poor. Richard Lacroix reported in a 1985 World Bank-sponsored study that loosely supervised project funds were filtered through so many layers of bureaucracy that very little arrived at the intended destinations. Lacroix says that program funds were spent to subsidize the political apparatus and noted that "the dedication of [administrative] personnel to the integrated rural development project is at times doubtful."[16] Lacking a coordinated accounting system, opportunities for theft were legion.

Aid-financed development projects, like all government programs, tend to take on a life of their own regardless of their stated goals. Many projects end up as costly boondoggles that add to a country's debt, and some cause widespread environmental devastation and dislocations that harm the people they are supposed to help.

Environmental and human rights groups have been particularly active in documenting the devastation wrought by development bank projects. Environmentalist Bruce Rich believes that "the single gravest global environmental impact of MDB projects may be the contribution of their agricultural policies and projects to accelerating deforestation of the tropics."[17] According to Rich, livestock projects, for which Latin American countries received $5 to $7 billion in loans during 1971–1977, have been particular offenders. Tropical rain-forest soils are unsuitable for agriculture or livestock grazing, as poor soils rapidly become depleted of nutrients once the forest cover is gone. Such projects produce few jobs and often turn former forested areas into wastelands.[18] The World Bank itself has acknowledged the high failure rate of livestock projects,[19] and in 1992 approved only one loan with a sizeable livestock component.[20]

In Latin America, the single most disastrous program, both from an environmental and social standpoint, is Brazil's Polonoroeste program. Another billion-dollar recipient of multilateral development bank loans, the program was designed to develop the Brazilian Amazon Basin. It has provided financing for roads, infrastructure development, hydroelectric projects, agriculture, and industrial development.

One Polonoroeste hydroelectric project alone has caused intense suffering. The Balbina Dam on the river Uatuma in Brazil, whose last floodgate was closed in October 1987, flooded 236,000 hectares of Amazon rain forest to generate only eighty megawatts of power. This was a notoriously bad project that the World Bank had earlier refused to fund. In 1986, a $500-million World Bank power sector loan was reportedly used by Brazil's Eletronorte, the electricity authority, to bail out the project along with another Polonoroeste hydroelectric boondoggle, the Tucurui Dam. Without placing a value on the natural resources lost, treated as costless by the bureaucrats of Eletronorte, unofficial sources put the total cost of the Balbina project at upwards of $1 billion.[21]

For the river-dwellers of the area, "the project has brought misery and despair,"[22] taking away their livelihoods and poisoning their water supply. Small farmers were not compensated for land flooded by the dam, and residents of the municipality of Presidente Figueiredo are now bombarded by clouds of tropical disease-carrying mosquitoes that proliferate in the shallow, stagnant lake. In 1989, residents of a small town 300 kilometers downstream from the dam organized a public protest against the dam, complaining that "the previously clean water now causes itchy skin and diarrhea when used for washing and drinking," and the fish in the river and nearby waterways, their main food source, "are dying and rotting in their millions." The local people pronounced the River Uatuma dead, and with it their hopes for a decent life.[23]

This story is repeated over and over. Development projects uproot the poor in communities that they are supposed to help, and inadequate resettlement programs result in hunger, disease, and death of the displaced peoples. Meanwhile, a host of new problems are created, and the cycle comes full circle as multilateral development banks approve loans to try to cure the devastation wrought by previous projects. For instance, agricultural projects finance the indiscriminate use of pesticides that poison water supplies, and then the World Bank announces a new focus on water supply projects.

Projects with the highest potential environmental and social impact tend to coincide with the World Bank's biggest lending sectors: agriculture and rural development, transportation, and energy, which together made up half of the bank's lending portfolio in 1994. The limits of space preclude the examination of all damaging development bank-financed projects, but the literature is extensive. One World Bank project, the Sardar Sarovar dam on the Narmada River in India, is so controversial that after it was seven years under way, the World Bank was compelled to commission a first-ever independent review of the project.

The World Bank approved $850 million in loans for the Sardar Sarovar Dam project and related canal works, part of a $3 billion scheme of Stalinist proportions on the Narmada River to build 30 major dams, 135 medium-sized dams, and over 3,000 small dams to provide hydroelectric power and irrigation to parts of four Indian states.[24] The entire scheme will displace more than 1.5 million people, mostly of tribal and minority origin. The first major dam to be constructed, the Sardar Sarovar, will cause the displacement of 100,000 people and submerge 31,500 acres of valuable forest land and 27,500 acres of rich agricultural land.[25]

Mass protests have taken place in India over the resettlement and environmental aspects of the project. The Commission, led by Bradford Morse, former Head of the UN Development Program, found that the projects were "flawed, that resettlement and rehabilitation are impossible under prevailing circumstances, and that environmental impacts were not properly considered."[26] No comprehensive Environmental Impact Assessment was ever completed.

Over the past few years, utter chaos has characterized the resettlement and rehabilitation plans for displaced people carried out by the World Bank and Indian state governments. There has been a lack of available land, a lack of a common policy for all three states, and little or no involvement of communities in the resettlement plans.[27]

Indeed, villagers were sometimes not informed about the dams until submergence was imminent. A few years ago, the New Delhi-based Multiple Action Research Group visited some villages to be submerged by the Sardar Sarovar dam and found that, in some places, villagers knew very little about the dam and its consequences. Six forest villages, scheduled for submergence, were completely omitted from resettlement lists. One of the forest villagers asked the MARG team: "Are we animals to be left to drown?"[28]

In June 1992, World Bank president Lewis Preston agreed that the report on the Narmada dam system had identified a "number of deficiencies in the bank's appraisal of the project, the borrower's implementation and the bank's supervision work."[29] Still, the World Bank president said the Bank planned to go ahead with the project, with modifications.

The Narmada controversy had a happier outcome than most damaging World Bank projects. International environmental groups successfully kept the spotlight on the project's defects until the Indian government cancelled much of a $450 million World Bank loan for Sardar Sarovar in March 1993 rather than subject itself to continued international scrutiny.[30]

Multilateral development bank projects rarely contribute to a country's economic betterment, but even development that is economically viable often adversely impacts the environment and threatens the interests of some while benefiting others. Private development is preferable because the assignment of private property rights provides incentives for people to take better care of resources. A market approach to resolving environmental disputes allows low-cost solutions to be found. All sides have a better chance of fair treatment if government money is not committed to projects. Throughout the world, countries with government-directed economies have by far the worst environmental problems.

With project performance admittedly poor, and the environmental impact of their projects often devastating, it can be said that multilateral development bank loans have, on balance, hurt the populations they were intended to help. When confronted with the reality of the lending record, senior World Bank economists sagely shake their heads and murmur "Oh yes, Colombia Transport," or "Brazil Power," or "Mexico Agriculture." Ill-conceived projects such as Polonoroeste, Narmada, and hundreds of others throughout the developing world are often approved because they serve the people who count. The international bureaucrats take their cut, developing country elites use the projects as slush funds to fatten their offshore bank accounts and provide grease for the patronage economy, international contractors and consultants win lucrative contracts, and political elites in donor countries are able to point to the loans as evidence that they are doing something about world poverty.

There have been some successes amid the sea of unproductive

multilateral development bank projects. However, those successes tend to be concentrated in countries that have established the institutional framework and business climate conducive to economic growth. Projects carried out in Chile are undeniably among the most successful of those financed by development banks. But such countries attract billions of dollars in private equity capital, experience rapid growth, and can afford to pay for the infrastructure they need out of general government revenues. Since the U.S. government does not send aid to Britain or France, there is no reason why U.S. taxpayers should have to continue to subsidize infrastructure development in other successful countries such as Chile, whose high level of domestic savings enables the country to finance its own infrastructure.

Moreover, even the successes are expensive compared to private-sector development. The cost per job created under international development bank projects has been as high as $900,000 per job, and is often in excess of $20,000 per job.[31] Such costs are exorbitant in countries with low per capita incomes, and when projects fail and are not maintained after international funding ends, the jobs disappear but the loans are still on the books.

The development loans created opportunities for another international institution, the IMF, which had been looking for a new role since the breakup of the Bretton Woods pegged-exchange-rate system in 1971. As early as 1979, it was evident that uneconomic projects were not producing the revenues necessary to repay the loans. Loan rescheduling was frequent beginning in the late 1970s, and by 1980 one of every two dollars borrowed was used to service existing debt. In 1980, the IMF stepped in with so-called "structural adjustment loans" that changed its focus from financing balance of payments crises to extending new loans to keep countries current on existing loans. In early 1980, an IMF decision raised borrowing rights to 600 percent of a member's quota, extended its lending periods, and imposed conditions on borrowers that would encourage fiscal restraint and foster exports in order to produce revenues needed in the short term to repay loans.

With the onset of the debt crisis, the IMF greatly expanded lending to heavily indebted countries at the behest of the United States and other donor countries. It provided fast-disbursing loans with longer repayment periods tied to a country's acceptance of a structural adjustment program. IMF lending hit new highs with the debt crisis, with loan approvals amounting to $29 billion during the years 1982 to 1984.[32]

Between 1985 and 1989, the IMF continued to pump a total of $25 billion into developing countries.[33] The outcome was nothing to cheer about, however, since there is no group of IMF borrowers that is showcased as IMF success stories. By providing ready resources to bloated governments, IMF lending served to slow the reorientation of economies to the private sector. Indeed, by advocating policies that served to choke private sector consumption and investment, the IMF helped to bring on Latin America's "lost decade" of the 1980s when living standards were forced down in order to make debt payments.

In the 1980s, officials and academics were forthright in declaring that developing country citizens would have to pay for the mistakes of their governments—and, we might add, the development banks. Stanley Fischer, an MIT professor and former Vice President and Chief Economist for the World Bank, who is currently First Deputy Managing Director of the IMF, met with approval when he told attendees of a 1987 World Bank–IMF symposium that wages would have to be cut and living standards reduced in order to generate export earnings with which to service debt.[34] Development ideas had come full circle; formerly Third World populations were told that they had to live in austerity to finance government investment projects, and now they were being informed that they had to further tighten their belts in order to bail out the unsuccessful projects.

IMF officials, like their World Bank counterparts, often cheerfully criticize and condemn past efforts of their own institution. In 1987, IMF historian Margaret Garritsen de Vries in effect admitted that since 1973, the IMF has been uncertain how to achieve its goals: "Since 1973 . . . an analytical framework for balance of payments adjustment, especially for industrial members but to some extent also for developing members, has been elusive."[35]

The IMF's lack of an analytical framework has not stopped the institution from making ever more loans at easier terms. Between 1986 and 1987, two mechanisms were created, the Structural Adjustment Facility (SAF) and the Enhanced Structural Adjustment Facility (ESAF), to help the IMF's sixty-one poorest members "restore and maintain payments viability, while changing the structure of economic activity to achieve high and sustainable rates of economic growth." These facilities have been no more successful than prior lending.

So much lending for so little result has left cynical officials presiding over hollow institutions. The views of one senior World Bank official, who did not wish to be named, are representative. This senior economist flatly stated that the past lending approach used by the

World Bank was a failure, and with a conspiratorial grin, told his visitor that he had no confidence in the World Bank's ability to "get it right" in the future either. Moreover, he said that he had no confidence whatsoever in the World Bank's internal project audit process or in World Bank economic modeling. That said, the senior economist announced that he would have to cut short the interview as he was preparing to head off for a three-week mission overseas to push World Bank policies.

On the fiftieth anniversary of the Bretton Woods conference, which founded the World Bank and the International Monetary Fund, critics from across the political spectrum aimed their guns at these institutions. Members of a coalition of leftists called "50 Years Is Enough" said that the World Bank is beyond saving and agitated for its demise. Free-market advocates reached the same conclusion in *Perpetuating Poverty: The World Bank, the IMF and the Developing World*, published by the Cato Institute in 1994. Pundits of different persuasions vented their criticisms in the *New York Times*, the *Washington Post*, the *Wall Street Journal*, *Business Week*, and the London-based *Financial Times*. No group was more influential in calling for change than the independent Bretton Woods Commission, headed by Paul Volcker. The Commission's report entitled *Bretton Woods: Looking to the Future* fell like a bomb on the development community. The study was critical of the performance of the IMF and the World Bank and recommended sweeping reforms to both institutions if they were to remain relevant.

The report contended that the IMF had strayed from its original mission of managing the global monetary system into providing financing for development, thereby overlapping the role of the World Bank. The report observed that at the behest of donor countries, the IMF has underwritten lending programs for the poorest countries and made a foray into medium-term adjustment lending in the 1980s. In the 1990s, however, the IMF should stop "duplicating functions" of the World Bank and focus on managing the global monetary system. The Commission seems to think that the IMF would have more success managing more complicated matters, but its criticisms of the IMF's Third World debacles are on the mark.

The Commission's criticisms of the World Bank were more pointed. The Bank had failed to adapt to a "world that has turned from public sector dominance towards private enterprise and free markets." While the report notes the World Bank's efforts to promote privatization and private sector development, it concludes that the World Bank's emphasis remains on building up the public sector and "it still supports too many state-owned enterprises." The World Bank should, but does not, direct its development assistance only at what the private sector cannot or will not do.

The report recommended deep-seated reform of the World Bank's organization and goals. The Bank should become a catalyst for private-sector development, channeling the bulk of its resources through its private-sector development arm, the International Finance Corporation. The Commission recommended that the World Bank itself lend more to the private sector under government guarantee. It should expand its guarantee authority for international private lenders as well. The report recommended that the World Bank continue to finance public-sector investment in vital areas, such as education, public health, and social safety nets, and other public infrastructure that the private sector will not finance.

The staff report that accompanied the main report contended that the Bank should apply a "market access" test to decide which countries should receive loans. That is, countries that have access to international private capital at reasonable rates, even if they are poor, should not be allowed to borrow from the World Bank.

A role was still envisioned for the International Development Association, the World Bank's soft loan window, but the Commission recommended that qualifying income levels be lowered to focus its lending only on truly needy countries.

The report attempted to deal with the World Bank's perverse institutional incentives. It advised the Bank to improve its loan portfolio by more carefully supervising its projects and implement the recommendations of the 1992 Wapenhans Report, which called for a complete overhaul in World Bank lending in order to maintain the institution's triple-A credit rating. The report recommended organizational streamlining to eliminate functions presently duplicated at other institutions and a reduction in staff time spent on internal matters. The Commission recommended significant staff cuts as the Bank becomes more efficient and the private sector takes over economic functions formerly monopolized by the government.

The Commission foresaw a shrinking need for World Bank lending "as privatization progresses and more countries can tap the international capital markets at reasonable cost." The report concluded: "The Bank should not resist this trend, of course, but encourage it."

The Commission correctly recommended that the bank curtail the scope of its activities and cease to crowd out the private economy. But it is the nature of bureaucracies to expand their activities, not to constrict them. Moreover, taxpayer-funded and guaranteed organizations lack the ability to apply a market test to their borrowers. To function successfully as a commercial lender, the Bank would have to be privatized.

In the 1990s, there is consensus on the left and right that government-to-government aid funneled into the statist development approach has failed to help the poor. Independent analysts conclude that developing country elites appropriated the aid to further entrench their control over economies.[36] As we have noted, the top-down development approach excluded the input of the so-called project beneficiaries, the poor populations that the projects were intended to help.

By fostering the growth of government, the development banks became one more obstacle for countries to overcome in order to progress economically. Now that countries such as Chile, Argentina, and Mexico have privatized and reoriented their economies to the private sector, it is pointless to continue a failed strategy. The development institutions should be closed down or privatized. Once, it was outside the realm of the plausible to suggest such a thing. In the 1990s, however, the debate has progressed to the point that Sir Alan Walters, former Economic Adviser to the World Bank (1976–1980, 1984–1988), suggested in a 1994 study that "the ideal solution would be to abolish the Fund and the Bank—wind them up and disperse their expertise to other activities."[37]

It has occurred to officials at these institutions that the private sector takeover of development leaves no role for them. At a December 1993 IDB seminar that assessed the IDB's lending program from 1979 to 1992, panelists were openly downcast at the fact that Latin American economies were improving. They were worried that there would be no more need for IDB loans and technical assistance if countries continued to privatize and attract investment capital. One panelist cheered up the crowd, however, by pointing out that there is such a long record of crisis in the region that eventually countries would get into trouble again and need IDB help.

In the 1990s, the World Bank and Inter-American Development Bank have produced numerous studies on the inefficiency and mismanagement endemic in government-owned companies and the need for privatization of many activities. In June 1992, the World Bank hosted a landmark conference in which it lauded the benefits of privatization in developing countries. Panelists discussed a study, "Welfare

Consequences of Selling Public Enterprises," authored by World Bank economists Ahmed Galal, Leroy Jones, Pankaj Tandon, and Ingo Vegelsang. The study examined privatizations in each of four countries: Britain, Chile, Malaysia, and Mexico. The sale of four airlines, three telecommunications firms, two electricity utilities, a road-freight transporter, a container port, and a lottery business were examined. Overall, the World Bank economists concluded that privatization does add to national wealth; according to their results, eleven of the twelve sales resulted in a net increase in wealth.

The study's methodology understated the benefits of privatization, but it was still an intellectual turning point. It exploded the myth long prevalent in the World Bank that a unit of capital in the hands of the state is as efficient as in the hands of the private sector and stripped the World Bank of its justification for lending to government agencies. Those familiar with development bank-financed projects easily spotted former development bank projects among the privatizations. For example, Chile privatized the Chilgener company, owner of the 160-megawatt capacity Alfalfal Dam, which received over $100 million in funding from the Inter-American Development Bank.[38]

The acceptance of private property and markets by some international bureaucrats is a welcome development. However, the studies' findings on the inefficiency of government and the benefits of privatization apply to the development institutions themselves. Indeed, the World Bank only installed a cost accounting system in the 1990s—almost fifty years after its founding. Where there is no bottom line and no accountability there can be no real development. At a May 1994 seminar, one World Bank economist rightly concluded that "government failure is worse than market failure to date." Now that poor countries have learned, at great expense, that markets are far more effective than governments at delivering the goods at reasonable cost, the international development institutions have outlived the statist era.

The loan portfolios of the development banks are not marked to market. Ultimately, U.S. taxpayers may be hit with their portion of a bailout of World Bank and IDB bonds. Four recent World Bank reports show that projects it has financed with bond issues are failing at a rate that would quickly lead to bankruptcy if the institution were a private commercial bank. The February 1992 report *Evaluation Results for 1990* assessed 359 projects at completion of World Bank funding, representing investments of some $43 billion. The report found that 36 percent of the projects had failed by the time their funding was completed, and only half of the remaining 64 percent would survive over time. In other words, the report projected a success rate of only 32 percent.

The following year, project performance was even worse. *Evaluation Results for 1991*, released in March 1993, evaluated 278 projects involving total World Bank investments of more than $32.8 billion. It concluded that 37 percent of the projects had failed by the time funding was completed. The report estimated that only 42 percent of the remaining 63 percent would survive over time. Thus, only 26 percent of the projects were deemed to be successful.

The March 1993 report noted that the 1991 results were part of an "overall downward trend in project performance" that had been observed over the previous two years. The report also pointed out that lending to the World Bank's best customers in Asia is declining while lending to Africa, the poorest performer overall, is increasing.

Another report, commissioned by World Bank president Lewis Preston in February 1992, was never released, but many details were leaked or incorporated into the March 1993 report. The report saw "a gradual but steady deterioration in portfolio performance." The report blamed the high failure rate on the bank's "approval culture" and described the internal push to approve ever more loans. It turns out that the best way to be promoted at the World Bank was to make a lot of loans, and the bigger the better.[39]

In June 1994, the World Bank released the next report in the series, *1992 Evaluation Results*. This time the bank reviewed 277 projects at completion, representing investments of more than $44 billion, and judged the performance of 67 percent to be satisfactory. The report estimated that 54 percent of those projects would be sustainable over time. Therefore, bank economists projected a success rate of 36 percent for projects reviewed in 1992.

The World Bank cautioned against a premature conclusion that its project performance had turned a corner, however. Aside from the fact that a 36 percent success rate is still failure however you look at it, the report projected a decline in the average ratings of projects in the near future, followed by modest improvement later.

The four reports themselves may be optimistic. The World Bank freely admits that its project monitoring capability is poor. Moreover, the bank's evaluation techniques would never survive scrutiny in a commercial operation.

The IDB's portfolio is as shaky as the World Bank's, although it refrains from publishing incriminating evidence. In 1994, the IDB asked for and received an expansion of taxpayer guarantees that boosted its capital to $101 billion, an increase of $40 billion. This large percentage increase was necessary to maintain a $6 billion per year lending level. Obviously, the IDB's lending process is not self-financing. Moreover, the IDB plans to dispense 40 percent of its new lending for social purposes and allocate 35 percent to smaller Latin American countries. In other words, the IDB is expanding its portfolio in the least creditworthy areas. Donors agreed to the capital increase with the stipulation that the institution would make up to 5 percent of its loans to the private sector, despite the fact that its existing private sector arm, the Inter-American Investment Corporation, has not been known for picking winners.

The IMF's portfolio is in no better shape, although that institution is likewise reticent about publishing studies that reveal that to be the case. Sizeable arrears have appeared on the IMF's books in the past few years, and there is a constant scramble in the IMF to reschedule loans in all but name. The IMF's greatly expanded lending in recent years to the poorest countries of Africa has downgraded its portfolio. As with the World Bank, top officers are keenly aware that if it were not for the periodic increase in Western taxpayer subsidies many loans would default.

In the past, the multilaterals dealt with bad loans by "round-tripping," which is the practice of lending money to pay interest. However, about $18 billion in bad loans to twenty-four Third World countries are too far gone to keep on the books. The World Bank is trying to hatch a scheme to create a new bank to be infused with taxpayer monies from the industrialized countries. This bank would be known as the Multilateral Debt Facility (MDF). Its function would be to buy at face value all the bad loans from the development banks in order to keep their books pristine. This way the multilaterals wouldn't have to impair their capital, and perhaps their bond ratings, by writing down bad loans the way commercial banks have to do.[40]

This scheme would introduce even more unreality into the lending practices of development banks. No decision, no matter how bad, could ever come back to haunt the banks, because the taxpayers would be standing at hand to keep the banks whole from their mistakes. If the MDF catches on, we are likely to see a proliferation of multilateral institution building rather than the phase out to which the failure of development planning points.

Development bank portfolios are in such bad shape because the projects financed were never expected to earn a market rate of return, despite apparently high projections. It has been taken for granted that project loans will be repaid out of general government revenues.

Moreover, World Bank president Lewis Preston himself has lamented the fact that no one is held to account for past failures.

The World Bank Articles of Agreement provide for the suspension of operations and the settlement of obligations. The provisions state, however, that a majority of the World Bank Governors, meaning shareholding governments, would have to exercise a majority of the vote to "permanently suspend its operations in respect of new loans and guarantees." This is not likely to happen.

A more feasible alternative is the unilateral pullout of a major donor country such as the United States. This could provide the stimulus to set in motion the closure of the World Bank. The bank's Articles of Agreement state that "any member may withdraw from the Bank at any time by transmitting a notice in writing to the Bank." Withdrawal would become effective on the date that such a notice was received.

On withdrawal, according to the Articles of Agreement, a country is liable for its share of outstanding loans and loan guarantees as long as any part of the obligations contracted before it ceased to be a member is outstanding. But it ceases to contract new obligations or share in the expenses and income of the bank. As of December 31, 1995, the United States was liable for about $30 billion in loans and loan guarantees of the World Bank.

If one major donor were to pull out, it would cut its losses and other countries would gradually be forced to assume a greater burden. Not wishing to expose their taxpayers to greater risk, other countries would probably follow the first and unilaterally withdraw. Remaining countries would likely demand a realistic asset evaluation to settle the departing countries' accounts with the bank. This would put an end to the World Bank's accounting fiction, and the process of deciding how to close down the institution could begin.

The World Bank's Articles of Agreement do not specify how best to close down the institution, leaving room for flexibility. The pertinent provision states that after suspension of operations, "the Bank shall forthwith cease all activities, except those incident to the orderly realization, conservation, and preservation of its assets and settlement of its obligations." The IMF and IDB charters have similar provisions regarding suspension of operations and the unilateral pullout of a donor country, and the United States could withdraw from all of them simultaneously and set in motion a consideration of alternatives to liquidating these institutions.

In analyzing how to close down these institutions, it is necessary to understand how they are financed. The World Bank's main lending arm, the International Bank for Reconstruction and Development

(IBRD), is owned by its 178 member countries,[41] who subscribe capital to the institution. Less than 10 percent of this capital is paid in, with the rest a "callable capital" guarantee to be relied on only in the case of necessity to meet the bank's obligation to its creditors. The bank finances its lending operations primarily by borrowing in the international capital markets based on the member country guarantees. For every dollar paid in, the bank generates another $200 in the capital markets. IBRD loans are made to better-off developing countries, generally have a grace period of five years, and are repayable over fifteen to twenty years. IBRD loans have variable interest rates, calculated in accordance with a guideline related to its cost of borrowing.

The IDB operates similarly to the World Bank and other regional development banks: a small percentage of capital subscriptions are paid in and the rest is a callable guarantee that the bank uses to raise capital in the international capital markets.

Unlike the World Bank and the regional multilateral development banks, the IMF is financed through member government capital subscriptions, known as quotas. The IMF's Articles of Agreement authorizes the institution to collect a pool of currencies in order to financially assist member countries confronting temporary balance of payments deficits. Membership quotas are assessed according to the relative wealth of the member and in the 1990s are set in terms of Special Drawing Rights (SDRs), the IMF's unit of account consisting of a basket of hard currencies.

As of April 30, 1995, the capital subscriptions of the 178 members of the IMF totaled $228 billion.[42] The IMF does not have this entire amount available to lend, however, for two reasons. Countries pay 75 percent of their quota in domestic currency and the remainder in foreign exchange. As most national currencies are not in demand outside the issuing countries, only half of the IMF's resources are available for lending.[43] Moreover, countries are only required to pay in 25 percent of their quota and the remaining 75 percent has to be called as the currencies in demand are used up. Therefore, the ratio of paid-in to subscribed capital varies.

Governments earn a below-market rate of interest on the currency they provide the IMF. The difference between the rate they receive and the market rate is a subsidy of IMF interest rates. The U.S. Treasury counts paid-in currency amounts as assets and for the IMF they are considered liabilities.

There are several options for winding down these institutions. Whatever method is finally adopted, undoubtedly the staff of these institutions will be called on to adjust. Some would say that is fitting, considering the painful adjustments they have imposed on member countries. Still, these institutions assume tasks at the behest of donor countries, and the failures were not any one person's fault.

There are good people at the international development banks, and they inspired enough confidence in the donor governments and world financial markets that they were given an abundance of resources. The size of the debt problem itself illustrates the fact that there was no lack of resources to try to make the development approach work. The staff did the best they could given the defects of the approach. It was an expensive lesson that served to teach us that development planning was not the way to approach development.

In the 1990s, the international bureaucrats should transfer their experience and know-how to the private sector to help the economic transformation. Some already have. They have good connections. It is a dislocation, but they are educated people and should be able to make the transition without undue difficulty. Perhaps a generous severance package could help smooth their transition.

As countries become more successful because of privatizations, the prospect of loan repayment improves, and the World Bank could become a coupon collector, retiring its bonds as its loans are repaid.

Alternatively, the World Bank and regional development banks could be privatized. The multilateral development bank loans could be stripped of their special status and the market could be allowed to determine the value of the loans and the bonds. The value of both will fall, at least in the near term, as it becomes apparent that the banks were financing failure. The World Bank and the regional development banks that are similarly capitalized could exchange their loans for equity and sell the shares to redeem their bonds or hold them for capital gains in order to minimize taxpayer expense. Privatization increases the value of assets, as experience to date demonstrates. Thus, by swapping debt for equity, the development banks might be able to redeem their bonds without calling on the taxpayers. Western governments could even forgive the debt in whole or in part in compensation for the damage they inflicted with development planning.

A 1993 study published by the IDB of privatizations in Mexico, Chile, Colombia, and Argentina concluded that while some privatized companies failed to thrive immediately (often as a result of government regulations and inflexibilities in the labor market), profits and output generally increased after privatization.[44] These positive results bode well for the post-privatization outlook for multilateral loans. As with commercial bank loans exchanged for equity, the value of the shares would rise as the privatized companies became more success-ful, keeping losses to a minimum.

Latin American governments are increasingly creditworthy, a good indication that the costs to U.S. and European taxpayers of closing the international agencies could be minimized. The value of Latin America's debt on the secondary market has risen substantially since 1989. Peru's sovereign debt, for example, which traded at a measly 5.75 cents per dollar in November 1989, had risen to 60 cents on the dollar by March 1994. Mexico's debt, trading at 35 cents in November 1989, traded at a range of between 74 cents and 97 cents in March 1994. The value of Argentina's sovereign debt had risen from a low of 13 cents on the dollar in 1989 to trade between 60 and 79 cents on the dollar in March 1994. Chile, at 59 cents in November 1989, traded at near full face value in March 1994, at 95 cents.[45] Substantial increases in value over the period were seen everywhere in the region, even in the Dominican Republic, Honduras, and Ecuador. In the aftermath of the Mexican peso devaluation at the end of 1994, Latin American debt val-ues fell but remained far above their earlier lows.

The World Bank and IMF portfolios have benefited from the fact that the commercial banks took the writedown, cleaning much debt from the developing countries' books and enhancing the prospects for wind-ing down the development banks without inflicting traumatic costs on taxpayers. The long experiment based on antimarket ideas has failed, and the bureaucracies spawned by that atmosphere need to be priva-tized or closed to prevent them from creating, like the IMF, a new job for themselves.

The window of opportunity is now. Many policymakers recognize that the development banks are no longer relevant, and the World Bank and its cohorts have not yet found a new task. They are gravitating toward becoming international welfare agencies, but the disillusion-ment with welfare in the developed world doesn't bid well for the sal-ability of this goal. To finance development was one thing, but to create international welfare dependencies is quite another. Taxpayers in successful countries can barely finance their own social services.

The World Bank and the regional development banks subsidized the growth of state sectors, while the IMF subsidized governments that mismanaged economic policy. The rationale for these counter-productive activities was that they would provide social benefits and the foundation for sustainable development. In fact, the development institutions were a concession to the anticapitalist intellectual mental-ity that ruled the postwar era. If the state did not own all the enterprises and make all investment decisions, then somehow monopolists would exploit the people.

These attitudes ruled out a private enterprise environment. Economic activity that was not sanctioned by government came to a halt or moved into the underground economy. The atmosphere that led to government dominance over the economy is gone, and privatizations are shrinking the state sectors.

The only kind of financing that has a role today is the kind that relates to risk and reward. The function of a private lender is to identify good loans that pay off and create long-standing business relationships. The different environment that exists in Latin America today is only compatible with private lenders and private investors.

In the new climate of intensifying international competition, countries can no longer afford to make policy based on the thinking that they can resort to international institutions, or to Uncle Sam, for a bailout. Policy failures, such as the Mexican peso devaluation, are expensive and set countries back when they need to accelerate their transformations. The Zedillo Government might not have devalued the peso if officials had not believed in the back of their minds that the United States and the IMF would come rushing to their rescue in the event of failure. The Mexican economy now has to divert resources from business creation and expansion to pay back loans that could have been avoided by better policy.

Capitalist success comes from attracting private capital flows, not from drawing up development plans to attract World Bank loans. Latin Americans can finance their own social infrastructure with domestic taxes once capitalism builds a tax base. Market forces can even be used to provide public services, thus further shrinking the rent-seeking arena. The international development institutions simply have no role left.

Notes

1. Roland Vaubel, "A Public Choice View of International Organization," in Roland Vaubel and Thomas Willett, eds., *The Political Economy of International Organizations: A Public Choice Approach* (Boulder: Westview Press, 1991; article first published in 1986), 27–40.
2. Bruno Frey, "The Public Choice View of International Political Economy," in *The Political Economy of International Organizations: A Public Choice Approach*, 19.
3. Ibid.

4. Vaubel, "A Public Choice View of International Organization," 27–40.
5. Frey, "The Public Choice View of International Political Economy," 7–22.
6. Ibid.
7. Michael Irwin, "Banking on Poverty: An Insider's Look at the World Bank," *Foreign Policy Briefing*, Cato Institute, 20 September 1990.
8. Ibid.
9. Ibid.
10. Employment figures for the World Bank Group, which includes the International Bank for Reconstruction and Development (IBRD), known as the World Bank, the International Finance Corporation (IFC), and the Multilateral Investment Guarantee Agency (MIGA).
11. World Bank, Staff Appraisal Report, Colombia: Third National Roads Sector Project, 3 March 1992. Marked for official use only.
12. Ibid.
13. World Bank, Colombia Public Sector Expenditure Review, 15 January 1991. Marked for official use only.
14. World Bank, Staff Appraisal Report, Colombia: Third National Roads Sector Project, 3 March 1992.
15. Riordan Roett, *The Politics of Foreign Aid in the Brazilian Northeast* (Nashville: Vanderbilt University Press, 1972), 116–40.
16. Richard Lacroix, *Desarrollo Rural Integral en America Latina*, No. 716S (Washington, D.C.: World Bank, 1985), 23, 26–27.
17. Bruce Rich, "Multilateral Development Banks: Their Role in Destroying the Global Environment," *The Ecologist*, Vol. 15, No. 1/2, 1985, 56–64.
18. Ibid.
19. "World Bank Experience with Rural Development, 1965–1986," 16 October 1987, World Bank internal document.
20. A $50-million Agriculture Sector Investment Loan to the government of Morocco is aimed in part to finance policy reforms in the livestock sector. World Bank Annual Report 1992, 160, 186.
21. Rogério Gribel, "The Balbina Disaster: The Need to Ask Why?," *The Ecologist*, Vol. 20, No. 4, July/August 1990, 133–35.
22. Ibid.
23. Ibid.
24. See Bruce Rich, "The 'Greening' of the Development Banks: Rhetoric and Reality," *The Ecologist*, Vol. 19, No. 2, 1989, 44–52; Stephanie Gray and K.K. Sharma, "World Bank Admits Indian Dam Flawed," *Financial Times*, London, 21 June 1992; and full-page ad placed in the *New York Times* by twenty-seven environmental groups including the Sierra Club, Greenpeace International, and three Indian groups, entitled "Why Thousands of People Will *Drown* Before Accepting the Sardar Sarovar Dam," 21 September 1992.

25. Claude Alvares and Ramesh Billorey, "Damning the Narmada: The Politics Behind the Destruction," *The Ecologist*, Vol. 17, No. 2, 1987, 62–73; Bruce Rich, "The 'Greening' of the Development Banks: Rhetoric and Reality," *The Ecologist*, Vol. 19, No. 2, 1989, 44–52; and full-page ad placed in the *New York Times* by twenty-seven environmental groups including the Sierra Club, Greenpeace International, and three Indian groups, entitled "Why Thousands of People Will *Drown* Before Accepting the Sardar Sarovar Dam," 21 September 1992.

26. Stephanie Gray and K. K. Sharma, "World Bank Admits Indian Dam Flawed," *Financial Times*, London, 21 June 1992; and full-page ad in the *New York Times*, placed by twenty-seven environmental groups including Sierra Club, Greenpeace International, and three Indian groups, entitled "Why Thousands of People Will *Drown* Before Accepting the Sardar Sarovar Dam," 21 September 1992.

27. Bruce Rich, "The 'Greening' of the Development Banks: Rhetoric and Reality," *The Ecologist*, Vol. 19, No. 2, 1989, 44–52.

28. Ibid.

29. Stephanie Gray and K. K. Sharma, "World Bank Admits Indian Dam Flawed," *Financial Times*, London, 21 June 1992.

30. A valuable study evaluating India's experience with large dams from a cost-benefit point of view is Satyajit Singh, "Evaluating Large Dams in India," *Economic and Political Weekly* (Bombay), 17 March 1990, 561–74. Singh contends that the true economic and social costs of dam projects have rarely been taken into account while the benefits have been greatly overstated. Singh concludes that uneconomic projects get built because they serve the interests of ruling elites who use irrigation and power generation projects to increase their own wealth and power at the expense of the population.

31. World Bank, *Tenth Annual Review of Project Performance Audit Results*, 3 volumes, 30 August 1984.

32. IMF Annual Report 1985, Table 19, 65, converted at average annual U.S. dollar/SDR exchange rates.

33. IMF Annual Report 1990, Table 1, 52, converted at average annual U.S. dollar/SDR exchange rates.

34. Stanley Fischer, "Economic Growth and Economic Policy," in *Growth-Oriented Adjustment Programs*, Vittorio Corbo, Morris Goldstein, and Mohsin Khan, eds. (Washington, D.C.: International Monetary Fund and World Bank, 1987), papers from a joint IMF-World Bank symposium held 25–27 February 1987, 151–75; see IMF research director Jacob Frankel's discussion of Fischer's paper, 226–36.

35. Margaret Garritsen de Vries, *Balance of Payments Adjustment, 1945 to 1986: The IMF Experience* (Washington, D.C.: International Monetary Fund, 1987), 284.

36. See, for example, Cheryl Payer, *The World Bank: A Critical Analysis*

(New York and London: Atlantic Monthly Review Press, 1982); David Korten, *Getting to the 21st Century: Voluntary Action and the Global Agenda* (West Hartford: Kumarian Press, 1990); Graham Hancock, *Lords of Poverty: The Power, Prestige and Corruption of the International Aid Business* (New York: Atlantic Monthly Press, 1989); Melvyn Krauss, *Development Without Aid* (Stanford: Hoover Institution/New York: New York University, 1983); and Peter Bauer, *Dissent on Development* (Cambridge: Harvard University Press, 1972).

37. Sir Alan Walters, "Do We Need the IMF and the World Bank?," Institute of Economic Affairs, London, 1994.

38. Inter-American Development Bank Annual Report, 1985.

39. Hobart Rowen, "World Bank's Preston Plans Shake-up of Lending Policy," *Washington Post*, 27 December 1992.

40. Patricia Adams, "A Troubling Deposit at World Bank," *Wall Street Journal*, 29 November 1995.

41. As of February 1996.

42. IMF Annual Report 1995, 244, converted at U.S. dollar/SDR exchange rate prevailing at the end of April 1995.

43. David Driscoll, *What Is the International Monetary Fund?* (Washington, D.C.: International Monetary Fund, reprinted June 1992, revised January 1992).

44. Manuel Sánchez, et al., "A Comparison of Privatization Experiences: Chile, Mexico, Colombia, and Argentina," in Manuel Sánchez and Rossana Corona, eds., *Privatization in Latin America* (Washington, D.C.: Inter-American Development Bank, 1993), 1–38.

45. Sources for secondary market debt trading figures: *International Financing Review*, 11 November 1989, 34; and *LDC Debt Report*, 7 March 1994, 3.

7

Implications of Latin American Capitalism for the United States

In the postwar period, the absence of competitors other than the Japanese and West Germans meant that U.S. policymakers could hamstring our economy with tax and regulatory burdens without dire effect. Not even state subsidies could offset the inefficiencies of socialized industries, and American industrial and agricultural products faced little competition. Moreover, there were few other places for people to invest their capital or pursue business careers. The growth of government under New Deal and Great Society policies was very costly to the economy, but other countries were much more mired in socialism and political favoritism than the United States. Now, an entire region is opening up to the south that welcomes foreign capital and ingenuity and is creating world-class competitive conditions to attract investment and entrepreneurs.

As Latin America and much of the rest of the world shed the policies that insulated U.S. business from suffering the competitive consequences of ill-considered government policies, our own policies will have to change. The implications of U.S. tax, entitlement, regulatory, and legal policies are inconsistent with the ability of the United States to be a global competitor. The current tax system raises the cost of labor with payroll taxes while reducing labor productivity with capital taxation. Unique regulatory burdens, tort liabilities, and legal uncertainty are helping turn the United States into a high-cost, high-risk place to do business relative to other locations.

The restructurings that began in the 1980s are now more or less completed, and there is little that U.S. businesses can do on their own to improve competitiveness other than to move more of their operations offshore. In global markets, no internal cost-cutting can offset disadvantages of domestic tax, regulatory, and legal policies.

The United States needs a tax system that does not discriminate against success and saving. The multiple taxation of investment income lowers our savings rate and retards capital formation. This puts us at a disadvantage vis-à-vis countries that encourage saving. Our policy of taxing capital gains as ordinary income discourages venture capital and keeps hundreds of billions of dollars rigidly locked into investments for tax reasons, slowing investors' response to promising new opportunities. A growing number of competitors have no capital gains tax at all, helping to facilitate business creation.

Almost everyone has heard of the double taxation of dividends, but saving is actually subjected to multiple taxation. As a result of this multiple taxation, the rate of return that an individual realizes from his or her investments is substantially smaller than the economic return of the investment to society. The amount of money a person has to invest is first reduced by the personal income tax. If after-tax savings are invested in a corporation, the return from this investment is taxed at the corporate level, and if the remainder is passed on in the form of a dividend, it is taxed as regular income at the personal level. If the remainder is instead reinvested, the return will be capitalized in the worth of the stock, adjusted for future corporate taxation. If the individual were to sell the stock and realize a capital gain, then this amount is subject to further taxation. These multiple layers of taxation are further compounded by such taxes as the property tax, with the end result being less investment and lower growth in labor productivity.

Progressive income tax systems make no economic or social sense. They are envy-driven and, at best, reflect the old Keynesian supposition (known as the stagnation thesis) that investment opportunities have dried up in mature capitalist systems, with the result that the savings of the rich cause permanent unemployment by reducing aggregate consumer demand. This view inspired by the Great Depression has long since been abandoned by economists.

Today the income tax system is widely regarded as an economically and socially inefficient way to collect tax revenues. The incentives of progressivity are perverse as they encourage leisure over work and consumption over saving. The attributes that lead to success are penalized, and there is no offsetting social gain. Redistribution, once thought to be dependent on tax progressivity, can be achieved through the expenditure side of the budget. Today economists understand that even regressive taxation can result in redistribution to the poor through the assignment of benefits. For example, a sales tax can be used to provide food stamps to the poor. Everyone would pay the tax, but only the poor would receive benefits.

In the United States today there are serious political proposals to eliminate progressivity and the bias against saving. Senators Sam Nunn and Pete Dominici advocate a consumption-based income tax that eliminates income that is saved from the tax base. House Majority Leader Dick Armey proposes a 17 percent flat rate tax that excludes investment from the tax base. Senator Lugar wants to abolish the income tax and replace it with a federal sales tax, an idea that also has the attention of Rep. Bill Archer, Chairman of the House Ways and Means Committee.

These proposals, unthinkable a decade ago, show a growing sensitivity on the part of policymakers to the importance in global competition of a country's ability to attract capital. Those that do a poor job of rewarding capital or that scare it away will fail in the global competition of the twenty-first century.

Until the collapse a few years ago of the Soviet Union and development planning in Latin America, the United States was the mecca for capital. Europeans kept money in the United States as a safe haven against Soviet gains in the Cold War, and the United States contained more of Latin America's private capital than the region did. As global capitalism becomes the norm, the United States's special advantages as a capital haven are fading away.

It is now widely understood that a tax policy designed to hold back "the rich" is not only unfair to the rich but also to labor and a country's competitive position. Everywhere there is a clamor for capital. New capital is a far more successful leveler than redistribution. New capital unleashes upstarts who bust up the status quo, create opportunities, and undermine protected enclaves. In achieving these results, new capital is more egalitarian than socialism.

Once it soaks in that the United States cannot continue to count on special advantages and is just another player in global competition, its economic policies will become more capitalistic. One obvious candidate for reform is the pay-as-you-go Social Security system that burdens employment with a tax while draining the country of savings.

A true pension system builds capital both for individuals and the country. It is a source of national savings that finances productivity-enhancing investments. The current Social Security system is nothing but an intergenerational transfer payment financed by an employment tax that reduces the income and savings ability of those who are working to provide income to those who are retired. The U.S. Social Security system is beset with demographic problems, and the government is already reneging on the promised benefits by subjecting them to income taxation.

Surveys show that only 9 percent of those between the ages of 18 and 34 believe Social Security will have the money to pay their retirement benefits—a smaller percentage than believes in UFOs—so it is only a matter of time before support builds for a retirement system based on equity ownership in lieu of tax-financed transfer payments. William G. Shipman in a recent study for the Cato Institute in Washington, D.C., shows that Americans would receive many multiples of their Social Security benefits if their payroll taxes were invested in the stock and bond markets. Social Security not only cheats retirees but also cheats the country out of needed savings and investment. It is a sacred cow that will fall to the pressures of global competition.

As Latin America consolidates capitalism, it will put the United States to the test whether we are ready or not. Entrepreneurs now often receive better treatment there than here. Hernando De Soto's 1986 account of how difficult it was to open a business in Lima, Peru, may now more closely describe the difficulty of opening one in parts of the United States. Peru has been deregulating its business sector, while in the United States would-be business owners confront a plethora of costly permits and regulations. For example, the Americans with Disabilities Act (1990) requires firms to make their buildings accessible to the handicapped and madates them to install bathroom stalls that accommodate the handicapped. Much money is spent to comply, yet the special facilities are seldom used by the handicapped. The Clean Air Act (1990) requires firms to spend billions of dollars to make marginal improvements in air quality. Landowners find their property taken by "wetlands" regulators without compensation. Others find themselves arbitrarily stuck with Superfund cleanup costs.

Thirty years ago most economists took it on faith that government needed to protect consumers from avaricious and unethical businesses with regulation. Since regulation was "good," the more the better. Regulatory agencies pushed regulation beyond the point where benefits equaled the costs. Regulation expanded until in some cases it was all cost and no benefit. For example, there are many small businesses whose physical plant consists of a single office adjoining sheds containing products that the business delivers. OSHA routinely harrassed businesses for not having the single door in and out of the single-roomed office posted with an exit sign. Business men and women struggling with truck maintenance and delivery schedules couldn't believe it when federal employees appeared on their thresholds to cite them for office safety violations.

These types of absurdities went on for a long time before many economists stopped taking the benefits for granted and began considering the costs. It took even longer for many economists to realize that regulation was not only a rent-seeking enterprise for the bureaucrat building an empire with unneeded and harmful regulations but also an activity that businesses themselves encouraged to protect a market or disable a competitor. In the United States today, regulation is infected with so much private interest that it is hard to find any public interest in it. Regulation has produced so many organized interest groups and such intense lobbying that American democracy currently responds to little else. An activity that was supposed to protect the consumer has instead enfeebled democracy.

Experience with regulation indicates that it doesn't take long before regulators lose sight of any sensible purpose. The Food and Drug Administration, for example, is so determined to protect dying people from possible harmful side effects that it delays the release of medicines and devices that could prolong life. Indeed, it is likely that the FDA's policies have boosted the mortality rate over what it otherwise would be. Without any doubt, the FDA has pushed up the cost of health care.

In today's runaway tort liability climate, the FDA is redundant. Every pharmaceutical firm and every manufacturer of medical devices has an immense interest in the safety of their products. Humans will always make mistakes, but the idea that drug companies must be deterred by federal regulators from making and selling harmful products indicates a paranoid distrust of business and an extraordinarily naive trust in government.

The dark side of regulation was not recognized by economists until after it had become a massive bureaucratic vested interest with strong private sector constituencies. Many economic studies show that regulation imposes a high cost on the economy, but despite the evidence little has happened that would redress the imbalance. The corrupt practices that characterize the American regulatory state are identical to those that Latin Americans are struggling to overthrow. If nothing is done in the United States, successful lobbying will become a more important element in a firm's success than any market test.

The most important lesson that the United States can learn from Latin America is that privilege is inconsistent with a rule of law. Privilege is a bending or removal of rules that apply to others. As privilege removes accountability, it leads to the rule of influence rather than the rule of law.

In Latin America, regulation was a primary creator of privilege. In the United States, regulations that bestow and require race and gender preferences have created inequality in the law. Proportional representation in the workforce cannot be achieved without reverse discrimination against white males. The regulations that comprise U.S. civil rights policy have disparate impact. They benefit groups defined as "protected minorities" and disadvantage groups without this designation.

Once privilege enters the law, it is difficult to contain. The allocation of government contracts by race and gender expands rent-seeking activity at the expense of competitive bidding as the market gives way to privilege. This nonmarket allocation of income-generating opportunities does not differ in principle or process from the dispensation of economic favors in Latin America.

Confronted with competition from countries that are shrinking government, the United States can no longer afford the cost of a government that has grown so large that federal, state, and local expenditures constitute a third of the U.S. GDP. The $1.5 trillion federal budget (1995) is as large as the GDP of France. Such a huge budget can stand a lot of cutting. Cabinet agencies, which were created basically to appease interest groups and reward political contributors and party operatives with Presidential appointments, can be closed: the Departments of Commerce, Energy, Education, Health and Human Services, and Housing and Urban Development are among those that can be abolished. Companies have been forced to restructure over the past decade; now it is government's turn. Like Latin Americans, we must stop looking to the government to solve every problem.

In a world of socialism, the United States could take for granted its ability to finance its large deficits. But as other countries clean up their acts and scramble to welcome private capital, it could become more difficult to market U.S. debt in the future. Domestic and foreign investors will increasingly diversify their portfolios as other countries establish their economies on a solid basis.

The United States has begun to respond to the global challenge. Politicians seem prepared to rein in excessive tort liabilities despite the clout of the plaintiff's bar's political contributions. The Republican electoral landslide of November 1994 was itself a response to a popular demand to reduce the size of government. The Republican Contract with America and the plan to turn welfare over to the states were efforts to scale down a monolithic central government. Capitalist developments in Latin America and the Far East will force policy changes in the United States.

The consequences of capitalism on a global scale are scarcely imaginable. It will literally change the face of the planet, as capital and human potential are freed from government inhibitions and channeled by market forces. With advances in technology and communications, it is already possible to disperse a firm's operations over many countries, utilizing the comparative advantages of each. Until recently, however, entrepreneurs have had relatively free reign only in the United States, limited parts of Western Europe, Japan, and Hong Kong. Yet the innovations generated by a small percentage of the earth's population have been astounding. If entrepreneurs are set loose all over the world, accelerating change will become the norm, and a major requirement for success will be the ability to swiftly adjust to changing circumstances. In this environment, the only people who will be secure will be those who are free and who have individually owned nest eggs.

Latin America's rent-seeking past and its dire consequences have much to teach North Americans. The United States is not free from rent-seeking. Much of the prime real estate in Washington, D.C., is occupied by special interest groups that lobby government for subsidies and privileges at the expense of both taxpayers and competitors. If the culture of inside-the-Beltway Washington became the culture of the country, the United States would find the efficient allocation of resources increasingly blocked by privilege and itself eliminated as a major player in the emerging global capitalist order.

On the one end of the spectrum, there are subsidies for the poor, and, on the other end, corporate welfare. Subsidizing poverty has been counterproductive, creating a permanent underclass dependent on the government. Equally bad, corporate welfare erodes competition and rewards political connections over market efficiency, thus jeopardizing the very existence of our free enterprise system.

According to a May 1995 study, "Ending Corporate Welfare as We Know It," by Cato Institute researchers Stephen Moore and Dean Stansel, U.S. corporations collect $87 billion annually in direct subsidies from the federal budget. The subsidies not only divert resources from economic to political activity, they often result in stifling domestic competition. For example, Moore and Stansel charge that the $100 million annually received by Sematech, a consortium of very large computer microchip producers, ostensibly to help U.S. chipmakers against foreign competition, is used to help the fourteen largest chipmakers fend off domestic competition. Other examples are taxpayer-subsidized Rural Electrification Administration loans that hold down the costs of running ski resorts in Aspen, Colorado, five-star hotels in Hilton Head, South Carolina, and gambling casinos in Las Vegas, Nevada.

Some U.S. farmers owe their wealth to unpaid loans from the Farmers Home Administration and not to farming. In March 1995, the *Wall Street Journal* cited $12.5 billion in farm loans written off since 1989. Among them was $17 million in debt relief for Gourmet Farms, a major California asparagus grower. Suzanne Enis, ex-wife of the former head of the company, told the newspaper that, "all he (her former husband) had to do is display a need, and they just gave him money. . . . I had it all—jewelry, furs, clothes." In September 1994, the Farmers Home Administration settled a $3.5-million loan to another California borrower for $800,000, leaving him with a home on a golf course and a meat processing company, among other assets. In 1991, the U.S. taxpayers forked over $2.9 million to advertise Pillsbury muffins and pies, $10 million to promote Sunkist oranges, and $465,000 to promote McDonalds' chicken McNuggets.

In 1995, Clinton Administration officials were still advocating "industrial policy" and "economically targeted investments" that would divert some percentage of pension fund assets into government-approved uses. Obviously, every government program would lobby for a share of private pension fund assets, to the detriment of the retirement income of pensioners. If government entities succeed in supplementing their budget allocations with private pension monies, rent-seeking will escalate with the government's regulatory control over investment.

Rents can be more rewarding than profits. Moore and Stansel report that Martin Marietta charged the Pentagon $263,000 for a Smokey Robinson concert, $20,000 for the purchase of golf balls, and $7,500 for a 1993 Christmas party. Ecology and Environment Inc., of Lancaster, New York, spent $243,000 of funds designated for environmental cleanup on "employee morale" and $37,000 on tennis lessons, bike races, golf tournaments, and other entertainment. Even universities get in on the act. In 1991, the Government Accounting Office exposed a pattern of high-living at Stanford University, complete with yachts, $70 wines, French antiques, and vacations at Lake Tahoe that were lumped in with $200 million in "research expenses" charged to taxpayers, including $7,000 for sheets for the Stanford president's oversized bed.

Rent-seeking has infiltrated scholarship. Megabuck research grants paid out of public funds and awarded by bureaucrats have reduced the independence of scholarly inquiry and elicit policy prescriptions supportive of government programs. Even science has been affected. In emotionally charged environmental issues, scientists skeptical of environmental apocalypses such as ozone depletion and global warming find it difficult to obtain research support. The resulting absence of debate has permitted extremist views to dictate public policy by press release. In the arts, humanities, and social sciences, the corruption of scholarship by public money is even more pervasive. The ability of program administrators to buy favorable research reports increases the difficulty of controlling public expenditures.

If the twentieth century's lessons of public sector failure are learned, the twenty-first century will see expanded individual responsibility, free markets, and private property. Fifteen years from now, the generation born amid the fall of the Berlin Wall will marvel at the credulity of people that permitted the ideas of Karl Marx and Gunnar Myrdal to be implemented on a global scale. It will be clear to all that without private property, individual incentive, and free enterprise, there can be no economic, social, or political progress.

Bibliography

Adams, Patricia. *Odious Debts*. London: Earthscan, 1991.

Alberdi, Juan. *Bases y Puntos de Partida para la organización Política de la República Argentina*. Buenos Aires: Editorial Universitaria de Buenos Aires, 1966; first published 1858.

Alemann, Roberto. *Curso de Política Económica Argentina*, 2 vols. Buenos Aires: Alemann S.R.L., 1981.

Anderson, Jack. "Mexican Wheels Are Lubricated by Official Oil, *Washington Post*, May 14, 1984; "Mexico Makes Its Presidents Millionaires," *Washington Post*, May 15, 1984; "Politics Dilute Anti-Corruption Effort in Mexico," *Washington Post*, August 24, 1984.

Appleby, Paul. *Public Administration in India: Report of a Survey*. Delhi: The Ford Foundation, 1953. Published by the Manager of Publications.

Arellano, José Pablo. "Elementos Para el Análisis de la Reforma Previsional Chilena," *Estudios Cieplan*, December 1981, pp. 5–44.

Arriola, Carlos. *Las Organizaciones Empresariales y el Estado*. Mexico City: Conafe, 1981.

Aubey, Robert. *Nacional Financiera and Mexican Industry: A Study of the Financial Relationship Between the Government and the Private Sector of Mexico*. Los Angeles: University of California Press, 1966.

Ayau, Manuel. *La década perdida*. Guatemala City: Manuel Ayau, 1989.

Bandow, Doug, and Ian Vásquez, eds. *Perpetuating Poverty*. Washington, D.C.: Cato Institute, 1994.

Baran, Paul. *The Political Economy of Growth.* New York: Monthly Review, Inc., 1957.

Barros Junior, Mario. *A Fantástica Corrupção no Brazil.* São Paulo: published by author, 1982.

Bauer, P.T. *The Development Frontier: Essays in Applied Economics.* Cambridge, Mass.: Harvard University Press, 1991.

———. *Dissent on Development.* Cambridge, Mass: Harvard University Press, 1972.

———. *Equality, the Third World and Economic Delusion.* Cambridge, Mass.: Harvard University Press, 1981.

———. *Reality and Rhetoric: Studies in the Economics of Development.* Cambridge, Mass.: Harvard University Press, 1984.

——— .*United States Aid and Indian Economic Development.* Washington, D.C.: American Enterprise Association, 1959.

Bentura Belena, Eusebio. *Copias a la Letra Ofrecidas en el Primer Tomo de la Recopilación Sumaria de todos los autos acordados de la Real Audiencia y Sala de Crimen de esta N.E.* Mexico City: Felipe de Zuniga y Ontiveros, 1787

Buchanan, Norman, and Ellis, Howard. *Approaches to Economic Development.* New York: The Twentieth Century Fund, 1955.

Bustamante, Jorge. *La República Corporativa.* Buenos Aires: Emecé Editores, 1988.

Caiden, Naomi, and Aaron Wildavsky (1974) *Planning and Budgeting in Poor Countries.* New York: Wiley-Interscience, 1974.

Campbell, John. *A Concise History of the Spanish America.* New York: Barnes & Noble, 1972; reprint of 1741 edition.

Cavallo, Domingo, Roberto Domenech, and Yair Mundlak. *La Argentina que Pudo Ser: Los Costos de la Represión Económica.* Buenos Aires: Ediciones Manantial, 1989.

Centro de Investigación para el Desarrollo, A.C. *Hacia una Nueva Política Industrial.* Mexico City: Editorial Diana, 1988.

———. *El Reto de la Globalización para la Industria Mexicana.* Mexico City: Editorial Diana, 1989.

———. *Tecnología e Industria en el Futuro de México.* Mexico City: Editorial Diana, 1989.

Coatsworth, John. "Obstacles to Economic Growth in Nineteenth-Century Mexico." *The American Historical Review*, Vol. 83, 1978, pp. 80–100.

Corbridge, Stuart. *Capitalist World Development: A Critique of World Geography.* Totowa, N.J.: Rowman & Littlefield, 1986.

Cosío Villegas, Daniel. *Historia Mínima de México.* Mexico City, Mexico: El Colegio de México, 1981; first edition 1974.

Cruchaga, Miguel. *Estudio Sobre la Organización Económica y la Hacienda Pública de Chile.* 3 Vols. Madrid: Editorial Reus, S.A., 1929.

de Escalona Aguero, Gaspar. *Gazofilacio Real del Peru.* La Paz: Editorial El Estado, 1941; fourth edition, originally published in 1647.

de Mora, Juan Miguel. *!No! Señor Presidente: La Realidad Nacional del Actual Sexenio sin Maquillaje Oficial.* Mexico City: Anaya Editores S.A., 1983.

del Barrio Lorenzot, Francisco. *Ordenanzas de Gremios de la Nueva España.* Mexico City: Secretaría de Gobernación, 1920.

Del Campillo, Joseph. *Nuevo Sistema de Gobierno Económico para la América.* Merida, Venezuela: Universidad de los Andes, 1971; first published 1789.

De Meira Penna, José. *O Dinossauro.* São Paulo: T. A. Queiroz, 1988.

De Soto, Hernando. *The Other Path.* New York: Harper & Row, 1989.

de Veitia Linage, Joseph. *The Spanish Rule of Trade to the West Indies,* translated by Capt. John Stevens. London: Printed for Samuel Crouch, at the Corner of Pope's-Head-Alley in Cornbil, 1702.

de Vries, Margaret. *Balance of Payments Adjustment, 1945–1986: The IMF Experience.* Washington, D.C.: International Monetary Fund, 1987.

Djilas, Milovan. *The New Class—An Analysis of the Communist System.* New York: Praeger, 1957.

Dobb, Maurice. *An Essay on Economic Growth and Planning.* New York: Monthly Review Press, 1960.

Ellis, Howard, ed. *Economic Development for Latin America.* New York: St Martin's Press, 1966.

Esteva, Gustavo. "Development: Metaphor, Myth, Threat." *Development: Seeds of Change,* Society for International Development, 1985, Vol. III.

Fatemi, Khosrow, ed. *The Maquiladora Industry: Economic Solution or Problem.* New York: Praeger, 1990.

Gil Díaz, Francisco, "Mexico's Experience with Foreign Aid," in Uma Lele and Ijaz Nabi, eds., *Transitions in Development: The Role of Aid and Commercial Flows.* San Francisco: ICS Press, 1991.

Glade, William, ed. *Privatization of Public Enterprises in Latin America.* San Francisco: ICS Press, 1991.

Godau Schucking, Rainer, and Viviane de Márquez. *Burocracia Pública y Empresa Privada: El Caso de la Industrialización Mexicana.* Austin: University of Texas, 1982.

Guissari, Adrián. *La Argentina Informal.* Buenos Aires: Emecé Editores, 1989.

Hachette, Dominique, Rolf Luders, and Guillermo Tagle, et al. *Seis Casos de Privatización en Chile.* Washington, D.C.: Inter-American Development Bank, 1992, Working Documents series, March.

Hancock, Graham. *Lords of Poverty: The Power, Prestige and Corruption of the International Aid Business.* New York: Atlantic Monthly Press, 1989.

Haring, C.H. *The Spanish Empire in America.* New York: Oxford University Press, 1947.

———. *Trade and Navigation Between Spain and the Indies.* Cambridge: Harvard University Press, 1918.

Heilbroner, Robert. *The Economic Problem*. Englewood Cliffs, N.J.: Prentice-Hall, 1968.

―――. *The Great Ascent*. New York and Evanston: Harper & Row, 1963.

Hellinger, Stephen, Douglas Hellinger, and Fred O'Regan. *Aid for Just Development: Report on the Future of Foreign Assistance*. Boulder and London: Lynne Rienner, 1988.

Hierro, Jorge, and Allen Sanginés. "Public Sector Behavior in Mexico," in Felipe Larraín and Marcelo Selowsky, eds., *The Public Sector and the Latin American Crisis*. San Francisco: ICS Press, 1991.

Higgins, Benjamin. *Economic Development: Problems and Policies*. New York: W. W. Norton, 1968.

Hirschman, Albert. *The Strategy of Economic Development*. New Haven: Yale University Press, 1958.

Hoselitz, Bert, ed. *The Progress of Underdeveloped Areas*. Chicago: The Univerity of Chicago Press, 1959; first published 1952.

Ickis, John, Edilberto de Jesus, and Rushikesh Maru, eds. *Beyond Bureaucracy: Strategic Management of Social Development*. West Hartford, Conn.: Kumarian Press, 1986.

Inter-American Development Bank, Annual Reports: 1970–1993.

―――. *Economic and Social Progress in Latin America*, series, 1982, 1983, 1985, 1987, 1988, 1989, 1991, 1993.

―――. *External Debt and Economic Development in Latin America*. Washington, D.C.: IDB, 1984.

International Monetary Fund, Annual Reports 1980–1994

―――. *International Financial Statistics*, series.

―――. *World Economic Outlook*, series, April 1987-May 1994.

Korten, David. *Getting to the 21st Century: Voluntary Action and the Global Agenda*. West Hartford, Conn.: Kumarian Press, 1990.

Krauss, Melvyn. *Development Without Aid*. Stanford: Hoover Institution/New York: New York University, 1983.

Lal, Deepak. *The Poverty of Development Economics*. Cambridge, Mass.: Harvard University Press, 1983, 1985.

Larraín, Felipe, and Marcelo Selowsky, eds. *The Public Sector and the Latin American Crisis*. San Francisco: ICS Press, 1991.

Lecomte, Bernard. *Project Aid: Limitations and Alternatives* Paris: Organization for Economic Cooperation and Development, 1986.

Levine, Barry, ed. *El Desafío Neoliberal: El Fin del Tercermundismo en América Latina*. Bogotá: Grupo Editorial Norma, 1992.

Lewis, W. Arthur. *Aspects of Tropical Trade 1883–1965*. Stockholm: Almquist & Wicksell, 1969

―――. *Report on Industrialization and the Gold Coast*. Accra: Government Printing Department, 1953.

―――. *The Principles of Economic Planning*. London: George Allen and Unwin, 1965; first printing 1949.

———. *Tropical Development: 1880–1913*. Evanston: Northwestern University Press, 1970.

López Portillo, José. "Sexto Informe de Gobierno," in *El Ejecutivo Ante el Congreso 1976–1982*. Mexico City: Secretaría de Programación y Presupuesto, 1982.

McKenzie, Richard, and Dwight Lee. *Quicksilver Capital: How the Rapid Movement of Wealth has Changed the World*. New York: Free Press, 1991.

Medina Macias, Ricardo, *Crónica del Desengaño*. Mexico City: Editores Asociados Mexicanos, S.A, 1983.

Meier, Gerald, ed. *Leading Issues in Development Economics*. New York: Oxford University Press, 1964.

Morgenstern, Oskar. *On the Accuracy of Economic Observations*. Princeton: Princeton University Press, 1963; first edition 1950).

Myrdal, Gunnar. *Asian Drama: An Inquiry into the Poverty of Nations*. The Twentieth Century Fund, 1968.

———. *Beyond the Welfare State: Economic Planning and its International Implications*. New Haven and London: Yale University Press, 1960.

———. *The Challenge of World Poverty: A World Anti-Poverty Program in Outline*. New York: Pantheon Books, 1970.

———. *An International Economy: Problems and Prospects*. New York: Harper, 1956.

———. *Rich Lands and Poor: The Road to World Prosperity*. New York and Evanston: Harper, 1957.

North, Douglass. *Institutions, Institutional Change and Economic Performance*. New York and Cambridge: Cambridge University Press, 1990.

North, Douglass and Robert Thomas. *The Rise of the Western World: A New Economic History*. Cambridge: Cambridge University Press, 1973.

Nurkse, Ragnar. *Problems of Capital Formation in Underdeveloped Countries*. New York: Oxford University Press, 1966; first edition 1953.

Olson, Mancur. *The Rise and Decline of Nations*. New Haven: Yale University Press, 1982.

Organization of American States. *External Financing for Latin American Development*. Baltimore: Johns Hopkins University Press, 1971, published for the Organization of American States.

Ospina Vasquez, Luis. *Industría y Protección en Colombia—1810–1930*. Medellín: Editorial Lealon, 1979; first edition 1955.

Payer, Cheryl. *The World Bank: A Critical Analysis*. New York and London: Atlantic Monthly Review Press, 1982.

Paz, Octavio. *El Ogro Filantrópico*. Mexico City: Editorial Joaquín Mortiz, S.A., 1979.

Pazos, Luis. *El Gobierno y la Inflación*. Mexico City: Editorial Diana, S.A., 1989; first edition, 1980.

———. *Hacia Donde Va Salinas*. Mexico City: Editorial Diana, S.A., 1989.

Pimentel, Francisco. *La Economía Política Aplicada a la Propiedad Territorial en Mexico*. Mexico City: Ignacio Cumplido, 1866.

Piñera, José. *El Cascabel al Gato: la batalla por la Reforma Previsional*. Santiago: Empresa Editora Zig-Zag, S.A., 1989.

———. "The Path to Privatization in Chile," in William Glade, ed., *Privatization of Public Enterprises in Latin America*. San Francisco: ICS Press, 1991.

Polanyi, George. *Planning in Britain: The Experience of the 1960s*. London: The Institute of Economic Affairs, 1967.

Prebisch, Raul. "The Economic Development of Latin America and Its Principal Problems," *Economic Bulletin for Latin America,* February 1962.

Rangel, Carlos. *The Latin Americans: Their Love-Hate Relationship with the United States*. New Brunswick: Transaction Books, 1987.

———. *Third World Ideology and Western Reality*. New Brunswick: Transaction Books, 1986.

Revéiz, Edgar. *Democratizar para Sobrevivir*. Bogotá: Producción Editorial: Poligrupo Comunicación, 1989.

Roett, Riordan. *The Politics of Foreign Aid in the Brazilian Northeast*. Nashville: Vanderbilt University Press, 1972.

Rosenstein-Rodan, Paul. "Problems of Industrialization of Eastern and South-Eastern Europe," *Economic Journal*, June-September, 1943.

Rostow, W. W. *The Stages of Economic Growth: A Non-Communist Manifesto*. Cambridge: Cambridge University Press, 1960.

Roth, Gabriel. *The Private Provision of Public Services in Developing Countries*. New York: Oxford University Press, 1987, published for the World Bank.

Salinas, Roberto. "Mexico, Markets, and Multilateral Aid," in Doug Bandow and Ian Vásquez, eds., *Perpetuating Poverty: The World Bank, the IMF, and the Developing World*. Washington, D.C.: Cato Institute, 1994.

Sánchez, Manuel, and Rossana Corona, eds. *Privatization in Latin America*. Washington, D.C.: Inter-American Development Bank, 1993.

Sapelli, Claudio. *Tamaño del Estado, Instituciones y Crecimiento Económico*. San Francisco: Centro Internacional para el Desarrollo Económico, 1992.

Schucking, Rainer and Viviane de Márquez. *Burocracia Pública y Empresa Privada: El Caso de la Industrialización Mexicana*. Austin: University of Texas, 1982.

Shaffer, Harry, and Jan Prybyla. *From Underdevelopment to Affluence: Western, Soviet and Chinese Views*. New York: Appleton-Century-Crofts, 1968.

Smith, Peter. *Labyrinths of Power: Political Recruitment in Twentieth-Century Mexico*. Princeton: Princeton University Press, 1979.

Tinbergen, Jan. *Central Planning*. New Haven: Yale University Press, 1964.
————. *Lessons from the Past*. Amsterdam: Elsevier Publishing Company, 1963.
Todaro, Michael, *Economic Development in the Third World*. New York: Longman, 1977 .
Tomassini, Luciano. *Estado, Gobernabilidad y Desarrollo*. Washington, D.C.: Inter-American Development Bank, 1993.
Ul Haq, Mahbub. *The Poverty Curtain: Choices for the Third World*. New York: Columbia University, 1976.
Van de Laar, Aart. *The World Bank and the Poor*. Boston: Kluwer—Nijhoff Publishing, 1980.
Vaubel, Roland and Thomas Willett, eds. *The Political Economy of International Organizations: A Public Choice Approach*. Boulder: Westview Press, 1991.
Véliz, Claudio. *The Centralist Tradition of Latin America*. Princeton: Princeton University Press, 1980.
Vera Ferrer, Oscar. *El Caso Conasupo: Una Evaluación*. Mexico City: Centro de Estudios en Economía y Educación, 1987.
Vicens Vives, Jaime. *An Economic History of Spain*. Princeton: Princeton University Press, 1969.
Villareal, René. *Mitos y Realidades de la Empresa Pública*. Mexico City: Editorial Diana, S.A., 1988.
Ward, William and Barry Deren. *The Economics of Project Analysis: A Practitioner's Guide*. Washington, D.C.: World Bank, 1991.
Waterston, Albert. *Development Planning: Lessons of Experience*. Baltimore: Johns Hopkins Press, 1965.
Williamson, Oliver. *The Economic Institutions of Capitalism*. New York: The Free Press, 1985.
World Bank, Annual Reports: 1970–1993.
————. Project Appraisal Reports (1980s and 1990s).
————. *Evaluation Results* series (1990–1992), Operations Evaluation Department.
————. *Tenth Annual Review of Project Performance Audit Results*, 3 Volumes, 30 August, 1984.
————. *World Development Report* series (1989–1993)

About the Authors

Paul Craig Roberts is Chairman of the Institute for Political Economy in Washington, D.C., Research Fellow at The Independent Institute in Oakland, California, and Senior Research Fellow at the Hoover Institution, Stanford University. Dr. Roberts was educated at the Georgia Institute of Technology, the University of Virginia, University of California at Berkeley, and Oxford University where he was a member of Merton College. A former editor and columnist for *The Wall Street Journal*, he is a columnist for *Business Week* and is a nationally syndicated newspaper columnist. In 1992, he received the Warren Brookes Award for Excellence in Journalism, and in 1993, he was ranked one of the top seven journalists by *Forbes's Media Guide*.

During the years 1982–93, he held the William E. Simon Chair in Political Economy at the Center for Strategic and International Studies. In 1981–82, he served as Assistant Secretary of the Treasury for Economic Policy, and he was awarded the Treasury Department's Meritorious Service Award for "his outstanding contributions to the formulation of United States economic policy." From 1975 to 1978, Dr. Roberts served on the congressional staff where he drafted the Kemp-Roth bill and played a leading role in developing bipartisan support for a supply-side economic policy.

In 1987, the French government recognized him as "the artisan of a renewal in economic science and policy after half a century of state interventionism" and inducted him into the Legion of Honor.

He is the author of the Independent Institute book, *Alienation and the Soviet Economy: The Collapse of the Socialist Era*, plus the books, *The New Colorline: How Quotas and Privilege Destroy Democracy* (with Lawrence Stratton), *Meltdown: Inside the Soviet Economy*, (with Karen LaFollette), *The Supply-Side Revolution*, and *Marx's Theory of Exchange* (with Matthew Stephenson).

Dr. Roberts has held numerous academic appointments and has published many articles in scholarly journals, including the *Journal of Political Economy*, *Oxford Economic Papers*, *Journal of Law and Economics*, *Studies in Banking and Finance*, *Journal of Monetary Economics*, *Public Finance Quarterly*, *Public Choice*, *Classica et Mediaevalia*, *Ethics*, *Slavic Review*, *Soviet Studies*, *Rivista di Politica Economica*, and *Zeitschrift für Wirtschaftspolitik*. He has further contributed to *Commentary*, *The Public Interest*, *Harper's*, *New York Times*, *Los Angeles Times*, *Washington Times*, *Washington Post*, *Fortune*, *London Times*, *Financial Times*, *The Spectator*, *TLS*, *Il Sole 24 Ore*, *Le Figaro*, *Liberation*, and the *Nihon Keikai Shimbun*. He has testified before committees of Congress on thirty occasions.

Karen LaFollette Araujo is Research Fellow at The Independent Institute and the Institute for Political Economy and President of Hemispheric Studies Institute. Trilingual, she has lived in Chile as a Rotary Exchange student and has traveled extensively in Latin America. She is the author (with Paul Craig Roberts) of the book, *Meltdown: Inside the Soviet Economy*. During 1996–97, she is a Visiting Fellow at the Universidad Nacional Andrés Bello in Santiago, Chile.

Mrs. Araujo has been a Research Associate at First International Corporation, a clearinghouse of information on development bank projects, where she developed and maintained an information data base of projects in planning in Latin America funded by multilateral development banks; wrote and edited articles published in quarterly reports informing client companies of the overall economic situation and investment climate of selected Latin American countries; and traveled to Peru, Chile, and Mexico to interview project directors and development bank representatives about upcoming projects open to competitive bidding.

Index

accountability, 67, 128, 129, 162, 175, 178, 191
Act of Bogotá (1960), 121
Aeromexico, 18
agriculture: and Argentinian economic transformation, 41; and Chilean economic transformation, 36, 37; collectivization of, 104; and development institutions, 166–67, 168; and development planning, 104; and legal system, 83, 85; and Mexican economic transformation, 24, 85; and Mexico as blocked society, 54, 58, 60–62, 83; in U.S., 193. *See also* Conasupo (Mexican agricultural supply company)
Aguila, Luis, 65
airlines, 18, 46
Alberdi, Juan, 156
Aldogaray, María Julia, 43
Alemán, Miguel, 65
Allende, Salvador, 34–35, 69–70
Alliance for Progress, 120, 121
Alsogaray, Alvaro, 43
Archer, Bill, 188
Argentina: austerity programs in, 42; as blocked society, 8, 87, 92, 94–95; civil war in, 42; Congress in, 47; debt of, 181; development planning in, 124; economic transformation of, 8, 41–45, 47, 48, 180; military in, 42; Pinochet as role model for, 41, 45; Radical Party in, 45; as rent-seeking system, 41, 42, 91–92; socialism in, 41–43; violence in, 9. *See also specific topic*

Armey, Dick, 188
Aspe, Pedro, 13, 14, 18, 19, 21–22, 26
Association of Exporters (ADEX) (Peru), 93
audiencias, 137–38, 140
austerity programs: and Argentina, 42; and characteristics of economic transformation, 48–49; and debt crisis, 171; and development planning, 117; and foreign debt, 49; in government sector, 48–49; and IMF, 27, 42, 49, 73; and Mexico, 27, 73; and taxes, 49
automobile industry, 41
Ayau, Manuel, 130
Aylwin, Patricio, 39
Azcarraga, Emiliano, 65

Baillerés, Raúl, 65
Baja California, 24
balance of payments, 34, 170, 171
Balbina Dam (Brazil), 167
Banamex (Mexico), 18
Banco de la Nación (Peruvian National Bank), 90
Bancomer S.A. (Mexico), 18
Bank of Credit and Commerce International (BCCI), 90
banking system: Catholic Church as, 152; in Chile, 33–34, 37, 39; and development planning, 109, 120, 122–23, 125–27; and legal system, 84, 85; and Mexican economic transformation, 12–13, 17–18, 24, 48, 85; and Mexico as blocked society, 71, 72, 84,